os Aires erupted as Pamela Walli[r]
[cover]ed her first year with Canada AM

BY TERRY POULTON

st anniversary as a
...ada AM news team
...a time she'll never
...e corks may not
...bullets and teargas
...d, as Buenos Aires
June riots following
...in the Falkland Is-
...e Canadian female
...ring the war, she
...herself a target for
...hysterical riot po-
...crew were shot at,
...ed, knocked to the
...rampled.

...to me at the time,"
...lightly shaky laugh,
...ite a dramatic way
...rsary." In fact, her
...was the kind of ad-
...nalists only get to
...was dying to cover
...allin, "and one day
...at four in the after-
...s to catch a plane
...xpect to stay about
...a time, everybody
...ey was about to fall
...four dresses into a
...up rotating them
...on't think I'll ever
...again."

...challenge was by-
...ng stories out of
...s who were entirely
...roviding them. "We
...here in Argentina
...he says, "so our
...describe another
...ther. For instance,
...ricans viewed (Ar-
...eopoldo) Galtieri
...t of Attila, he
...s considered a
...nding ways to
...ross, when the
...rief [g]nding information
...the [s]ite a job. You
...ably] and some-
...nd on what

night-
If you... come up
...ap me, ...idiences
...es of get-... a lot of
...s had to d[r]... V net-
...arance. For ...crew
...ed and make-... and
...sy.

...s sent down ...ly
...over the Falk... y
...r with Britain, [I]
...ameras...ere her
...going on,
...emselves in
...and wound-
...rs."

...n Buenos
...er kudos
...at CTV, her
...ly the kind
...xpected of
...k for Cana-
...tawa corre-
...e toughest
...wing Pierre
...well (Wallin
...natch) that,
...r Scott re-
...Wallin was
...her as co-

...as already
...essive jour-
...in Wadena,
...ors degree
...niversity of
...ial work at
After some
...adio, Wallin
...ing career,
...open-line
...progressing
...CBC radio
...katchewan
...a morning
...moved to
...'s Sunday
...up with a
...As It Hap-
...y into print
...espondent
...cializing in
...urn led to a
...ticians on
...d later her
...a AM. Wal-
...might fell a
...pare time.
...a night, is
...about 4:30
...d then
...p.m.

...s too much
...its to an
...one so far,
...ed embar-
...ast year's
...awa. When
...ce of West
...hmidt, his
...ff Wallin's
...inus three

'One day the office
called me
at four in the afternoon
and said I was to catch
a plane at 6:15
and could expect to stay
about a week.
I threw four dresses
into a suitcase
and ended up rotating them
for five weeks.'

so frank on TV. While we just fc
for granted that our job was to a
rately report whatever was goir
they were falling all over themse|
competing with each other and
up acting as their own censors."

Although Wallin's work in I
Aires obviously earned her
among the powers-that-be at C
professionalism was exactly /
of thing that's come to be exp
her. She kicked off her work I
da AM (initially as the Otta
spondent) with one of the
assignments of all: interview
Trudeau. That went so w
says she's eager for a rem
when Canada AM's Gail
signed last December, '
quickly chosen to replace
host with Norm Perry.

Not yet 30, Wallin I
managed to pile up imp
nalistic credentials. Borr
Sask., she earned an h
in psychology at the
Regina and briefly did r
the prison in Prince Alb
moonlighting on CBC
decided on a broadc
beginning as co-host
radio show in Regina r
to being producer c
program there called
Today. She then pro
radio show in Ottaw
Toronto to work or
Morning. She follow
stint as national ed
pens and then mad
journalism as the
for the Toronto S
political reporting.
regular spot gri
CTV's Question F
fulltime position c
lin's daily schedu
lumberjack, leav
She sleeps only
routinely at her
every morning
returns to work

Anxious not
of a paragon
occasional go[r]
she says wit
rassment, o...
summit meeting outside O...
she mentioned the presence of West
German leader Helmut Schmidt, his
last name somehow rolled off Wallin's
usually precise tongue minus three

U.S. colleagues. "I was broadcasting
one evening over the facilities we all
shared," she says, "and, as usual, I
was simply describing what we had all
seen. Suddenly, there was dead silence in the room. I had repeated in
English what the crowds in the street
were calling their president, which
was 'a son of a bitch.' The Americans

T here's no doubt it was a
bit embarrassing. There I
was hanging, not very
gracefully, over the railing
trying for the umpteenth time to
get Joe Clark's attention. From
my precarious and quite undig-
nified perch, I shoved the microphone into his face, cajoling him
to utter some truth, some intimate thought. What I didn't
realize was that the microphone
was live and the cameras were
rolling, capturing for posterity
my professional entreaties.
Fortunately, the humiliation —
all part and parcel of the joys of
live television — was fleeting.

It was Saturday, June 10,
1983, a day the weather was
sweltering. For all the weeks of
waiting, months of meeting and
days of dress rehearsals, this
Progressive Conservative federal
leadership convention had a life
and will of its own.

It's the same with any leadership convention. When the red
camera lights go on convention
morning they stay on until a new
party leader is chosen or an old
one re-confirmed — whenever
that may be.

Conventional wisdom

**Triumph, pain and embarrassment — it's all
in a Grit-ty day's work for a TV
reporter at a leadership convention,
writes CTV's Pamela Wallin**

Ottawa's Civic Centre comfortably seats a thousand or two.
Unfortunately for all, there are
more than 5,000 reporters, camera crews, candidates, delegates
and assorted political hacks and
hangers-on jammed into the airless hall. Crowded is an under-
statement; so is airless, there
being no air conditioning.

We (the electronic press) are
weighed down with pounds of
electronic gear, not so neatly
hidden under suit jackets (definitely not needed for warmth!).
The wires for the complicated
system of headsets, microphones, walkie-talkies and tele-
phones run up logs, down backs,
through belts and around necks.

Amidst the heat and deafen-
ing roar of the hockey stadium
— now fully draped in banners
and balloons — the CTV reporters are balanced atop two wood-
en boxes no more than two feet
square, battling to maintain
their turf. A CBC reporter is less

than an a
between o
dozens of
ers. And ca
objective: to
his handlers
and only you
Unable to
ferret out the
tics of the
camps. We a
speculate. The
ing are the offi
but the obviou
asked. The cand
with false brava
bit, smiles a lot a
imminent victory.

But despite t
punditry and the
one really knows
when this story will
ers and candidates
the fickle hands of t
It could take all day
with a miracle, be c
one, decisive ballot. S
reporter wants that
would be no suspens
time for deal-making.

Striking deals is the
sence of conventions and
CONTINUED O

been ...
lowed. When I'm ...
one job I move on to the
next ...

the story back ...

Weighed down with electronic gear, Pamela Wallin and Craig Oliver keep a sharp eye on events at last year[...]
convention. They'll be at the Ottawa Civic Centre again this week for the Liberal convention, along with a c[...]

THE GIRL FROM WADENA

Staying in touch with her roots in
Saskatchewan, where 'people are
open and frank', and listening to the
opinions of others, especially her parents, have helped CBC superstar
Pamela Wallin keep in touch with the
real world.

By Joyce Singer

*"One of the joys of working on
television is that you feel as if
you've got friends everywhere."*
— Pamela Wallin

W hen the Canadian
Broadcasting
Corporation effected its
radical programming cutbacks and
changes a couple of years ago, one
of the most talked-about events
was the cancellation of *The
Journal* and the launching of
Prime Time News at 9 p.m.. The
fact that the CBC had stolen
CTV's sparkling intellectual main-
stay Pamela Wallin made the
whole brouhaha even more exciting.

For Wallin, who now clearly
ranks as one Canada's most
admired and trusted television personalities, man or woman, it was
like going home again. Over 20
years ago she had worked with her
Prime Time News co-host, and fellow Westerner, Peter Mansbridge.
As well, she earned her early jour-

deserve kudos for their daughter's
success. Both retired now, her
mom Leone was an English teacher. Pamela says, "She used to say,
make sure you can express yourself, because if you can't express
yourself you can't communicate,
and if you can't communicate you
can't succeed." Since retiring she
has taken up art and several of her
scenic paintings adorn the walls in
Wallin's office. The evocative pictures portray the idyllic atmosphere near Pamela's hometown.

Her dad Bill was an X-ray technician. He also made his mark as a
mover and shaker in local politics,
as a campaign manager for the
Social Credit Party. "He used to sit
around after dinner and read the
encyclopedia. And when we kids
would ask what things where all
about, he'd tell us to look it up!
My parents just gave me the skills
that I now use every day in my
work." Wallin explains that she
feels her parents represent the
heartbeat of the country, and the
current interests of an older generation. So whenever she needs to

Since You Asked

Since

You Asked

Pamela Wallin

Random House of Canada

Canadian Cataloguing in Publication Data

Wallin, Pamela
Since you asked

Includes index.
ISBN: 0-679-30946-2

1. Wallin, Pamela.   2. Television journalists – Canada – Biography.
3. Radio journalists – Canada – Biography.   I. Title.

PN4913.W34A3 1998   070.1'95'092   C98-931199-6

"Unfortunate Coincidence," *The Portable Dorothy Parker*, © 1928,
© renewed 1956 by Dorothy Parker. Used by permission of
Viking Penguin, a division of Penguin Putnam Inc.

Cover and interior design: Gordon Robertson
Cover photograph: © Gabor Jurina

Permission to reprint *Chatelaine* cover courtesy of *Chatelaine* magazine
© Maclean Hunter Publishing Ltd. and Jim Allen.

Permission to reprint *Maclean's* cover courtesy of *Maclean's* and Peter Bragg.

Permission to reprint the photograph by Bruno
Schlumberger granted by the *Ottawa Citizen*.

Printed and bound in United States of America.

10 9 8 7 6 5 4 3 2 1

Acknowledgments

To examine one's own life is frightening, daunting, sometimes even disappointing. But the process also provides some missing definition, shining a light on moments long forgotten that explain so much today.

I am grateful to Gary Katz, a friend and a writer, who helped me find an objective voice to tell this very subjective story. To make the mundane memorable, he patiently cajoled, threatened, pried and extracted memories that had faded and facts that had disappeared into the recesses of a brain crammed with information. He even pretended he was interested. Thanks for the lies and your deft pen. I could not and would not have even begun this without you.

That did not alleviate the need for the patient advice and endless hand holding. Bill Fox, Bonnie Brownlee and Michael Decter were my salvation. Michael is the remarkable love in my life. And despite the pressures of writing his own book at the same time, he was and is always there for me, convincing with his words and reassuring with his steady, loving hands on my shoulders, living up to a promise we once made.

My love to my sister, Bonnie George, for her instinct and insight and for her unfailing support in this and many other of life's endeavours.

And to Jack Fleischmann, Toni Stevens, Peggy Taylor, Rick Muller, Lou and Rhonda Clancy, Hugh Segal, Bruce Philips, Michael Kirby, David MacNaughton and Terry O'Sullivan, my thanks for always being there and being who you are.

The details of a busy life can disappear with time, so I am indebted to Malcolm Fox, Craig Oliver, Carol Goar, Sheila Moore, Patsy Pehleman, Elizabeth Gray, Shelley Peterson Bull, Laine Drewery, Alan Fryer and my family, who willingly and repeatedly jogged my memory and helped fill in the blanks.

The writing of this book required many sacrifices by those around me, especially "the girls." These four women, a most extraordinary group of friends and colleagues, have worked tirelessly and selflessly to make my dreams come true. Anne Bayin, Mary Lynk, Wendy Bryan and Rebecca Eckler defy the odds daily and create extraordinary programs in spite of their sleep-deprived host, who was either distracted by the trauma of being a first-time author or by the endless juggling that's required to run a business and be a public person. Their talent and wit and style is unparalleled. My thanks, too, to Janine Blanchard, Graeme McCreesh, CatherineTamas and Mark Landells, who always seem to be able to work miracles.

To my editors Sarah Davies and Doug Pepper, thank you for taking me on—pun intended—and for your confidence that this project was worth doing. I am grateful for copy editor Tanya Trafford's sharp eye. And thanks to David Kent for the "motivation."

To my friend and protector, Perry Goldsmith, who on more than one occasion saved me from myself, thank you for making me do this against my will.

This book is for my Mom and Dad and for Wadena.

Pamela Wallin
July 1998
Toronto

Contents

Introduction 1

ONE: The Centre of the Universe 7

TWO: Social Work 37

THREE: The Brown Envelope 61

FOUR: The Hill 79

FIVE: As It Happens 97

SIX: Byline 113

SEVEN: Lights, Camera, Make-up 133

EIGHT: War! 149

NINE: The Dawn to Midnight Shift 165

TEN: Two Deaths 191

ELEVEN: Prime Ministers I Have Known 201

TWELVE: Settling Down 229

THIRTEEN: Prime Time 243

FOURTEEN: From Prime Time to My Time 263

FIFTEEN: Pamela Wallin Lives 275

INDEX: 291

Introduction

I SOMETIMES FORGET how fortunate I am. In the course of doing my work, I've met many of the most intelligent, creative people in the world. As my path has crossed theirs, my own life has been shaped and altered. So this book is about the forces, like family, that have guided me. It is also about my encounters with the famous, the powerful and the immensely talented, all of whom have helped carve our collective Canadian character.

I was reminded of one such encounter recently when I was invited to the home of Rob Prichard, the charming and persuasive president of the University of Toronto. The university had just bestowed an honourary degree on a former premier of Alberta. Rob asked me to say a few words about a man whom I now call a friend but who wasn't always one. The warmth of genuine affection for the guest of honour filled the room, but as I began recounting the story of my first run-in with him, I could almost feel the biting chill of that wintery March air of 1980.

At the height of the "let those Eastern bastards freeze in the dark" days, I had hopped a plane to Edmonton. I had been dispatched by

The Toronto Star to what it considered enemy territory to confront Peter Lougheed, the blue-eyed sheik of a new oil-rich kingdom called Alberta. He wasn't much taller than I, but behind a desk on a raised stage at the front of the room holding court he seemed larger than life. And in full control of a captive press corps, who had learned it was better for their journalistic careers to speak only when spoken to.

Always immaculately turned out, the handsome, one-time football star and Harvard-educated businessman was now, as his grandfather had once been, the premier of Alberta. And Peter Lougheed was in battle mode. The rich resources of Alberta would be the spoils of this war.

Telling the story of our own "battle" some seventeen years after the fact at Lougheed's tribute dinner got me thinking. Almost absent-mindedly I made the calculation I make more and more these days—it was *how* many years ago? It occurred to me that, with any luck at all, I had as many years ahead of me in my working life as I now had behind me. This sparked both fear and relief. The fear came from asking, "What have I accomplished? Have I really made a difference in my life or in the lives of others?" The relief came from the knowledge that there was still time if I hadn't. But I couldn't know the answers until I asked the questions—of my self.

I have always been a curious person with an abiding interest in how things and people work, and in the process of finding out. I am afforded the rare privilege of being able to invite interesting people into the studio every night and ask them questions, sometimes very intimate questions. And since we're on national television when I ask, they generally oblige me with an answer. Over the years that's hundreds, perhaps thousands, of people and certainly hundreds of thousands of questions.

Over the next few days, my simple "behind me–ahead of me" calculation became an idea that refused to flee. Before I knew it I was into that reappraisal of my life that seems to be a necessary part of the landscape of one's forties.

Everybody's mid-life look-around starts from a different place. For some it's the numeric magic of the fortieth birthday, or a dramatic personal event or crisis, and for others a general dissatisfaction with the way their lives have unfolded. Mine had little to do with any of these.

I live on a very pleasant street in downtown Toronto in a home that is ruled by a particularly adorable chocolate-point Siamese called Kitty. She lets me come and go pretty much as I please and throws temper tantrums only when I spend too long on the phone.

I have a "gentleman caller" who is smart and loving and whose own full life, which includes two teenage children, enriches my own. And I have great friends and a job that inspires and intrigues.

No, my dissatisfaction came from a simple and, I'm afraid, very common feeling that my future was suddenly quantifiable. And that raised in me a resolve that I wanted to be more present in my future than I'd been in my past.

Let me explain.

I'm a runner. I don't mean in the gym or up and down the streets of my neighbourhood, but metaphorically, from minute to minute, from event to event, from chapter to chapter of my life. I often feel I'm running a bit too quickly to notice the scenery.

Not that I haven't always made my own decisions and enjoyed or suffered their consequences. And not that I believed at all that I'd been swept unwittingly along through my life. But I began to feel that I'd never slowed myself down enough to turn my natural curiosity inward in the way I so enjoy turning it on others. I knew, in some respects, more about "formative influences" as a line of interviewing than as a personal experience. Once the idea of "the mid-point" had taken root in me I knew I had to address it. This book is the result.

What follows is my attempt to prepare myself for the second half of my life by answering the questions I have asked writers, scientists, performers, humanitarians and politicians, among others:

How did you get here? What were your influences and epiphanies? What have you seen along the way? Where are you heading? It's a personal journey, but I'm pleased you're coming along. It will help keep me honest. And I trust that along the way I'll answer some of the questions many of you have asked me over the years.

In the pursuit of self-knowledge some people turn to astrology to explain the world they were born into. They analyze the relative positions of astronomical bodies at their birth and find, in the cosmic mosaic, some indication of the influences that will rule them for life. For me, reading David Halberstam's book *The Fifties* was like having my chart done.

I was born on April 10, 1953. Six weeks later, on June 2, everyone in the country, especially anyone fortunate enough to have a television set and a transmitter close by, was riveted to the coronation of Queen Elizabeth II. She'd been monarch for more than a year since her father, King George VI, had died, but the event was still big news. And it was the first-ever coronation to be televised. The advent of television may have been the most indelible fact of the time, but it was just part of a chronological package.

The Fifties was an era of prosperity and hope, a time in which it was easy to feel that almost anything was possible. Though I credit my parents for raising me with a sense that I could do what I chose to do with my life, the times conspired to prove them right. Halberstam declares it an "orderly" time. The Baby Boomers were being born and raised, though no one had yet coined the phrase. The ferment of the Sixties may have been predictable to the prescient, but except for the odd Beatnik—and you'd have to travel far from Wadena to find one—there wasn't much evidence of it.

Besides the coronation, 1953 was the year Edmund Hillary and Tenzing Norgay conquered Mount Everest, John F. Kennedy and Jacqueline Bouvier were married and an armistice ended the Korean War. Joseph Heller, whom I recently met and interviewed, was writing, longhand, the first chapter of his now-classic novel, *Catch 22*.

Introduction

The big movie was Disney's *Peter Pan* and my father's favourite base-ball team, the New York Yankees, won their fifth consecutive World Series. Jean Beliveau signed with the Montreal Canadiens, Marilyn Monroe (whose likenesses you can find scattered throughout my home) starred in *Gentlemen Prefer Blondes*, and women swooned for Burt Lancaster and Frank Sinatra in *From Here to Eternity*.

It was a good time to be born, a good time to absorb the exalta-tion of a growing understanding of the world. But it was also a world that was so much more complicated than I could have imag-ined. In 1953, an unknown, lower-middle-class girl with French-Canadian roots named Grace Metalious sent her manuscript to publishers. She had penned a hot and steamy novel that would even-tually become *Peyton Place*, though it didn't hit the bestseller lists until 1956. Using her own experiences and fears she conjured up the sad story of Betty Anderson, a girl from the wrong side of the tracks.

Metalious chronicled the lust, sexual intrigue and loneliness of a fictional small town. One of the characters, a teacher, laments the wasted effort of teaching the children of the "sad little town" about the Roman Empire, knowing that the boys will spend their lives milking cows and the girls will use their basic math skills to count the months of each pregnancy. When I was older I would think of the Bettys of the world and of the teachers, like my mom, whose mission must have been so frustrating at times.

Some have even traced the roots of the modern feminist move-ment to Metalious' blunt descriptions of sexual politics and the problems affecting women in the rapidly changing modern world. They may be right. It certainly made me think about what I wanted my future to look like. Then again, 1953 was also the year Hugh Hefner started publishing *Playboy* magazine and Harvard doctors were beginning to explore the idea of a contraceptive pill. Canada's Roman Catholic bishops responded by condemning the practice of teens "going steady." I was, as the Chinese curse says, born into interesting times. And I am grateful for it.

Recently, Mark Kingwell was a guest on my program, *Pamela Wallin*. He's a thirty-something philosophy professor at the University of Toronto and, in my opinion, one of the best young minds in the country. He observed that in the media madness about the inevitable millennial moment, we have yet to declare a slogan to sum up the Nineties. The Nineties was supposed to be the decade of responsible individualism, a kinder, gentler response to the fear and greed of the Eighties. It's not.

Mark's theory is that the Nineties is simply the decade in which we remember, sometimes nostalgically, the preceding four decades, which make up the Boomer's reference point. The Nineties, he contends, has been about sampling the politics, the styles, fashions and memories of simpler times—because we know or perhaps fear we may be about to face massive changes in the world.

Writing this memoir is a sampling of my life over the last four decades. I can only hope that those who have gone down the forty-something road ahead of me are right when they contend that there's plenty more "prime time" to be had.

But back in 1953, while suburbia was a new but spreading concept, rural culture was still dominant. I was part of that rural culture and, though I couldn't have known it at the time, I'm sure that even Wadena had a bit of Peyton Place in it.

1

The Centre
of the Universe

To thine own self be true.
—WILLIAM SHAKESPEARE

OR ME, the centre of the universe will always be Wadena, Saskatchewan. And even though I live in Toronto, the city that smugly claims that title for itself, I will always see the world through the prairie lens. I never read between the lines of a breaking news story or scan the research for an interview without looking at the facts and the feelings involved from that born-and-bred prairie perspective. So when the inevitable question arises, "Would they care about that in Wadena?" I never hesitate to make a phone call.

My parents are still there, and so is my sister, Bonnie, and her husband, Steve. They are my touchstones. I always test my thinking against theirs, my instincts against their reality. And it's not just about their take on the prime minister's latest gaffe or some bureaucratic bungle. It's about what matters.

My father is a legionnaire, a longstanding member of a dwindling club of those who fought and served. I remember a conversation I had with him as he was preparing to attend a national convention where the hot issue was the wearing of turbans in the Legion clubhouse.

Some Sikh veterans had been turned away by a local Legion chapter in British Columbia and it had set off a national media frenzy. I called home, ready to chastise my father, knowing his very traditional views of the proper dress code. He was always a stickler for detail when it came to the November 11 ceremony or the funeral of a comrade.

I broached the topic with my assumptions in full view and his response was a sharp and pointed rebuke.

"First," he said, "as a citizen of this country I will defend our freedoms and rights and those who protect them."

"Second," he continued, "if the Sikhs were good enough to be recruited and brave enough to fight and die for this country, then who gives a good goddamn what they have on their head?"

So, long before the ballots were ever cast or counted, I had a sense that the convention vote would support the Sikhs.

The basic decency and fairness of my father's views are very much a part of the place I come from. I may not live in Wadena, but it'll always be home. It's where I go for Christmas.

If all the residents of Wadena, Saskatchewan, man, woman and child, went to a baseball game together at Toronto's SkyDome, they would barely fill the first two rows.

It's certainly not true that the most important thing about Wadena is its smallness; but its size, or lack of it, allowed my childhood to unfold in a manner unknown to most city kids. It was a little like the *Leave It to Beaver* years some of us look back on with nostalgia. As children in Wadena, we walked in a cloak of security.

That's not to say we didn't resent the "know it all, see it all" town busybodies who never hesitated to call our parents if they saw us riding our bikes hands-free or cruising Main Street with the wrong kind of boy. Bonnie always laughingly concedes that all the nosiness that drove us crazy back then is exactly the reason she decided to move back to Wadena to raise her children.

In the booming Fifties, suburbs, strip malls and television antennas were dramatically changing North American landscapes. But you could hardly tell in Wadena that the post-war future had arrived.

As kids, we would run errands without any concern for our well-being. We'd be sent off to the Red and White store to pick up groceries because Bob and Mary Somers, the owners, were neighbours who'd also make sure we left with the right goods. Mina and Hartley Graham did the same at their grocery store at the other end of the street. Wes Ottmann, a friend of Dad's and fellow legionnaire, ran the meat market. He loved kids and always let us sneak a peek into his big cooler at the back of the shop. Of course, this was long before *Rocky* made such scenes famous, but my sister and I were horrified and fascinated by the animal carcasses suspended on vicious-looking hooks.

Wilf Vellacott was another story. We were convinced he was the male version of the wicked witch and perhaps even had some little kids chained in the basement of his dingy and dusty general store that doubled as the bus depot. He scared the daylights out of us, but that didn't stop us from tempting fate or his wrath. It's amazing what horrors kids can conjure up in their heads and how that totally contrived sense of danger can outlast the youth that created it.

There's no denying Wilf was a little eccentric, but when I went back into his store as an adult, the man I discovered all those years later was warm and gentle and shyly confessed that he never missed a chance to watch me on television. He was proud, he said, that I had done so well.

As kids, we didn't need the pagers or cellphones that seem a must, especially for urban kids, these days. If Mom was in search of a tardy child or husband, she would simply call any of the shop-keepers on Main Street and they'd stick their head out the door, spot us and tell us to come on inside and call home. Wadena was one big Neighbourhood Watch.

The other comforting and convenient aspect of small towns is that businesses run in families. We have our own rivals for the Eaton family dynasty. The Banadygas ran the general store that became a Macleod's franchise, and then a Home Hardware, which is now run by their son Perry and his wife, Cindy. Even though Perry was still in grade school when I left town, I can call him from Toronto and ask him to pop over to Mom and Dad's to help them reset their VCR.

Displayed on the wall above my desk today is a framed piece of prose about the Wadena we grew up in, written and cross-stitched for me by my sister. It says in part:

> You know you're in Wadena when . . .
> You don't have to signal at Wesa's because everybody knows
>   that's where you turn.
> You can't walk for exercise because every car offers you a ride.
> Third Street is on the edge of town,
> and you can dial a wrong number and still talk for fifteen minutes.

By the mid-fifties, Wadena was home to about a thousand and a half souls and there was a good chance that anybody you passed on the street would be a friend or neighbour. It was a place where adults and children had little to fear. And if you were ever in need, you could count on someone being there for you. At the time, I didn't particularly value the town's enfolding community because I had no real understanding that life was different anywhere else. But that implicit security allowed me to grow up with a sense of self and place and confidence that has been invaluable to me.

I'm not about to start a movement, literal or figurative, to herd us back to rural towns as a means of making our own lives, or our children's, richer and safer. It would be difficult to be entirely convincing, since I live in downtown Toronto and, at least for now, I like it that way—despite the wailing sirens and pollution and lack of space.

But I do believe that the values of small-town Saskatchewan had much to do with the fact that in places like Wadena there are few strangers and, as a result, fewer dangers. It's hard to think of a better place to be a child. If I'm looking for formative influences, then one is my hometown—Wadena, Saskatchewan. The other, of course, is my family.

Though I believe very strongly that each of us must take responsibility for our own path, I never forget that in the catalogue of life's blessings, at the top of the list is a fortunate birth, and I was very fortunate.

I'm warning you now. What follows may read like a travelogue for a town or a paid advertisement for the family, but as far as I'm concerned, it's the truth. I feel I had a close-to-perfect childhood. That doesn't guarantee happiness or success, but it at least eliminates many of the obstacles that so many others find fatal to their aspirations.

Wadena is in the middle third, top to bottom, of a province most people know only from side to side. The name Saskatchewan usually calls to mind the view from the Trans-Canada Highway, which cuts straight through the southern part of the province, with dozens of little towns and hamlets and grain elevators on either side that you'll miss if you blink as you speed along.

The one city you will see is Regina, but even that you can easily by-pass. Wadena is about 200 kilometres northeast of Regina and about the same distance east of Saskatoon. It's at the intersection of highways 5 and 35. The name Wadena, which translates into English as "little hill," was suggested to CN by the Tolen family, who took the name from a town in Minnesota named after a Chippewa chief.

In the summer I still marvel at the physical beauty of the place. From the air, it looks like an elaborate patchwork quilt. From the ground, the quilt has depth and colour. Blue flax fields against the yellow of the canola or the gold of the wheat. The black patches of summer fallow that allows the land a season to breathe. I'm obviously no W. O. Mitchell, so I'll spare you further pale imitations of his evocative genius, but when I go home there is no better feeling than jumping behind the wheel of a car and spending a couple of hours just soaking up the scenery. Sometimes you can drive for an hour and never see another human being.

One of the many things I miss about Saskatchewan, now that I'm an urban dweller, is the big sky and the sound you can hear only when all others are silent. W. O. described it as the "hum and twang of the prairie harp"—the music of the wind as it glides along the miles of telephone wires.

There's plenty of good farming around Wadena, but there's little of the bald prairie about it. It's known as the Parkland. The top third of the province is almost unpopulated except for trees and lakes and remote native communities.

In the south where my uncle, Don Macfarlane, farms there is more of a sense of that *Jake and the Kid*–type prairie that's so well known, but that is a very different place from where I lived.

Even in my earliest memories, the sun is always shining from a bright blue sky. That's because Wadena is blessed with an incredible amount of sunshine, winter and summer. It can also have relentless weeks of brutally cold days and nights, but if the sun shines, somehow you can cope.

The town of Wadena had nine churches and a Jehovah's Witnesses' Kingdom Hall, two railway stations, two schools, a curling rink, a skating rink, a movie house, a Legion hall and three Chinese restaurants. It still has no traffic lights. Nothing was really missing for me as I grew up, though whenever I visited my grandparents in Moose Jaw I rode the one-floor escalator at Eaton's like a ride at Disneyland.

My parents moved to Wadena in 1952, the year before I was born. My father, Bill, was the chief x-ray technician at the Wadena Union Hospital, a handsome man with jet-black hair and skin that tans the minute the sun hits it.

My mother, Leone, was a teacher in the high school. She had a beautiful head of red hair and fair skin that freckled after just one day in the garden or at the ball diamond. She and Dad both played ball and loved to dance. In fact, they'd met at a dance and she'd fallen head over heels for the man in uniform—even though she was engaged to someone else at the time.

She was thirty when they settled in Wadena and Dad was a few years younger. It's been a never-ending family joke that he was her "younger man."

Doc Rollins, the town doctor, was a good friend and mentor to my dad. Doc had come to Wadena as a newlywed years before and, as many country doctors did, he'd survived by often taking goods in return for his services. Medicare was still years in the future. Since small-town life quickly makes generalists out of specialists, my dad shared as much of the hospital load as he could. He was essentially on call seven days a week. He wasn't a medical doctor, but he should have been. However, there was no money for that after the war so he took the x-ray technician training instead. Still, he could diagnose better than most.

Both my parents were attracted to the small-town life, and the fact that they're still there, forty-odd years later, supports their belief that it was the right choice. They were young and active in the community and since they both held positions of crucial importance in everyone's lives—the care of children and the care of the body—they were accepted into the social fabric quickly.

We were a two-income family, though neither paycheque was particularly large. My father was in a "management" position so he wasn't eligible for overtime pay, no matter how many hours he worked. My mother's teaching salary was slightly larger than his (a rare anomaly in those dark ages) but not by much and it didn't reflect the endless extracurricular hours she put in.

Our first home, a tiny two-bedroom house that my father did much of the work on himself, eventually had running water but no plumbing. It sounds somewhat nineteenth century, dragging the slop pail out to the honey wagon twice a week, but, like everything else in a contented child's life, the lack of modern conveniences wasn't a particular hardship. Sharing a bedroom with my older sister was, though, because age and the power of intimidation gave her the upper hand. Somehow, we've become better friends now than we could have dreamed of being then.

The truth is, as kids we never stopped fighting. Name a topic and we fought over it. Had I stolen her 45's ? Had she unearthed and read my secret diary? And who would get to use the electric rollers first?

Bonnie still carries the scar on her arm from a wound I inflicted deliberately just a day before a big date on which she was to wear a new sleeveless dress. She had to borrow a shawl to hide the unsightly act of revenge.

Bonnie was more outgoing, more social when we were kids. I won the points for studiousness, no small matter in our household with a teacher for a mother and a father who read voraciously. I was deemed by the powers that be to be "smart" and in those days, the system responded by moving us forward faster.

There were six of us who took grades four, five and six in two years. What that meant was that we were left to our own devices, expected to amuse ourselves and do our assignments without being goaded or cajoled. And, of course, we were the teacher's pets because we were, relatively speaking, easy to deal with. I'm sure this provoked resentment from the other kids, but we enjoyed our special status nevertheless. We ran errands for the teachers and were allowed to go off to the library. The downside was that I missed some basic math along the way and never really did grasp algebra years later. Fortunately, this mathematical black hole has seldom caused a crisis in my life and never seemed to hamper my ability to cover a federal budget. But one wonders about those who write them. Maybe they skipped a grade.

While Bonnie was becoming interested in the local male population I still thought of boys as being strange at best and repulsive at worst. As the older one, Bonnie had the tough task of breaking ground in the eternal struggle between maturing children and vigilant parents.

By the time I had to do battle for my independence, it was a considerably easier fight than Bonnie had faced at a similar age. But then again, she always pushed the limits and I seldom did. And, fortunately for me, I didn't have an obnoxious little sister tethered to my side.

My parents had concluded rightly that I would make a convenient chaperone for my sister—perhaps deterrent would be a better description—and as a result our relationship deteriorated.

When Bonnie had friends over or went out on dates she was also, simultaneously, required to babysit me. It wasn't an arrangement either of us liked, but for her I'm sure it was grounds for the tortures she imposed.

To this day I blame her for cementing my fear of the dark. One of the ways she contrived to rid herself of me when her boyfriend Steve (now her husband of thirty years) was visiting was to chase me into the bedroom onto the bed and then shut off the light switch next to the door and slam it closed. She knew full well I would be too scared of potential monsters under the bed to make my way across the room in the dark and turn the light back on, so it all but guaranteed I would stay shuddering out of her way for the remainder of the evening.

Bonnie and I are now best friends, and business partners too. Together we own the local beauty salon, The Special Effects Spa on Main Street, which only goes to show that the passing of years has a way of separating what's important from what seems to be. Her daughters, Erin and Meaghan, were and are the children in my life, even though they are both now in their twenties and Meaghan has kids of her own.

When they were old enough to get the joke, I always teased them that they had been my best form of birth control. A week with them and I'd happily return to my eighteen-hour workday just for a rest!

I remember one night when the girls called to announce breathlessly that they had seen me on TV. I was puzzled at their excitement as they'd grown quite blasé about Auntie Pam appearing on a television screen. "Well that's good," I said, because that's where I work." No, no, they insisted. They had seen a show that was all about me, or at least about my life as a television journalist. In fact what they had just seen was their first episode of *Murphy Brown*.

Meaghan Dawn carries my middle name, which for the first ten years of my life was the name I was known by at home and at school. It was only when I started to bristle under the accusation that I had a boy's name—I was named after my uncle Don—that I decided unilaterally to adopt my first name, Pamela. I'm not sure my parents quite approved of the sudden switch from the familiar, but they sympathized with my need to make my own decisions and didn't try to dissuade me.

Meaghan and Erin were wonderful kids, confident, well mannered, and our adventures together took us to places like New York City and Disneyland, and they occasionally came on their own to Toronto to visit. Aunts have an easier time saying and hearing things that parents can't.

Erin and Meaghan brought me great joy, but they also brought Bonnie and me together. We talk several times a week now and despite the distance, she is a person with whom I can and do share even my troubles and doubts. And our relationship, as friends and entrepreneurs, is yet another point of connection with my community.

Besides my parents and my sister, family close to me included my grandmothers, though neither lived in town. They both lived, by prairie standards, close by, and they and their husbands were a familiar presence in our lives. It was only years later, when I was introduced to feminism in the wave of passion and political theory that university life promotes in young people, that I realized I had been surrounded by feminism in its most practical form all my life.

My father's mother, whose last name was Piper by the time I knew her, lived in Tuxford, near Moose Jaw, where she and her second husband, Archie, ran the service station. My relationship with her, at least the most intense part of it, was still to come, but even as a child I knew that her life had been hard and I respected her.

Her first husband, my biological grandfather Wallin, was a Swede who first landed in the U.S. but then followed the cattle and the horses north to Alberta. He was an itinerant cowboy who eventually disappeared, leaving her alone to raise the six children he had fathered.

Grandma became a short-order cook and scrubbed floors in the local hotel in Granum, Alberta, to feed her kids. It was the Dirty Thirties. My father tells stories of how he and his siblings helped out by earning nickels and dimes doing farmhand work for the neighbours.

Grandma's new husband, Archie, appeared to me, compared with his predecessor (whom, of course, I never knew but had heard about), to be a good step up.

My maternal grandmother, Clare (we called her Nan), had been a homesteader in her younger years. At the turn of the century she had travelled with her husband, Colin Macfarlane, from her comfortable home near Peterborough to the "Wild West," where they built a life from scratch. The distinction made later between a working mother and a stay-at-home one was, to say the least, irrelevant for the pioneer woman.

Family history, perhaps apocryphal, says they bought land near where the railway was intended to run but that backroom dealings (backrooms in the East, that is) resulted in moving the tracks miles from their chosen location. The Macfarlanes' life was made much more difficult as a result. Mistrust for large financial institutions and the disregard of eastern-run big business were recurring themes as I eavesdropped on adult conversation. They're built into the western worldview.

Nan and her second husband, Russ—Bub to Bonnie and me— had retired to Moose Jaw. She and Bub had been married after my biological grandfather, Colin, died. Bub had been a bachelor and neighbouring farmer.

On many a Friday, right after school, the four of us plus Bubbles, our cocker spaniel, would load up the big black-and-yellow Pontiac and head south to Moose Jaw to visit Nan and Bub. My parents would be dead tired from the week, but family was important so we'd make the four-hour trek.

It was exciting for us kids. The winter trip through the icy hills of the Qu'Appelle Valley was treacherous, but Dad always had blankets, flashlights and enough food stored in the trunk that we could have survived for a week in the Arctic.

Eating in a restaurant or at a truck stop was still a rare treat and we always lobbied and whined until our parents agreed to pull in for a snack or a bathroom break. If that bathroom break became an emergency you could always use the ditch or the side of the road. On Saskatchewan highways the cars were few and far between.

It was always a thrill for me to see the bright lights of the big city of Regina suddenly appear in the night sky. Across the open prairies you could see the city's halo a fair way off. It meant the trip was more than half over. But there was also the lure of all the activity and people. And I loved the neon signs. I would, I knew, live in the city one day. But for now, just visiting was enough.

Each of my grandmothers was remarkable in her own way. And each introduced me to a different facet of the female experience and left me with a different entry point into what I would later identify as my feminist ideals.

Grandma Piper was philosophical—live and let live—in her approach to life, while Nan was both pragmatic and religious, though perhaps her religious side might be better termed as spiritual.

Each of them played a key role in my later life, but as a young girl, I knew only that they were strong, self-reliant and contented women. From both of them and from my own mother I learned that a husband is a partner, not a protector, and that you ought to choose a man because you love him, not so you can abdicate your own responsibilities.

And I learned that hard work has an intrinsic value beyond being the beginning of satisfaction. Learned only from books, these are ideas that can so easily become cant. Observed in action, they have an intense and inarguable truth.

Let me tell you one quick Nan story. Among my most prized possessions is her wedding ring. As a young wife she worked hard carving out a home and a life in the harsh, untamed prairies, and it was to her that the wives of the other homesteaders often turned in times of need. One of her many roles was that of midwife. She told me stories of how she would comfort and distract the would-be mothers by using her wedding ring to predict the sex of the unborn child, an act she performed by suspending the ring from a strand of the mother-to-be's hair, dangling the ring over her stomach and observing the direction of swing. To my knowledge, she was never wrong in her determinations.

When she bequeathed the ring to me it hadn't failed yet and it hasn't since. I have performed the "ring test" on many a pregnant friend.

Superstition, witchcraft, nonsense? Maybe, but not to me. Then and now I think of it rather as a form of deep sensitivity to forces you don't learn about in science class. Just reconciling her strong belief in what could be called intuition with her hard-headed, practical nature was an important step for me into a world that contained the possibility of quite different kinds of perception than I was used to.

Nan was convinced that a pregnant woman has an unscientific but sure knowledge about the life growing inside her, an understanding that could be transmitted through a strand of her hair to a person willing and capable of hearing the message.

Her sixth sense was always strong. It was uncanny, but throughout my life Nan always seemed to know when to call and what question to ask when one of us was in need. And she always did. I grew up believing in women's intuition and in the certain knowledge that some aspects of being are uniquely female. Economics might be one aspect of female concern, but Nan's ring was another. Men and women could be equal, it was saying, but that didn't mean they weren't different in many important ways.

As kids, Bonnie and I saw the Pipers less frequently. Grandma Piper was tall and dark and a handsome, though not pretty, woman. Archie was a short, round, red-faced, hot-tempered Scot. His accent sometimes made him incomprehensible, especially when he was yelling. But despite all the bluster, he seemed to like us, and he always gave us free run of his gas station in Tuxford, which meant access to the chocolate bars and Cheezies and pop. Our two cousins Barb and Deb also lived in Tuxford and they were the same age as Bonnie and I so we had instant companions.

But even more important than the unlimited candy and the freedom for the four of us girls to run wild was that Archie would let me play with the cash register and the real money inside. I was so taken with this amusement that Mom and Dad gave me a toy replica for Christmas and I made change to my heart's content.

But Tuxford was even smaller than Wadena, and kids have short attention spans. So the trips to see the other grandparents held more appeal.

Among all the wonders of a visit to Moose Jaw, the highlight was surely being chauffeured like royalty to the Dairy Queen in Bub's big green Buick with its pristine interior usually protected by plastic except on important occasions. He trusted me so much that he even let me hold the ice cream on the trip back to the house, although had I spilled on those seats I'm not certain his good nature or my young life would have lasted. The DQ forays ranked as high as a trip to Joyner's Department Store, where the business transactions were conducted by sending cash and bills of sale around the store and up to the cashier in little boxes that looked like miniature rail cars that ran on cables suspended from the ceiling.

Sometimes Bub and I would watch wrestling on TV or maybe the evangelists preaching to the sinners. It didn't matter much what we watched, just that we did.

Though it's impossible not to make them sound noble, it has to be said that my grandfathers, like their wives, also laid groundwork for my later forays into feminism. They, as well as my own father, showed me that men could be kind, loving and generous, which helped me to come to sexual politics from concern with the issues rather than from rancour. They were all good role models before the phrase was in vogue.

Needless to say, my relationships with my parents were more complicated. Grandparents don't have to dispense discipline. Parents do. And both my mother and my father were hard-working and busy. That's the kind of people they are to this day.

They were both in a line of work that drew them into after-hours participation, and so much of the activity in a town the size of Wadena is community-based and self-generated. If the parents went, the kids went too. If my mother was in charge of the lunch at a funeral at the church, then I'd be around somewhere serving tea and sandwiches with their crusts cut off. If she was putting on a play down at the hall, then I was a willing gopher.

My mother's love of teaching had a profound effect on me, though I must say that it was my father who imbedded in me the primary rule of education: "Look it up." It was always his first response to questions prompted by our homework assignments. He was approachable on any topic but only after we'd satisfied him that we'd met that first requirement. Our family collection of books rivalled the tiny town library, an annex attached to the firehall. At home, we had the bright red set of the children's *Encyclopaedia Britannica* and the wine-coloured grown-up version as well. Dad often sat and read the volumes, as engrossed as if he were reading a novel. So I picked up the reading habit quite young. And, fortunately, I've never lost the pleasure of looking things up.

My mother taught English and literature at the grey school. It was the high school, but we called it the grey school because of its slate siding. The elementary school across the street was always referred to as the red-brick school. Much of Mom's activity revolved around her sincere attempts to communicate a love of the subject to reluctant pupils.

She would sometimes recruit Bonnie and me to help out marking the multiple-choice exams for her. It was easy to do—I just compared the test paper with the key. In the process, I felt not only her passion for teaching, but a sense that she knew I could be trusted with such an important task. Those are the gestures that help build a young girl's self-esteem.

Being in my mother's class though, which I was for just one subject (thankfully) in grade nine, was an unabashed pain. I felt the burden of public judgment, as if doing poorly at school would be broadcasting an insult to my mother all over town. I suppose it's comparable to being the child of a minister perhaps, or the town policeman. The standard of behaviour was higher. And there were always the taunts of my classmates that I scored good marks because I had prior access to the answers. The allegations angered me because it wasn't in my nature to cheat and my mother certainly wouldn't have been party to it. The truth is, I did well in school because it was important to me. I wanted to please my parents and that seemed like the most direct route. I laugh as I look back at the report cards that Mom has saved. I was always "industrious" and "attentive," and the only consistent criticism was that I talked too much. Now there's a news flash.

Much of what my parents taught me was about the core values that shape how you see the world. One virtue my mother instilled in me, by example mostly, was despising the sin and not the sinner, at least when the sinner is a child.

Many children from the surrounding area were bussed into town for school. Often I would hear my mother's regrets about the farm kids who would appear only after harvesting in the fall and would disappear again at seeding time in the spring, often failing school because of their absence, cutting off their options and pinning themselves for life. She lamented the perpetual absence from class of many of the native kids from the nearby reserve who were supposed to come into town for school but who never seemed to arrive. The few who came were often badly fed and Bonnie and I were always given an extra sandwich in case someone at lunch needed one.

My mother never let us forget that there were obstacles in place that made these kids' lives harder than our own. And if they were rough or angry, she reminded us, their behaviour was only a small bit of a story, with its biggest part hidden.

Wadena was definitely not a town without problems or problem people. But Mom constantly reminded us to blame the situation more than the child. She cared very deeply for all the young scholars under her care and never forgot their vulnerability to their circumstances.

Many of these insights I gleaned by osmosis or indirectly from casual conversation. Most Saturdays, after we cleaned our rooms and finished household chores, Bonnie and I would spend time in the kitchen, helping Mom with the baking. I learned a lot of culinary skills in that kitchen and I still love to prepare meals, but like my mother I seldom glance at a cookbook.

I also learned a little about life. Bonnie and I would ask about teachers or parents or rumours that were going around town and share our opinions and theories. And through our mother's responses we always learned the intended lessons.

Only once did she chastise me. One of our grade-school teachers was fondling our budding breasts during class and Mom was reluctant to believe my charges against one of her respected colleagues. She said, and I suppose it reflected the times, that I should explain to the other girls that we should sit in such a way as to make his unwanted groping impossible. We did and simply waited for year's end so we would move on to the next grade and out of his reach. Today, his actions would have cost him his job. But we all seemed to survive the experience without emotional scars.

In terms of spending time alone together, I was often with my dad, just the two of us. I think that's why I have always felt so at ease with men and have so many good male friends. Dad liked to hunt and fish and putter around. He had no sons, and Bonnie was totally uninterested in outdoorsy pursuits, so I would hang around with him and we'd go off to the lumberyard or hardware store for whatever was needed.

He taught me how to play crib and I even became a sometime hunting companion. I'm not talking about shooting moose or even geese here but gophers and other small things generally agreed to be a pain in the pasture.

There was a small shed in our backyard where my dad had once tried to raise chinchillas as a source of extra income. When the project proved to cost more than he could make, he soundproofed the walls and converted the space into a room of his own where he stored his guns and practised his aim.

We spent long hours out there together and, in a warm privacy that contained (in a way I later learned to think of as very male) few words, I learned to load bullets. I may be the only person I know in my current social circle who can make that claim. Although, the skill appears to be no more useful than algebra.

My father hunted to fill our deepfeeze with meat for the winter, and since he kept guns around, he believed we should know about them, largely for our own protection. And I do. I know enough about guns to know I don't ever want one in my house as long as I live in a city. But I'm not sorry to have felt the heft of a rifle or to have felt it explode against my shoulder, if only to have a clearer idea of why the idea of them touches me so viscerally.

I feel fortunate to have had the opportunity to experience an aspect of the rural life that's usually restricted to male children. And that sensibility informs my views today on issues like gun control. As my father is quick to point out, the laws for city folk simply don't make sense on a farm. He's right.

The anchors and centres of activity of town life were the church, the Legion hall and, from fall to spring, the curling rink. Our own church was the United and besides the usual Sunday business there were potluck suppers, teas to serve at, various charity events, rummage sales and, of course, the weekly meetings of c.g.i.t.—Canadian Girls in Training—our town's answer to Brownies and Girl Guides. The church basement, or rather the many church basements, provided a lot of what passed for entertainment in the town. Bake sales, post-funeral wakes, even bridal and baby showers, were often held there.

But it was the curling rink, conveniently located at the end of our street, where you could have plain fun with no pretence of seriousness. Becoming a curler was a rite of passage into adulthood, but before that the rink was simply a place where a young girl might be sure that the guy she had her eye on would likely appear. Bonspiel time was like a holiday. For two or three days over a weekend the rink was filled with kids running around or grabbing a hot dog or each other while mom and dad were otherwise cheerfully engaged.

The Legion hall was also an important place of community. Of course, the Remembrance Day service was the big event, but most wedding suppers and dances were held there and the New Year's Eve dance was such an event that my bachelor uncle Don—generally considered a "good catch"—would drive up from his farm south of Moose

Jaw just to survey the local scene. He always had a car with fins. And it was always exciting to see Uncle Don, not least because Bonnie and I thought he was rich. After all, he'd been to Vancouver and Hawaii.

He gave us transistor radios one Christmas, one red, one green. Of course we could only tune in one station (sometimes two if the weather was clear), but that didn't matter because we were the first kids in town with this new leading edge technology.

Uncle Don, Mom's only brother, was an important figure in our lives. He and Mom were close and so we became his surrogate kids. In the summer, Bonnie and I would sometimes go down to his farm to visit and "cook" for him. We loved that chore because it meant taking lunch out to the field and that meant we could climb in behind the wheel of his relic of a farm truck long before it was legal to do so. Before I could even reach the pedals, I was manoeuvring that old '53 blue Chevy down the back roads. Driving is one of those forbidden but irresistible freedoms when you're a kid.

Don had a way with animals—maybe he'd inherited some of those powers from his mother, Grandma Nan. In minutes he can teach any animal to do almost anything. His dog Kingo, a beautiful golden lab, had learned to survive life with a bachelor owner. If hungry and forgotten, Kingo would go to the cellar and bring up a can of food and drop in it your lap as a gentle reminder. Don loves to tell the story—although he swears it happened when a friend was dogsitting—about the time Kingo brought up an entire winter's supply of food, can by can, and placed it on the bed until his hungover master finally responded.

Outside of my family circle there were two women, both close neighbours, who remain vivid in my memories of growing up in Wadena. Grandma Smale lived next door and I knew her house as well as my own because she was my daycare when my parents were at work. She was paid for her efforts, but it wouldn't have been much and my dad did work around her yard and house doing such things as shovelling coal for the furnace. For my first several years

I would be at Grandma Smale's for much of the day and when I started school it was to her home that I went after classes.

Lily Smale was very old to my young eye and had retired in town after a life of farming. Her tiny box of a house always seemed dark to me, crowded with heavy furniture covered with her handiwork. She tried—and failed repeatedly—to teach me to crochet. Her home often smelled of baking and my first forays into the kitchen were under her watchful eye. I remember her for her gentle patience.

Then there was Mrs. Fair, Grandma Smale's back-up as a sitter, who lived across the street and down a house or two and helped inspire my first fantasies.

Mrs. Fair was a British war bride from the First World War and I strived to adopt her accent, without success. Though she didn't live in anything resembling opulence, I always found her house quite intriguing. She had kid gloves from Paris, France, that she let me wear, but only in the house. Years later, I bought a pair just like them with my very first paycheque. Her influence was one of the reasons that this kid living in small-town Saskatchewan grew up wanting to go to Paris, a dream I satisfied as a university student.

A widow whose son was miles away, Mrs. Fair loved to tell me stories of events, people and places more exotic even than Vancouver or Hawaii. She had a piano, and though our family did too, hers was about music, while ours was about lessons and endless hours of practising scales. She lived alone in a two-storey house that I remember as, like Grandma Smale's, always dark. She tried—and failed repeatedly—to teach me to knit. I was not destined to be the happy homemaker.

Mrs. Fair had a trunk in which she kept, among other old treasures, large photograph albums. We could easily spend an hour or more turning the heavy pages slowly as she told me about people I'd never met in places I'd never seen. She and Grandma Smale, each in a different way, helped a small-town girl think both distant thoughts and about the importance of home.

I lost touch with Mrs. Fair as I grew up and adolescent concerns replaced old associations, but even after I left Wadena for good I'd try to see Grandma Smale each time I returned for a visit. She, like my real grandmothers, was a woman who had worked long and hard and probably missed the farm desperately. I know that my visits filled her heart and were probably as important to her as she was to me. The elderly have a useful role to play in the community and can keep their spirits young by keeping in touch with those who are. Hillary Clinton captured the notion with her book *It Takes a Village (to Raise a Child)*. That's what happened in Wadena.

In her final years, Grandma Smale went back to the farm but not in the way she would have liked. Old and frail, she moved in with her son so the family could take care of her.

Every Christmas of my life she had presented me with a new pair of knitted mittens. The last time I saw her, on one of my visits home from university, she was barely able to move, but she had a pair of mitts for me, white and beige with red trim. I still have them.

One of the things I loved most about Wadena was my best friend, Shelley Peterson. She was dark-haired, pretty, taller and skinnier than I was. We met at a preschool day camp and became inseparable from the age of four. We wanted to be Siamese twins but settled for the next best thing—we spent every possible moment together. We tried to dress identically as often as possible, although the results were not always what I'd hoped. One year, probably around age nine, we bought matching gold, black and white bathing suits at the Robinson Store to wear at summer camp.

I had formed the opinion by then that taller and more slender were better so I was horrified to discover that I looked like the Goodyear Blimp beside her. She still threatens to blackmail me with the picture that captures the horrible truth. We were so intent on sharing everything that Shelley even tried to give me the wart on her index finger so we would have matching ones. We spent hours rubbing our fingers together but it simply wouldn't take.

Every day after school we went to her house, where her mom had fresh-baked brownies or buns with butter waiting for us. We read and reread every Nancy Drew and Trixie Belden book ever printed, we had our Razzle Dazzle secret decoder rings and we talked pig latin on the phone, convinced our parents were stumped by our top-secret communications.

Shelley was the youngest of a large family, and, perhaps because her mother and father were well beyond the overprotectiveness of the less-experienced parent, her home felt luxuriously lax to me. If I slept over at her house we didn't have to sneak out at night. We used the front door. Shelley, on the other land, felt a certain exotic security in the more parentally overseen routines of the Wallin household. It was a fair and satisfying exchange.

Shelley and I did adult things together. We saved our allowances so we could go out to the Wadena Cafe for Chinese food and discuss life, boys and our futures. We went to the movies on Saturday afternoons, where the Gidget or Elvis film was to us what the western flick had been to young matinee-goers a decade before: an essential weekly event. And we prided ourselves in noticing mistakes in the continuity and, if you can believe such a thing possible, holes in the plot!

One of the less-adult things Shelley and I did was to contrive, one gentle spring evening, to run into Kelly Peace and David Russnel, two very cute schoolmates, in the playground beside the red-brick school.

We had, as best friends do, negotiated the details of the school-yard entrapment. We staked our claims in advance, she on David and I on Kelly, but after a bit of hanging out we all seemed to think that a switch was in order, and David Russnel eventually became my first boyfriend. That summer, out at the lake, on the road behind the cabin my dad had built, David kissed me for my first time.

These were such great moments and provided endless fodder for Shelley and me as we imagined dating and weddings and practised writing our first names with the boy's last. My family approved of our innocent romance. Our fathers were good friends and were, conveniently, neighbours at the lake.

I now own the compact little A-frame cottage on Fishing Lake that Dad had built, with telephone poles and great difficulty. Shelley and I spent many summers there creating our fantasy futures. She was almost always with me. Among the many things we discovered about life during those long summers was a whole new language from some deaf kids who spent the summer at a cabin up the road and who spoke only with their hands. Shelley and I used sign language back at school that fall, frustrating the teachers to no end. They couldn't really tell us to shut up, now could they?

Shelley and I have never lost touch. We remained friends through university, and though sometimes one or the other of us has dropped her end of the thread that joins us, we've always been able to pick it up again as if no time has passed. She stood up with me at my wedding and I am godmother to her daughter Meagan, whose middle name is also Dawn. I call her Meagan Jr. and our time alone together is very special. She loves the cabin as much as her mother and I did and now she brings her friends to the lake.

For many years, wherever either of us was living, Shelley and I sent a birthday card to the other—and I mean the same birthday card. I think we picked up the idea from a book in which two friends had started a tradition of sending a single card back and forth between them and had continued doing it all their lives. Though Shelley and I both lived in the same town only a few blocks apart, it was an idea that appealed to our desire to prove the importance of our friendship. We kept the correspondence up through university and beyond.

I chose the card initially—it was white with a red rose on it—and whoever had it would sum up her year in one line and mail it off, knowing she'd find it back in her own mailbox when her birthday came up. Over time the card followed Shelley to Texas and me to Ottawa and Toronto. One year, because we were struck by the weight of history the card contained and felt sharply how terrible the loss would be if it ever went astray in the mail, Shelley sent it by courier. They lost it. We cried long distance. We begged the courier company to find it. We threatened legal action. They promised to reimburse us for the value of the card, but I pointed out that the purchase price of ten cents wouldn't ease the pain. Actually, I was far less polite than that. I still don't trust couriers. Despite the post office's bad reputation for speed (or lack of it), at least they hadn't lost it. Shelley and I have never instituted a replacement, but we're very careful now not to let our communications lapse.

Although Shelley was my constant and most intimate companion, it was with another friend, Bev Franks, who lived across the back alley from me, that I experienced an important lesson of adolescence. Bev's family was Catholic—mine was Protestant—and we were about thirteen when she invited me to come to Mass with her.

Though I'd been in every church building in town, I'd never been to a service at any but my own. So I was curious to know what could be so different. My mother, I remember, was dubious.

I think kids are always a bit older inside than their parents know (though a bit younger than they think of themselves), and my mother's fear was probably that I wanted to go merely as an entertainment. In the end she let me go with Bev, but not before I gave my solemn promise to take it as seriously as I might my own service, and to remember that I was not a participant but merely a guest at someone else's mystery. I kept my promise. And I found that my mother was absolutely right. It wasn't frivolous entertainment but the beginning of an understanding about difference and sameness in both the form and content of other people's personal places. Wadena is a small town but not too small to learn some of life's lessons.

The underside of the smallness that encourages caring is the limitation of possibilities. An evening's entertainment as a teenager was largely restricted to driving up and down Main Street doing swooping U-turns at each end of the run. "Making your own fun" meant that some of my school friends were pregnant at sixteen and local judgment on them was instant and harsh. Some of the girls compounded their mistake by marrying the father because that was offered to them as a moral solution. My parents' response to these incidents was always practical rather than philosophical. Whatever future I had in mind, they would remind me whenever the opportunity arose, having a baby at seventeen wasn't likely to enhance it. They were very convincing. I would be saving myself for the right guy at the right time.

So, was it a perfect childhood in a perfect place? To me, Wadena was friendly and safe, a wonderfully protective cocoon from which I could later emerge to confidently fly off to Moose Jaw, Regina and beyond. It wasn't so, however, for every child in town. From my father I heard about parents from the reserve who would feed their young children soap whenever a government cheque arrived so the hospital would babysit their "sick" child for a weekend while mom and dad partied. I remember the rape of a local native girl and the subsequent disinterest in prosecuting the white boys—whose identities, it appeared, were known to many. I remember the small building beside our school where the ten or so kids from the area with mental or physical disabilities were taught and remember that all of us kids, with no apology (or even a thought that one might be needed), called it the "RE-tard School."

These are not pleasant memories and they certainly don't define the community. But our response to these darker aspects of life did help define some of the issues that all kids have to confront: tolerance, difference and the idea that life isn't fair.

Can you learn tolerance, or teach it to your children, in a place where everyone seems the same? There's more diversity to the small community than might appear to a big-city eye, and my parents never let us forget how privileged some people, ourselves included, were compared with so many others.

Wadena was a community of immigrants, Ukrainians, Swedes, Norwegians, Poles and Germans, but the mosaic was more a melting pot. The only black person who came to town during those years, a nurse at the hospital, married a local man and quickly and easily became a part of the community. There were three families of Asians; each ran one of the three Chinese restaurants and the kids were separate from us more because of the unimaginable amount of work they did between school and the family business than for any other reason. The half-dozen denominations of Christians (I didn't meet my first Jewish person until university) managed to co-exist quite well.

So yes, I still find a tolerance there that amazes me.

Take my sister, Bonnie. I see in her life and in her work the kind of values we were taught as kids. Against the odds and those old notions about difference, she has integrated a real workplace, not a workshop, for the mentally and physically challenged into the community, along with the group homes where the clients live and learn life skills. They don't just make baskets. They run, among many other projects, a catering service for weddings and banquets, a shoe repair, the dry cleaners and a furniture shop, and manage the town's recycling efforts. It wasn't always an easy battle, but Bonnie made her converts, one at a time, by proving the mentally challenged could be contributing members of the community. Despite their own disabilities, they willingly lend a helping hand to the elderly or those less fortunate or more vulnerable than themselves.

Bonnie does more real and valuable work in a day than most and gets less credit than her more famous sister. But Bonnie believes in making a difference, or at least trying to. And she is the proof that a caring community is not just possibility but a must.

When *The Globe and Mail* asked me recently to write a brief article on my thoughts on Canada as we approach the millennium, what I wound up writing about was my fear that we might lose the values that my sister lives and practises. With the decline of community we may not have much reason left to actually like and care for one another in the future. I sometimes feel part of a society where civility is eroding and tolerance is fading. Urbanization is creating a kind of social amnesia where no one is anyone's keeper. Our "gated" lifestyle has broken our faith, loyalties and trust in one another.

Individual values and shared practices collectively equal a community. But those values and those practices are harder to share in these more driven, self-centred times. And the situation is exacerbated by government funding cuts to services that many have come to expect and certainly need. We may have balanced the books, but have we rebalanced the social contract to sort out who will be responsible for filling the void and meeting the needs of the needy?

Small towns are not perfect communities. They are flawed and not spared the petty politics that you inevitably find at the office or in the cabinet room or permeating the bureaucracies we've set up supposedly to help those in need. But at least it is still possible to extend a helping hand in the Wadenas of the world.

There are no homeless, because everybody has somebody or at least somewhere to go. And personal needs and foibles are more easily accommodated. If you know that Mrs. Smith doesn't drive quite as well as she used to, then you make a point of giving her a lift more often or a clear berth when you see her car coming down Main Street. And if you know the recently widowed Mr. Jones could starve to death before he figures out how to use the microwave, then you, and all the others, will be at his door with dinner until he learns.

In the city, it's so much easier just to send a cheque to some charitable organization fronted by a celebrity than to help your neighbours, especially when the celebrity is sending you his or her message in well-produced, thirty-second bursts several times a night and your neighbour is silent and invisible.

Caring, I know, can't be legislated. But it bothers me that when we send that cheque, the government recognizes the act and even pays you back some of it in the form of a tax refund, but when my father builds a wetlands bird sanctuary, or my mother makes and delivers a meal for a neighbour, or my brother-in-law answers a midnight call from someone who has fallen off the wagon, or my sister takes a lonely client into her home because his or her family won't, the government gives them neither recognition nor compensation. This is the behaviour that should be recognized and rewarded.

Today, living as I do in the largest city in the country, my return trips home are a reminder of what's been lost as urbanization and galloping technology redefine the concept of community. I don't dispute that one can care and be cared for in the middle of a metropolis, or that an isolated person who finds friendship on the Internet has an improved life. But I do worry that being surrounded by strangers makes it easier to remain—and feel—invisible and unresponsible, and that the anonymity and distance that come with technological association can do the same.

We are living in a multi-channel universe where the whole world can come together as a community of mourners for a beautiful princess none of us knew, but do we watch the channel that shows us the hungry or the war-mangled or the lonely? And if we do, do we consider them as part of us? The kind of personal, face-to-face talk about local issues that was once a staple of town post offices, community halls and corner stores has been replaced by a worldview fed by the talk-show vision of vituperation without responsibility.

Wadena was hardly a perfect community, but it gave me safety, confidence and a wide-enough range of experience to fill my growing lust for knowledge and newness. From my parents I learned, among much else, curiosity, an appreciation for hard work and the habit of concern for others' lives.

I learned a lot growing up in Wadena, Saskatchewan, and I'm glad the town is still there, at the centre of my universe, as a reminder of what really matters most.

2

Social Work

Any education worthy of the name is bound to be dangerous.
— L. NEIL, a teacher

I N TOWNS and small cities all across the country there are young people laying plans for escape. I was never one of them. I always knew that I'd go to university, which, obviously, meant "away," but I was never determined to get out or stay out, nor were my fantasies necessarily set in the big city. It wasn't about where; it was about what. And I was so absolutely positive about my future career. By a quite early age it was set: I was going to teach French.

The idea of being a French teacher took hold when Bonnie and I were visiting my uncle Don on his farm near Viceroy, south of Moose Jaw and just north of the U.S. border. We were out driving one day and Uncle Don took us to the abandoned building where he and my mom had gone to school. There, in the damp, long-deserted cellar of the old one-room schoolhouse I found a mouldy, mice-eaten French textbook. Something about it captivated me, some mix of the mysteriousness of the surroundings, the exoticism of the text.

In a way I had been prepared for this moment by Mrs. Fair and those kid gloves from France. That day in the musty cellar connected in some way with my earlier ideas of the grown-up world and its possibilities. Anyway, there and then I chose my career, a plan that remained unchanged until university.

As it turned out, the decision to leave Wadena, even before university, was made for me. Just as I was finishing grade nine my mother discovered that she would have to upgrade her teaching qualifications. She had gone through teachers' college—normal school, as it was then called—but that qualification was no longer enough for her to be guaranteed a job teaching high school with reasonable pay. She needed a university degree. My sister, Bonnie, had set the family precedent by attending the girls' school in Moose Jaw and living with our maternal grandmother. Now that Mom was going to be away five days a week, my parents agreed that I'd be under more of a watchful eye with both my mother and my grandmother to share the duties than if I stayed behind in Wadena with my father. I didn't agree. I fought against it, as my mother says, like a "blue steer." Alternately I threatened to run away and promised to be good and do exactly what Dad said if I could only stay, but I lost the battle. So that was that. My mother and I moved to Moose Jaw. The plan was that we would live there with my again-widowed grandmother Nan. My mother would commute the sixty-five kilometres to and from the Regina campus daily and on weekends we would return to Wadena.

Initially I went back with her on Friday evenings, but before long I had a job to go to on weekends, and even though I had a father, a boyfriend and my pal Shelley to tempt me back, I was slowly being pulled into my new universe. Even in the summer I didn't go back that much because earning money became too appealing.

Central Collegiate Institute in Moose Jaw, where I started grade ten as soon as we were settled, had inside its walls the equivalent of half the population of Wadena. All teenagers. It was intimidating, to say the least, and I took a wrong turn or two in trying to fit in. My snappy, paper tent dress—it was made of a J-Cloth-like fabric, a gift from my American aunt Fran—failed to impress, as did my zebra pants and white go-go boots. But I kept at it. And it didn't take long to find what every teenager is obsessively drawn to: a group and a social life. The catch was that to earn my spending money I needed a job. The Co-op in Moose Jaw was a combination bakery, grocery store, cafeteria and social hall. I spent Thursday and Friday nights and all day Saturdays there, first in the bakery and then, by the next year, in the cafeteria. If there was a function happening in the hall on Friday or Saturday evening, I often waitressed as well. I resented the effect this inconvenient obligation had on my life, especially since I was the only one of the kids I hung around with who had to work, but I loved the income and the independence that the job afforded. Not to mention that from time to time it provided a much-needed excuse to say no to a date that might have been embarrassing or filled the void when a date was not to be had. Funny that girls didn't think they could say "no" to a date, even if the guy was completely uninteresting.

But I also truly enjoyed the camaraderie with my fellow workers, who were quite different from any of the other people in my life. Most of the people I worked with at the Co-op were adults with full-time jobs, supporting families—very unlike the students who worked, if at all, on weekends for spending money. However much one gripes at the time, in retrospect, of course, it's much easier to see the imposed responsibilities of teenagehood as valuable when one does finally join the real world. It's a combination of adult perspective and smug self-satisfaction that makes it easier for us to recommend such responsibilities to the next generation.

What I missed by working weekends were two of the most common recreational activities shared at the time by my peers: driving up and down Main Street, and going dancing at Hernando's Hideaway or Temple Gardens, a dance hall where live bands from the area performed. Even when my mother was young, the Gardens was definitely the place to go on a Saturday night. Though I did go the odd time after my shift, I was usually in the wrong mood for it, after serving a couple of hundred suppers at the Co-op. And I always smelled like kitchen grease.

But there was another activity that I didn't miss out on and it's more problematic to talk about. I was a precocious, curious teenager at a time when you could watch the Vietnam War like a mini-series on your television over supper. On my fifteenth birthday, in April of 1968, Martin Luther King had been dead less than a week and, as I blew out my candles, four American cities were still burning in the aftermath of his murder.

In June it was Bobby Kennedy's turn. In August the whole world could watch the Chicago police at the national Democratic Convention smash the heads of people not much older than myself with truncheons until they bled, all captured by the camera. Nineteen sixty-eight was also the year that Pierre Trudeau, so remarkably different from Lester Pearson or John Diefenbaker, rode triumphantly through Moose Jaw in a convertible, with the car-hops from the A&W, dressed in their orange-and-brown uniforms adding local colour and enhancing a reputation Trudeau would strive to maintain for decades.

I'm not trying to say that I was a teenage news junkie or political activist. Quite the contrary. I didn't pay any more attention to the situation outside my immediate community than did most young people, but the events set the tone. The social turmoil that pervaded the times produced an environment that permeated every community that was wired.

It was a backdrop that included everything we now sweepingly refer to as "the Sixties," and even in Moose Jaw, "grass" was almost as easy to find as beer. The choice, or so it seemed then, wasn't between smoking pot or not smoking pot. It was between smoking pot or drinking alcohol. Not that the two groups didn't overlap, but there was a temperamental difference between the smokers and the drinkers, and the easiest way for me to characterize it is to say that each had a very different idea of what constituted a party. The drinkers—most of whom were sports-minded, either football players or cheerleaders—got together, played the stereo loudly and danced. The smokers—less likely to be prom king or queen—got together, played the stereo loudly and talked (or tried to over the din) about Issues.

I wasn't predisposed to becoming a drinker for a number of reasons. Alcohol didn't have much of a presence in our house when I was growing up, I didn't like the taste and I believed that it made people—and this, I think, is especially true of teenagers—too often act crudely and irresponsibly. On the other hand, I've always loved to talk.

I'm not going to argue that when the group I hung around with talked we were on a par with an Oxford debating society. Shakespeare said (though, admittedly, in a slightly different context) that drink "provokes the desire, but it takes away the performance." He might just as well have been talking about marijuana and deep talk. There isn't a budding writer from that time who hasn't had the experience of committing profound ideas to paper after one of those intense discussions only to find, in the morning, that the profundity has fled in the night and been replaced by drivel. I was no exception.

Drugs didn't make us any smarter, but the circumstances and the company may have made us a little more thoughtful. I learned that there were some very large questions out there, and felt the pungent pleasure of trying to address them.

As well, the "scene" brought me into contact with a group of people who were generally a bit older than I was. Even though the events depicted nightly on the television news were not very real to them either, it was through that crowd—the music we listened to and the conversation it sparked—that I was first awakened to the political ferment bubbling outside the city limits: the war and the draft, the sexual revolution, social inequities and, perhaps the biggest of all because it included, it seemed, everything else, the place (and the power) of the young in a rapidly changing society.

One of the more long-lasting effects on my life of my flirtation with pot—besides learning to enjoy asking new and enormous questions—was, as I said, that I found myself among people who were older. That environment led to every parent's nightmare, at least every parent of a daughter. I fell for a boy who was "older" and, by any mother's standard, bad.

It was, in its Elvis way, extremely romantic and it changed my life, or at least guided it down an alternate route. I was at a party with a group of people in their early twenties. I was not yet sixteen. A good friend of mine, Joan Miller, was dating one of them and I had come along with her. Since I didn't really know anyone, I was sitting alone on a staircase, watching the room, listening to Janis Joplin belting out songs filled with her unique brand of pain. She was screaming her most well-known hit, "Piece of My Heart," an emotional plea from a masochistic woman to her cheating lover to break her heart again (and again and again), when he threaded through the room toward me.

He was tall, dark, handsome and obviously Bad. I was mesmerized and flattered. John, he said his name was, and he told me that he'd been watching me across the proverbial crowded room, that he found me attractive and that this would always be our song. John and I stayed together for over three years, a third of it dating, a third of it living together (after I went to university) and a third of it with me visiting him every Saturday morning in the provincial jail. Every mother's nightmare, indeed. And yet, in so many ways, an absolutely pivotal experience for me.

My attraction to the idea of the "bad boy" is an intriguing one for me to look back on. I suppose any shrink would say that it all starts with one's father. Mine could hardly be characterized as the outlaw type but he is very masculine and a little mysterious. He's muscular and fit, likes to hunt and fish and can fix almost anything, in addition to being sensitive, intellectual and knowing his way around a kitchen. And that was my idea of what a guy should be: a mix of the macho with the thoughtful—but who also appeared to have lived in a way that my teenage male contemporaries hadn't. I liked boys with an edge to them. They were invariably older than I was by several years, had cars of their own and exuded masculinity but with a tinge of introspection. Macho but caring and sensitive.

John was one of those guys, though some of his behaviour could have caused us a lot of grief. Although he worked, he and his buddies used to do a little shoplifting from time to time. When I found out, after we'd been together for a short while, I was morally troubled, but I have to say it fit the bad-boy mythology perfectly. And there was always something Robin Hood-ish about his excuses for stealing: there was a need and never enough money.

Perhaps that's how I justified it to myself. It was never gratuitous or for profit so I never refused his gifts, though I always had my suspicions about where they came from. Legalities aside, he suited the tone of the times. He was clearly a rebel against convention and I liked that.

I'm glad to say I've grown out of that particular attraction as it relates to partners. But I'm also amazed that it hasn't completely lost all its appeal. When Julian Austin, the brawny and talented country singer who has done his fair share of time in jail (where he had time to work on the muscles) was a guest on my program, I instantly felt a connection with him. And despite his initial reluctance to talk, the meeting caused me to remember, quite fondly, my earlier days with John.

Some girls I knew, even back then in high school, were always appraising potential boyfriends in terms of their future prospects or earnings. I was more interested in what I could share with them in the present. My attraction was always for the guys who were the most interesting and not the guys voted most likely to succeed.

Fortunately, a highly developed sense of duty and obligation, and of right and wrong, nurtured by my parents was always there as a balance.

There were, of course, different draws on my attention than just my social life. My mother and I were living with my grandmother, who was well into her eighties by then. On weekends and during summers I was alone with her, and with my mother away so much, I was responsible for most of the day-to-day household chores. Of the three of us, I had the most time and energy, so I shopped, cooked and cleaned. As I grew closer to my grandmother I was growing more able to see her as a real person with a history. Grandparents always appear in a child's life already "old." Sometimes it is hard to remember that they too once were kids, or young and in love, or capable of mistakes.

Kids often find it impossible to talk to their parents openly. But grandmothers—well, that's a different matter. I could tell Nan almost anything and confess almost any doubt or fear, of which there were many in those teen angst days.

In my last year of high school, my grandmother and I spent a good deal of time together as Mom had returned to Wadena. Because it was often just the two of us at home, it was during this time that she became truly three-dimensional for me, rather than the kind of unexamined stick figure that relatives can be to a child.

It was also during this period that I began to sleep with one eye open, always attentive for evidence Nan was okay, or at least not in need of me. This was the beginning of chronic insomnia that has never really abated. I give Nan credit though, because I probably wouldn't have accomplished half of what I've managed to in life if I had become accustomed to eight hours of sleep a night.

Nan and I liked each other immensely. However, I was aware, even at that self-involved time in my life, that having a teenage girl around was a pleasure that might wear thin when a visit stretched into a joint tenancy. I knew she worried about me, so I intentionally kept her anxiety level as low to the ground as possible. Occasionally that called for some philosophical manoeuvring. I knew I was involved in activities that would concern her, but I excused myself by doing them, as much as possible, at home so she'd at least know my whereabouts. Nan worried most when I was out of "our" house, but she was always prepared to welcome my friends. That gave me room to let my friendships flourish and gave Nan the comfort of knowing where I was. The fact that Nan was also a bit hard of hearing was to everybody's advantage. So my high school days continued, pulling me with equal force in two directions.

One direction compelled me to gaze outward toward the future, political and theoretical, stamped with the curious blend of optimism and cynicism that characterized the times. The other direction brought me, through a growing understanding of my granmother's personal history, to a deeper connection with the past. My relationship with Nan grew even stronger after I left to attend university and acquired a deeper sense of the "real" world and of the particular place of women in it. It's too bad we're not always ready for our grandparents and what they have to offer until so late in our lives.

In the summer between high school and university my mother insisted I leave Moose Jaw and return home with her to Wadena. The reason, of course, was the boyfriend. Just as my grade twelve year was ending, John was stopped by the police while driving on the highway between Moose Jaw and Regina, and during a search they discovered some marijuana in his car. He was sentenced to a year in provincial jail in Regina. I certainly couldn't argue with my parents' concern, although I was convinced they simply didn't understand. But I was indignant, both at his punishment, which seemed extreme, and at the conditions I saw in the jail when I went to visit him. The following year, my first at university, that indignation was to mesh cleanly with a much larger sense of injustice about how the world around me worked, and it would change my plans considerably.

But that summer I reluctantly quit my job at the Co-op, said my farewells and did as I was told. My parents had been saving baby bonus cheques all my life in anticipation of this coming autumn. I would go to university, an option that had eluded both Mom and Dad, who were sure it would also elude me if I continued down my headstrong path. That fall I moved to Regina to go to the University of Saskatchewan and live, according to my parents' wishes, at the YWCA. I was sixteen years old.

I registered to take many of my first-year courses in the French language section of the Faculty of Education. My plan to become a French teacher remained, I thought, unchanged. By halfway through the year it became evident that I needed a new plan. My reading had shifted easily from Malraux and Gide, in whose world I felt a foreigner for more reasons than just language, to Friedan and Greer, in whose company I felt comfortable and whose stories, in spite of all the obvious differences, felt remarkably familiar. What were then quaintly termed "women's issues" became my new centre of interest.

I came to feminism purely because the issues women were trying to publicize and solve were so obviously valid, and not because I had any personal demons to exorcise. I was raised in a home where my mother not only had a full-time job but actually made more than my father, I had no brother to compete with, and I never even heard about battered wives until I was a teenager. John, my first adult relationship, was sensitive, open-minded and, despite our choice of "song," a wonderful, caring guy. As a woman I had no gripes.

What moved me, what stirred the C.G.I.T. soul in me, was the number of women who did. I hadn't suffered in any obvious way by being female. Instead I began to recognize in the lives of my mother, my grandmothers and so many of the women around me, those shadowy effects of sexual discrimination that are now commonly referred to as "systemic." It was no accident, I saw clearly now, that my mother had been passed over for promotion so many times.

It was also in first year that I went to my first protest march and I have to say I enjoyed it thoroughly. Political talk, though we never referred to it as such, had been a common occurrence around our house when I was young.

My father was involved in health care, so one of the greatest political battles in our national history, the fight over medicare, was a constant presence at our supper table. And my mother worked in education, a perpetual political mine field, no matter who was in power. And there was always talk about how the eastern powers didn't understand us, were ignorant of western dreams and desires and dismissive of prairie necessities. You didn't have to be a farmer to know what the Crow Rate was or how you felt about it. This youthful training prepared me for the activism all around me at university.

The Regina campus was a hotbed of radicalism in the early seventies, at least compared with Saskatoon's, which we dismissed arrogantly as the traditional, more conservative factory for doctors and lawyers. And that was the subject of my first sit-in: independence. The Regina students wanted our campus to separate from Saskatoon and go it alone.

When a group of us occupied the president's office the police were called in, but mostly for effect. All in all it was pretty tame stuff but very heady for a political neophyte. And it was so satisfying to be heard or at least to think we had been.

My routine was fairly regular during that first year. I had a room at the Y where I kept my possessions, but I lived mostly with my girlfriends from high school, Joan Miller and Marilyn Douglas, in an apartment on Retallack Street. I visited John at the jail on Saturday mornings and then I'd take the bus or hitch a ride back to Moose Jaw to take care of things at Nan's house. The transience was no fun—but it was then, as I was forming strong opinions about so many different issues, that Nan's history took on even greater depth for me. I was pulled, as before, in two directions, though, thankfully, not opposing directions.

As I worked with others on women's issues at the university, I was learning more and more from Nan and her life why the work I was devoting myself to needed to be undertaken. Nan had something for me that left-leaning, American and mostly male professors, however articulate and erudite, couldn't match. She had been a prairie midwife. When I tentatively raised the issue of abortion with Nan, a devoutly religious woman, I wasn't sure what her views would be. However, she smiled knowingly, as elders do when they watch their offspring rediscover the wheel. She told me simply, "We had our ways." That's when I understood that women's issues have been around as long as there have been women.

Every day at university was a revelation as I met more and more bright, involved, thoughtful people, both students and professors. And big-city living was suiting me well too. Regina is to Moose Jaw as Moose Jaw is to Wadena.

If only John hadn't been living behind bars. There's something about visiting someone you love in jail, about being frisked when you enter, about seeing him enclosed with people the sight of whom is chilling, that inspires an active desire to bring about social and political change. The combination of women's issues and a boyfriend in jail was a potent cocktail. I also had another learning experience that year that was potent as well—and I'm glad it was.

One weekend a group of us hitchhiked to Calgary to go to a Ten Years After concert. They were a well-known American rock group. We decided to drop in unannounced at a place where several friends from high school were staying. Lots of young guys from Moose Jaw had gone west to find work. We finally found the place, hoping we'd be able to crash there after the concert. What we saw was a horror show.

The house was filthy with garbage and excrement everywhere and it stunk to high heaven. The poor dog, obviously forgotten for days, had out of desperation relieved himself repeatedly all over the house. A couple of guys lay passed out on couches. One of our friends was sitting on the floor of the bathroom, with his head almost in the toilet. He'd thrown up all over himself. And there was a needle hanging from his arm. Within a couple of months, that friend was dead.

They had apparently been on a binge, drinking and shooting up for days. We were afraid to call the police because we'd get them into trouble—and there were no drug crisis hotlines to call. We made sure everyone was alive, and we left. It was a decision I've always regretted. If we had called an ambulance or the police our friend might still be alive. Then again, maybe not. These were the days when addiction was perceived as a character flaw—not an illness—and one that required punishment not treatment.

In the spring of that year—on May 4, 1970, to be precise—at an obscure university in Ohio, the National Guard shot into a crowd of students protesting American bombing raids on Cambodia. Four people my own age were killed.

The Kent State killings resonated particularly on university campuses and cemented the feeling among left-leaning students and staff that the world required changing. By the end of the school year, Career Plan B was emerging: I would become a social worker. And if I could save the world at the same time, well, that would satisfy me too.

That summer—between the first and second year of university—I went to study at the Collège de Bandol on the beautiful south coast of France. The trip had been planned since the previous autumn, when it had seemed to fit in so well with Plan A. As it turned out, the trip was still an unforgettable experience, just not as originally conceived.

A group of students, me included, lived in France for six weeks, studied the French way of government and immersed ourselves in French culture. In other words we spent as much time as possible in bars and restaurants and trying, unsuccessfully, to get tickets for the Rolling Stones concert in Marseille.

That month and a half was a truly mind-expanding time and it whetted my appetite for travel. I met students from across my own country and from around the world. And, predictably, I formed pompous conclusions about the world that only a naive seventeen-year-old could on her first trip away from home. The Parisians, I declared, were snobs, while the quaint French villagers who still hand-seeded their crops and hauled supplies with carts and horses were clearly "happier than we'll ever know with all our hustle, bustle and progress." Mom saved one of the letters I wrote home that summer and it was filled with such prosaic comments about the lifestyle of the French and their love of food and wine, followed by a critique of our "alleged progress" that had robbed Canada of such simple pleasures.

And if Mom and Dad hoped I would meet and fall in love with some nice young boy and forget the one I'd left behind, they were out of luck. I dismissed the potentials as spoiled brats shipped off for the summer by busy and distracted parents. They were "too high-class" or worse. I described one suitable boy who sort of liked me as "tolerable as long as he keeps his mouth shut." But, I declared with disgust, "he's an egotistical capitalist."

That summer marked the end of an intention I had carried, unquestioned, for years. I struggled with the choice of a new direction only in as much as I'm not a quitter and was never allowed to be one, despite my pleading over the unjustness of, for instance, unwanted piano lessons.

What replaced my childhood intention of becoming a French teacher, however, was stronger and more fitting and reflective of my new interests. By the second year of university I was studying, in English, toward a psychology degree, with an eye to social work. My experiences as a very concerned observer at the provincial jail gave me a new focus. As well, I found myself drawn to some of the many charismatic left-leaning professors—some of them draft dodgers from the States—and indulged my growing political passions: student politics and the women's movement. School itself, the actual passing of the courses, was made as easy as possible. There was a built-in contempt for "old-fashioned" education and we were subjected to few rigorous examinations. The term paper ruled and allowed a great degree of latitude for eccentricity. In some instances classes were an extension of those late-night conversations about the meaning of life, at least in terms of the topics we thrashed around. So many of the professors, it seemed, had a new take on things, a new way of seeing, of interpreting, of understanding. University was a boiling pot of talk, ideas and new perceptions and it caught me at the perfect time.

One teacher, just to pick an example, Bill Levant, gave an elasticity to my mind for which I am still thankful. His subject was psychology, but his text was not Freud or Jung or Skinner. It was Charles Darwin's *The Origin of the Species*, a seminal work first published in 1859.

The survival of the fittest and the struggle over the means to survive in nature was the perfect metaphor for capitalism and the psychology it creates. He used the book's revolutionary effects on Western thinking about where we had come from and how we'd evolved to illuminate the prevailing world view. In the process, he was teaching political science and philosophy, as well as sociology and biology.

Much of my university life is a blur. I never stopped running. The novel and sometimes bizarre hothouse atmosphere of a campus and of the times was formative and turbulent and fun.

John was eventually released from jail and we and a few others moved into a house together. One of our housemates was, like John, just out of jail. But Ray finally decided that life on the outside was too burdensome and he put himself back in again by holding up a store and waiting for the police to arrive. John, while certainly not that buffaloed by life in society, seemed a bit awkward in the midst of my student world. He loved to read and to deal in ideas as much as the rest of us, but it was clear that academia and formal studies and my budding feminist activism were redefining our future. Ultimately this would come between us.

My parents, despite their displeasure with my choice of mate, often stopped in Regina to visit and bring care packages, but my living arrangements were never openly acknowledged. I remember one occasion when my mother dropped in to one of our temporary abodes and I proudly swept open the doors to our large double closet as part of the house tour. Without a word or a sign, my mother quickly closed the door to the side where John's clothes hung, commenting that yes, it certainly was a good-sized closet.

During my university life I was also one of a group of remarkably energetic young women, including my friend Shelley, who had stayed in Wadena for high school but who was now in university in Regina, that opened the University Women's Centre.

We started small by asking for an office in the Student Union Building and we got it. It included a phone and maybe even a typewriter. We sent away to the States for some books and pamphlets on "radical" topics such as women's health. Soon the office was crammed with women who needed—or who wanted to provide—the kind of information that you can find with no difficulty today but that, at the time, you almost had to wear dark glasses and a trench coat to search for. It turned out that women had body parts, and very important ones, that some of us didn't even know we had. And there was, in the absence of reliable, accessible information, so much misinformation. I'll never forget the poor young woman who arrived one day in a tremor of anxiety. Could she be pregnant, she wondered, from what she described as heavy petting? She'd had no one else to ask, knew of no place to even look for an answer.

Though it wasn't impossible for a woman to get an abortion in Canada in the early seventies, it still was terribly difficult. Hospital boards passed binding judgment on a woman's level of need for the procedure, and the boards often included members openly antiabortion either for political or religious reasons. We tried to help women navigate that maze of hospital-board bureaucracy or, if necessary, suggested they go elsewhere, where the rules were less onerous. But above all we offered women information and education, an oasis in an environment that didn't appear to value them, at least where their health and reproductive freedom were concerned.

My political passion also led me to take a spot on student council. As academic chairperson my job was to book the speakers we brought onto campus. I used this opportunity to invite some influential woman to our university.

Robin Morgan, the radical lesbian and feminist poet from New York, raised many male eyebrows (and not in appreciation). The two witches—and I mean real, practising witches—caused even more criticism. But I soon learned it was the number of women and not so much the content of what they were saying that steamed some of the guys, even though the usual line-up consisted of a non-stop stream of men. It wasn't fair then and it's not fair now.

Though I never received any formal complaint from the university for the speakers I was booking I did receive a few grumpy comments from the leftist males who seemed to think that the ghost of Karl wouldn't approve. It gave me the feeling that the lefty guys were mostly guys first and lefties second.

Every woman who came to speak to us broadened our range of understanding and increased the reputation of the Women's Centre. And some of them gave us ideas as to what publications were out there. Just a year or so earlier, in 1971, the Boston Women's Health Book Collective had published *Our Bodies, Ourselves* in an attempt to give women more control over their health decisions. The more militant among us would have described it as "wresting control over our bodies from the patriarchal, male medical establishment." It was a must-have and we ordered it for the office. As well, we supplied literature on birth control and on that most contentious issue of all in women's lives: abortion. It had been completely legal to offer birth control information in Canada for only about a year at that point. Hard to believe. And the abortion battle had barely begun.

On the personal front, by the end of second year John and I had split up. It was a very sad event, but there was no acrimony. There was no one particular thing that caused the split. We were just going different places. During the nearly three years we spent together I'd experienced an emotional and intellectual growth spurt. It was a time of constant motion—small town to big city, high school to university, idealistic talk to feminist action—and I had landed in a place I felt comfortable. I was sure of my politics and committed to my vision of social engagement. For me the days, wonderful as they were, of sitting up all night talking had been replaced by a whirl of term papers and activism and any all-nighters were more likely spent with my women friends than with John.

One day, after much agonizing, he loaded his half of the closet into his car and headed west to find work in Calgary. He was my first real love and I had believed we would be together always. Instead, I found myself standing on the street, watching him drive away. I wished him well and I'm sure my mother wished him godspeed.

I saw John only a few times after that. Today, my memories of our time together are washed with affection. He taught me a lot about life and love, but we haven't kept in touch.

That summer, between shifts working as a cashier at the Economart—a job I quite enjoyed, believe it or not, because I liked the process of making change (no pun intended)—I joined the usual suspects in setting up the Women's Health Centre, courtesy of an O.F.Y. grant. Opportunities For Youth was the federal Liberal government's attempt to provide summer jobs for the young (and in the process plant the seeds that would sprout, with luck, into grateful Liberals). We sent in our proposal, it was accepted, and a group of us received the princely sum of $90 a week each to take our university office into the community.

When the grant ran out in the fall, we moved the community office onto the ground floor of our latest house. We called ourselves a collective and intended fully to dedicate ourselves to the feminist cause. We learned—and then taught—genital self-examination and experimented with radical birth control ideas and technology.

Meanwhile, at university, I met another in the line of strong, intelligent and politically aware female role models that have punctuated my life. Ann Gustin was an American who had come to Regina with the wave of professors who left the States in political anger over American policies in Vietnam. She reminded me of Mama Cass from The Mamas and The Papas. She was both the advisor to the campus counselling centre, where about-to-graduate students learned the practical aspects of social work, as well as my honours-paper advisor. It was a standard practice for graduating psych students to work in the mostly student-staffed clinic in order to gain some practical experience and I put in my share of time there. My work at the Women's Centre had already taught me the difference between textbook learning and actually applying it to people's most intimate problems and concerns.

My honours paper—the mini-thesis that I needed to complete my degree—was on melancholia and the difference between the way depressed men and depressed women were treated by the medical mental health establishment. In a nutshell my premise was that men were treated as having a problem that needed solving, while women were dismissed as crazy. It doesn't seem like a new idea now, but it certainly was contentious at the time.

I chose the topic because I believed the research needed to be done and because it was the type of inquiry that Ann promoted. But I was also drawn to the idea of the word "melancholia" because it was so rich and strangely attractive.

Ann made no secret of the difficulties she was having with her partner, another of those lefty men who seemed to believe in equality among social classes but not necessarily between genders within them. She never despaired that progress could be made in relations between men and women or between rich and poor, and her hope in the face of difficulty was an inspiration to me, though not everyone agreed with her optimism.

My friend Joan made another kind of choice. Dissatisfied and distressed by what she saw as the impossibility of a truly intimate relationship with a man, she chose to become a lesbian, even though she had been living an active and decidedly heterosexual life up until then. Today, Joan is living happily with her longstanding female partner in California. As for Ann, I can only hope she's still spreading insight and optimism among young people on a campus somewhere, but I don't know for sure.

It was in this context—having worked with women in both the Women's Centre and the student counselling office—that I was first invited to appear on the radio, an accidental event that still reverberates for me. I'd spoken on a few occasions on campus and in the community at that point. Sometimes a church or community organization might call the Women's Centre and ask for someone to speak to a group on the new area of "women's issues" and I was often the one to go.

So when Lorne Harasen, a popular and much-listened-to local radio show host, called wanting a "feminist" to field calls with him live on air, I volunteered and Joan agreed to come along. For one hour we sat in the studio and responded to callers and to the host himself, who had very strong opinions on "women's issues." Harasen's basic position, as I recall, was that birth control turned women into sluts, though he may have contradicted himself by suggesting that any unmarried woman who even wanted birth control was already a slut. On abortion he was considerably less liberal. Most of his callers, predominantly women, agreed with him. The whole experience verified for me what an enormous amount of work needed to be done. It wasn't a new idea to me, but hearing so much uninformed—and often quite nasty—comment reinforced it.

I'd like to say that my appearance on the radio was a magical happening, that I came off the air exhilarated, drunk with the power of the electronic soapbox, knowing secretly it was my destiny.

The truth is, it seemed so incidental that I hadn't even alerted my family to listen to the program. I didn't really understand yet what you could accomplish with an audience so large, an audience that was with you by choice. It should have seemed obvious, but it wasn't: if you want to save the world it's easier if you don't have to do it one person at a time.

Over the next while I did a few radio spots whenever I was invited, as well as more public speaking, and I always came away somewhat satisfied. If I faced vituperation it reminded me of how important this all was. If I found agreement I felt we were making progress.

By the end of my third year I'd squeezed in four years of courses and graduated with a B.A., Honours, with a major in psychology. I intended to finish my Master's degree, but money was now a real issue. Despite the baby bonus cheques and the savings from my part-time work, I had racked up some daunting student loans. So I headed for the world of work, armed with an education and some of life's lessons learned—lessons about friendship, love, activism and learning. My time at university had been a political and emotional awakening. But the experiences were just as important as the degree. University may well be wasted on the young but not entirely. I learned how to think for myself.

When young journalism students write or call to ask for direction I often find myself reluctantly offering contradictory advice. It's a tough competitive business; the pyramid for promotion is steep and slippery. Go get yourself a journalism degree because that's how the big networks cut the thousands of wannabes down to a shortlist of those who might make it. But I can never stress strongly enough the importance of the lectures in political science or economics or history. As a journalist you report on how the world works. You need to know the rules by which the game is played.

And those psychology classes are just as important, because fundamentally those who make the rules or break them are human beings. Journalism is about divining human nature to find out not just what people do but why people do what they do.

These are important tasks and they impose an enormous responsibility on the journalist. Despite all the motives attributed to us, journalists seldom set out to uncover human flaws or scandal just for the sake of creating pain, or embarrassment or defeat. But we do quite deliberately look for contradictions and incompetence, which sometimes leads us to uncover the aforementioned. And I'll challenge those who would question our pursuits and our legitimate curiosity about those who seek to lead us to explain why, as citizens, the less we know the better able we are to make choices.

It's a hobby horse I ride relentlessly. Be informed, stay informed, become media literate. We must understand the filters through which we see the world and television is the predominant source of information for the majority of people. Decry the fact if you will, or shut the TV off if you think that that will help. But don't raise the cry to censor what you see, without first thinking whether you could instead teach kids how to learn from it. As keepers of the on-off switch we have a responsibility to the next generation to make them wiser and more critical users and thinkers.

But in the greater scheme of things, what's really important in life, above all else, is people. Many of the friendships I formed at university, and some from earlier school days, have lasted a lifetime. And they take at least as much effort and energy and time as a romantic relationship. The old saying that the only way to have friends is to be one makes complete sense. I have throughout my life nurtured friendships, and although the older we get, the more difficult it is to make new friends, I have always tried.

Perhaps because the nature of journalistic work is collective, I have always been fortunate enough to find like-minded people in the workplace. And because of the long hours and the forced confinement of airplanes and edit suites, studios and newsrooms, many colleagues have become lifelong friends. A collective voice is louder than a single voice crying for change. So my mission in life, to make change, has always been made possible by those who hear the same siren song.

On love, well, no one ever stops learning about that. I am a wiser person for loving those I did, even though the objects of my affection often puzzled friends and family. Still, as I grow older I must say I'm feeling a little more cynical. Dorothy Parker, whose acerbic wit, humour and painful honesty set her apart as a writer more than fifty years ago, is just as relevant today. Her work seems to have withstood the test of time. I read and reread her all the time, I guess because her words mirror my own thoughts on love. She once wrote a funny little poem about love, which she called "Unfortunate Coincidence":

By the time you swear you're his,
Shivering and sighing
And he vows his passion is
Infinite, undying—
Lady, make a note of this:
One of you is lying.

When my relationship with John ended it was about loss, but it was also about growing up. Breaking a heart causes as much pain as having your heart broken. It's just the price of admission to the adult world.

3

The Brown
Envelope

Words without actions are the assassins of idealism.
– HERBERT HOOVER

I HAD PUMPED GAS, sold encyclopedias, waited tables, baked bread, cashiered and proffered psychological advice—all for money. But my first real job after graduating still seemed to be an important beginning. I didn't know it would be but a brief stop.

It was 1973, an exciting time to be entering the working world. To my politicized eye there was so much that needed doing, and people appeared to be listening to the rising chorus of young voices that were calling for a chance to try. As soon as I graduated I went to work for the Saskatchewan government.

Henry Ford once said that work does more than get us a living; it gets us our life. Little did I know just how true that would be for me. My work, for better or worse, defines much of who and what I am. And that was true when I was hired at HURDA, the Saskatchewan government's Human Resources Development Agency. It was a bit like O.F.Y. for adults and I don't mean that as a criticism.

Governments were recognizing that an unprecedented number of young, idealistic, educated people were out looking for work— "meaningful" work if they could get it—and pools of government money were being set up to turn that energy into action. One of HURDA's particular areas of focus was working with native people on natural resource projects. I might not have considered this kind of work as a first choice of things to do when I graduated, but as it turned out, I had a contact there. Though I've never been a party-political type of person, many of those I hung out with in my student days were. And the party they all seemed to favour was the Waffle. The Waffle started in the late sixties as a splinter of the New Democratic Party by those who thought that the party wasn't left enough. The Waffle was the left wing of the left wing. They were proud socialists and believed in, among other things, throwing out American owners of Canadian industries and taking them over as public property. They were very active on campuses across the country and supposedly pro-feminist. It was through those Waffle friends that I was directed to Larry Sanders, who was in Prince Albert working for HURDA. I called him, told him that I'd just graduated and was ready to take my energy and political resolve out into the world.

Given my experience in counselling both on campus and in the community, as well as my academic qualifications, he was quite sure I could get a job with the agency. He was right on. I jumped in my blue Chevy and by the summer of 1973 I was installed in a basement apartment in Prince Albert, Saskatchewan, a small city of about 30,000, halfway up the province, working out of the tiny HURDA office.

The city itself is not particularly attractive, although it's set in some of the most beautiful countryside in the province. Located on the south shore of the North Saskatchewan River, Prince Albert, named for Queen Victoria's consort, is only a stone's throw from

Batoche, where Gabriel Dumont convinced Louis Riel, the champion of the Métis cause, to make his headquarters in the late 1880s.

The air was often filled with sulphur from the pulpmill or the characteristic aroma of the slaughterhouse. The town is home to a maximum-security federal prison.

As for my apartment, all that sticks in my mind about it was that I had to weave behind the furnace in the dark of the cellar to get to my door. My mother, when she saw the set-up, turned white with fear, predicting there would be an explosion and fire that would block the apartment exit with devastating consequences. I spent so little time there that even if that had occurred I probably would have missed it.

I went to Prince Albert as a "community development worker," and at the beginning we worked with the local native and Métis groups who were setting up a forestry co-op. Natives were organizing to make claims on the land and its resources, and we were helping them plan negotiations with government and the corporations, which, needless to say, were less than thrilled at the prospect.

I had known native and Métis kids back in Wadena, but the Métis people I worked with in Prince Albert might as well have been from a different planet. The kids I'd known were reserve kids who lived in poverty, with alcohol and abuse. They were supposed to be bussed into town for school, but they didn't show up very often. As a result, most were several grades or more behind where they should have been and were, therefore, usually bigger and older than the kids in their class. They were ridiculed in the classroom for a variety of sins, including the fact that by tradition, they took the name of their mother's current mate and it seemed to change with regularity, something the school system could not abide. Others were sent off to residential schools and that was considered the right of the privileged. Little did we know. They seemed sad even as children. The truth is that the idea of the natives I had known running their own affairs was not plausible.

The people I was meeting now were different. They were more aggressive, educated and entrepreneurial and their actions gave credence to the importance of native rights. They were, needless to say, angry at the paternalistic forces that had deprived so many aboriginal people of the skills, confidence and resources they needed to conduct their own lives successfully. And now, so was I. As I settled in to the place and the work I found myself—not surprisingly, given my history and inclinations—becoming increasingly involved with native women and their issues.

It didn't take me long to discover that just about every one of them had a man—husband, lover, father, son—in the penitentiary, and it was a small jump to the conclusion that one way to help the women was to, somehow, help their men. I had already had some very close encounters with the prison system, and though I knew that going back through the barbed-wire fences, past the searchlight towers, into the barred buildings, would be reminiscently spooky, it was also an opportunity to scratch an old itch. It seemed the perfect opportunity to do good works in jail.

Things seemed somewhat simpler to me then than they do now. One of the prices one pays for maturity is facing the complex shades taken on by things that once seemed so clearly black or white. Federal penitentiaries are very different from provincial jails. The latter, like the place where my old boyfriend did his time in Regina, house people whose sentences are under two years—the often-heard "two years less a day" is the maximum. The former hold everyone else. You don't normally find pickpockets in the pen; you find murderers and rapists. Just getting permission for a woman to be admitted to speak to a gathering of inmates was a major campaign. Told I was a security risk, I was, perhaps, too naive to agree. At this age you always feel somehow invincible. And I suppose I was also making a political statement.

I'm not sure how the inmates saw me, but the authorities evidently thought of me as a hostage incident in blue jeans. In any event, I was eventually allowed to organize a meeting and was ready to reinvent the system.

The first meeting with the inmates was tense for a number of reasons, not least because an armed guard was posted almost beside me. Not surprisingly, he made the men reticent. I, admittedly, was already a bit on edge just from the trip in. The effect a prison can have on you can't be exaggerated. It's a huge warehouse full of cages, two storeys high, and it feels miles long. Every sound echoes. The paint is peeling. The air is cold. Every door clangs closed behind you as you pass through. Every door ahead of you is barred and bolted. But, in time, it stopped rattling me quite so much.

What doesn't change is the constant sense of "there but for the grace of God go I." One young prisoner I came to know eventually explained why he was in prison. Manslaughter was the charge. He would spend most of the next fifteen years paying the price. Fair enough, except that his story was one I had heard and even witnessed myself on countless occasions. A bunch of guys drinking in a bar. Someone insults someone else. They take it out on the street. One guy lands a drunken punch; the other falls. But in this case he doesn't stagger back to his feet. It turns out he has hit his head against a parking meter. He's DOA. One night's excesses—one life is gone; another is lost. Many of these guys were normal people to whom abnormal things had happened. Many were gentle but had countered violence with violence. That's why I didn't really fear for my life.

After a few more get-togethers with the ad hoc Prisoners' Association, with absolutely no sign of any trouble or danger, the guard began to wait just outside the door. That's when things really started to buzz. Many of their beefs were about the petty restrictions on mail and phone calls and other ways to keep in touch with their family. But I found the men totally receptive to the idea of trying to find a way to make a real contribution to their families. We proposed setting up a small woodworking project inside the prison that would pay them a small income that could be sent directly to their wives and kids. In the end, I hoped, the women would have more money and the men would regain the pride they felt in being some support to their families. It would have the longer-range outcome, we all believed, of maintaining the connection between the men inside and their families outside.

Personal contact was always difficult because it required money (lack of which was a constant problem) for the families to visit, and so keeping up relationships was an almost insurmountable problem. But there's an enormous difference in attitude and behaviour between a man with someone on the outside and a man without.

Though the inmates were quite optimistic about the project, it wasn't the first time that some do-gooding outsider had tried to make life better. What they knew better than I was that translating intention into action is never easy and the phoning, writing, explaining and justifying to the various government departments involved would be frustrating.

I also spent a lot of time on the road, commuting back to Regina to keep my love life alive. I had a brand-new government car at my disposal because our work involved daily travel out of the city. (It drove my father nuts that a kid just out of university was given such a perq, not to mention a paycheque that rivalled his. I should have been more sensitive. My dad had worked hard and long, only to discover late in life that his third pension plan, like the first two, had gone bankrupt.)

When I moved to P. A. I had left a boyfriend behind in Regina, so I grabbed every opportunity to visit with him and all my old friends. True to form he was "older"—nearly ten years—and also named John, in this case Deverell.

We met when he was hired as the business manager for the Student Union and I was on student council, spending money on those controversial feminist speakers. We fought quite viciously over that, but eventually a mutual attraction replaced the budgetary battles and our professional involvement turned into a personal attachment.

I sometimes felt as if I were living in two places at once, with each home feeding a different need. Between the prison project and the continuing connection with my old attachments in Regina, my life that year was very full. I was satisfied that I was making a difference in the world, helping to make things better for a group of people who needed all the help they could get. It was in the late winter of 1974, when everything appeared to be rolling along smoothly with no surprises on the horizon, that Hollywood called. Well, Regina, actually.

The call came from an acquaintance, John Ridsdell. He'd moved from university to a job at CBC Radio in Regina, where he was the producer of the lunch-hour show known, not surprisingly, as *Radio Noon*. His host was sick and was going to be out for a while, maybe a month or two. He knew I'd been on the radio a few times and could certainly hold my own as a public speaker, even with a hostile audience. Could I get a short leave of absence from my job to come down and help him out? Without a second of hesitation I agreed.

I kept my apartment in P. A., since I intended only to be away a short time, and lived a nomadic life with what I had with me. I began hosting the second hour, phone-in segment of *Radio Noon* with more confidence than experience, since my entire broadcasting resume up to that time included fewer than half a dozen guest appearances on various talk or phone-in shows.

It was within days of stepping into the old CBC building on McIntyre Street that lightning struck. This is what I had been looking for. If you were on a mission to improve the world, if you believed in your own message, then what better place to spread the word? (Let me not leave the impression that my "message" was party propaganda. This was about righting wrongs, not converting partisans.)

Radio appeared to be my natural calling. Somehow, until that moment, that calling had fallen on deaf ears.

The place itself should have been condemned. A three-storey building filled with ratty little cubbyholes called offices or studios. In the winter, there were some rooms where you had to keep your coat on, the floors creaked, the roof leaked. But I didn't seem to notice. I had found the place, if not the building, I would call home.

The career that would take over my life began uneventfully. *Radio Noon* was essentially divided into two parts: the first hour was made up of farm-market reports, while the second was a phone-in on a topic that the host and the producer would choose. We would then invite a guest expert—a cabinet minister, for instance—to respond to the callers' comments on our topic of the day.

From time to time the discussion would be fuelled by a mini-documentary on the issue at hand. I found myself in the midst of a crash course in journalism and it made the adrenalin flow. I discovered quickly that I enjoyed engaging the people who phoned in.

I believed then and I still believe now that people from Saskatchewan have a born-and-bred feeling for and an interest in politics and the political process that are the strongest in the country. Whatever the topic, I was always impressed by the thoughtfulness of the callers, by the quality of the calls. The programs were wide-ranging and considered questions such as "What do you think of the two-price wheat system?" or "What is the future of rural Canada in the wake of massive rail line abandonments?" Also, the government was nationalizing the potash industry and around that same time a precedent-setting court case involving a farm wife who wanted half of the family property after her marriage dissolved was making the news. It was fascinating work and I couldn't get enough of it. In a matter of a few days I felt that I'd been tried by fire. I was pleased to discover I'd passed.

Prince Albert was feeling farther away every day. Then, as if to erase any doubts I still might have about my future direction, the brown envelope arrived and there was no turning back.

Whatever the colour or form of the container, a "brown envelope story" is what I later learned to call investigations initiated by an "informed source" who wants, or needs, to remain anonymous while revealing crucial facts. It usually starts with a package of information of unknown origin appearing as if by magic at your door or on your desk. Often the trick is to decide if the story is likely true and worth investigating or if the informant's real motivation is spite, malice or personal gain. My first brown envelope story emanated from a very reliable source, even though the sender wasn't obviously identified. I knew who had sent the package, but since it wasn't signed I could ignore that fact. "Plausible deniability" is the ponderous phrase that merely means you can convincingly claim not to know something if you don't know it officially, however strong your suspicions are. Politicians use it all the time, but it's also a valuable tool to a journalist, even as we recognize and try to neutralize it in those who use it against us. Like a budding Woodward or Bernstein, the journalistic duo who broke the Watergate story and have kept their deep-throated source secret ever since, I'll go to my grave not revealing my source. But my deep throat, D. P., is a good friend, has a brilliant mind, and he's still stirring the pot.

My informant made a very serious allegation based on a series of conversations with insiders in the province's health system. My source claimed that some anesthetists working in at least one Regina hospital were double- and triple-booking operations to maximize their incomes. This was resulting in a sort of round-robin care, as anesthetists jumped from one operating theatre to another, giving each patient a fraction of the time and attention that should have gone with the serious circumstances. The source reported that patient lives were on the line because of this practice. And then added the dire prediction that someone was going to die if this behaviour was not stopped. My first response was shock and indignation. My second response was paralysis. What could I do about it? It was clear from the material that even though the evidence was local the situation was likely provincial. This was a big story, and I had little experience. Left entirely to my own devices I might have simply gone on the radio the next day and made outraged allegations. Thankfully, I wasn't, and I didn't.

Fortunately, Ridsdell explained one of the most basic rules of journalism to me: outrage and an unnamed though reliable source weren't enough to warrant immediate exposure of the story. We needed to put together a persuasive bundle of independent evidence and then and only then drop it publicly into the lap of someone who could do something about it.

Over the next few days we made dozens of phone calls, talking off the record with nurses and other workers at the hospitals as well as bureaucrats. They all had stories and suspicions, but no one dared to speak on the record. The doctors were a powerful lot and to cross them would be, as they say, career limiting.

We knew we didn't need a case that would stand up in a court of law, only a credible list of contentions and allegations that would force a powerful person to listen and, hopefully, to act. Finally, we had gathered enough information to make our claims publicly.

We invited the provincial minister of health, an NDP stalwart by the name of Walter Smishek, to the program, raised the allegations, and the minister responded with due dismay. The SMA, the Saskatchewan Medical Association, needless to say was quick to deny and as they often do attacked the messenger instead of the problem. In private, I'm told they swore they'd get "that bitch" (me) off the air.

But the pressures and the story continued to build. The public was pretty uniformly against the practice. The minister swore that the government was committed to protecting the safety and health of every citizen and that his department would swing into action immediately, investigating the situation and correcting whatever needed correction. He appeared to me to be making a sincere statement of intention. And we, through the power of radio, had made him do it.

If there was any doubt about what route I was going to pursue in my professional life, that experience settled it. This is how one could make a difference and actually right a few of those wrongs.

By the time the red "on" light switched off at the end of that show I was, if not a journalist, then certainly an aspiring one. The power of broadcasting had hit my passions square in the face. We had made a government accountable to the people, as they were supposed to be. It was immensely satisfying to watch both journalism and government work as they, in my opinion, ought to do.

I knew that we had, in some small way, been responsible for saving lives, lives of extremely vulnerable people. As outraged as I was when I first read the allegations of malpractice, that's how elated and satisfied I was when I saw the positive result of our work.

That the government might have been using us for its own purposes did occur to me, but it didn't impinge on my sense of satisfaction, since I was so pleased with the apparent outcome. I knew then—and have had it confirmed over and over again during the course of my career—that governments sometimes like to be made to act. They often prefer to answer a righteous call to arms—to be seen to be leaping into some breach or other—than to take big chances of alienating citizens (read "voters") or powerful lobby groups (read "doctors") by acting on their own initiative. We may have succeeded only in making the minister do what he wanted to do anyway. Regardless, we all got what we wanted. That affirmed, rather than tainted, my faith that the system often worked quite well. And it made understanding life in Ottawa, which I would have to do before much longer, considerably easier.

My fill-in job at *Radio Noon* ended shortly after that life-defining event, but I never went back to Prince Albert, except to collect my personal possessions and say my farewells. I now wanted to be a journalist for the same reasons I had previously wanted to be a social worker. I wanted to be part of social change and now I finally had the tools I needed.

At the time—1974—Sheila Moore, who ran the morning show, was the only woman working in an editorial position in radio current affairs at CBC Regina. Except for the host—a staff announcer—Sheila *was* the morning show. I still don't know how she swung it, but she managed to hire me as her assistant. I wasn't yet twenty-one when I began my first real job in journalism as a radio producer at *Saskatchewan Today*. My job title was actually "story editor." That meant you did the research and assisted the producer but got paid less. I constituted fifty percent of the entire female producer staff at the station. I had never worked so hard in my life.

In a small station like CBC Regina, the people who hosted radio programs often were not journalists. They were announcers. Sheila, the producer, was the one with the killer instinct for a story. And under her tutelage, I honed my own.

We went on the air at 6:00 every weekday morning, a time of beauty and peace in May, of biting cold and impenetrable darkness in February. Most nights we were still on the phone at eleven. And then back into work by 5:30 A.M. for the last-minute preshow preparations.

There was an added wrinkle. I wasn't permitted to have my own key to the station. Only technicians and announcers were allowed to have one and one icy winter morning the technician and the host locked me out and left me shivering on the fire escape until the program was well on the air. The cold might have killed me, except that the anger and frustration set my blood boiling. The boys thought it was a joke, but it was an event filled with significance for me. Despite my long hours and hard work, in the end they felt it necessary to prove they could do the show without the "girl" producer. It was tiresome and juvenile, but I had already learned that lecturing your male workmates on feminism was not the way to go. Actions speak louder than words, so just do the job so damn well that they can never challenge your ability. However, that wouldn't stop them from challenging your authority.

The incident led to my first encounter with management and in the end I got a key to the station. It was a small but important victory along the way and it taught me the value of keeping a cool head under siege.

These pivotal battles aside, I was having the time of my life. I had no regrets about not being on air. In fact, I learned about the secret power of the producer. I learned the crucial skill of directing an interview through the talkback that feeds a producer's voice directly into the host's earpiece, and I became quite adept at encouraging the host to ask exactly the questions I thought were necessary.

Now that I'm on the other end of the talkback, I have mixed feeling about the process, like all other on-air interviewers I'm sure. Sometimes my producers can save me by whispering important facts. Sometimes I just wish they'd leave me alone to follow the interview path I already have mapped out in my head. But two heads are usually better than one.

A few months after the provincial election, Sheila took a radio job at CBC Winnipeg, an important step up in career terms. So her job was up for grabs and I grabbed. Not that there was really much (if any) competition for the spot. The pay was bad, there was certainly no glory, you got up before dawn and you worked yourself silly all day and all night long. But by then I was smitten and there was no place else I wanted to be.

My feelings on being treated with respect at work haven't changed since my days at CBC Regina. I didn't and still don't believe that women make useful inroads in an industry like broadcasting by carrying placards—even metaphorical ones—or by being aggressively confrontational on the gender front. Ultimately, the most effective way for me to earn respect has been to do my job as well as it could be done by anyone. And while there have certainly been some people I've worked with who might dismiss me as an aberration— a woman with balls—there are others who have been forced to confront their own prejudices.

I think that's how things change. But it's true that if you're going to change minds by example, you have to get in the door in the first place—and it was Sheila who had made that happen.

It was my mother and father who taught me that the measure of your contribution lies in the number of people whose lives you've made better rather than in how much credit you get. Like much that I learned from my parents, I learned this more from their actions than from their words. My mother, for example, had been passed over for promotions that went to others who seemed less qualified and competent, but her students have made her successes tangible. A few showed up at my parents' fiftieth wedding anniversary just to make the point. Many others, now grown with children and grandchildren of their own, drop in to say hello whenever they pass through Wadena. And because people know where to find me, I get letters from time to time saying that through her teaching my mother had saved them or encouraged them not to give up. It's the kind of legacy we'd all like to leave.

As I settled into and learned my new job, I felt the weight of the large mantle that Sheila had passed on to me: trying always to balance the public's right to know with the accountability owed them by those in power. The problem was, while I had replaced Sheila, no one had replaced me. I was my own lackey. For the better part of a season I put a show on the air five days a week about anything from politics to potholes. And, of course, the Crow Rate.

It was not long after I took on my new and expanded duties that my boyfriend John got a job as a book editor in Toronto. Naturally, I considered going along with him but two things held me back. Any job similar to the one I had in Regina would be out of my reach in Toronto. I still didn't have a great deal of experience at that point and Toronto was the magnet for almost every aspiring broadcaster (on air and behind the scenes) in the country. The second reason was that I didn't hold Toronto in very high regard.

I've already mentioned that I was raised amid a great deal of supper-table talk that I only later learned to identify as "political," and that the content of much of that talk was that "the East" was not a place I could ever call home. I am still a westerner in spirit, but having lived between Ottawa and Toronto for nearly twenty-five years now I've lost some of my admitted prejudice. Back in 1974, however, I thought of Toronto rather like the Book of Revelations Babylon, so though John moved away I stayed in Regina.

Later, during my first trip to visit him in Toronto, John's downtown apartment was broken into while we were out. We came back to discover the place a mess and to find, among other disarray, clear evidence the burglars had been rifling through my underwear. It was not an event designed to alter my opinions of the quality of life in T.O.

After John left, I moved into a house with Heather Bishop, a singer/songwriter friend from university who remains a good friend and a beautiful singer. Her roommate had just vacated, so it was an ideal situation for both of us. My work at the station took up so much of my time and energy that I had little left over to socialize, so I eventually moved into my own place—a small bachelor apartment a stone's throw from the CBC. It was yet another firetrap and once again my anxious parents arrived, this time with a care package from the deep freeze and a rope ladder that my father had fashioned that I could toss through a window and flee to safety in case of emergency.

Once again, in workaholic's terms, my life seemed settled and stable. And it was—for about six months. By then, John, with whom I still had an ongoing, albeit long-distance, relationship had moved again, this time to Ottawa to work with the Canadian Union of Postal Workers.

I went there to visit him and attend a women's conference as part of the United Nations–declared Year of the Woman. It was there that I met the person who helped to set in motion the next big change in my life. Elizabeth Gray, whom I only knew at that point from her on-air work and reputation, was my idea of a journalist. I was thrilled to find her in the flesh exactly as I had imagined her. Dark-haired and deep-eyed, casually dressed, a cigarette constantly clutched in an animated hand, she is brash, aggressive and daunting. She is also funny, warm and completely dedicated to her craft.

She personified journalism and, more than that, political and social activism. It was for me as it might have been for an aspiring writer to meet Margaret Atwood or for a young actor to meet Jessica Tandy.

I had accidentally on purpose run into Elizabeth outside a radio station one day when Stephen Lewis, the Ontario NDP leader, was being interviewed. I introduced myself to the formidable Ms. Gray and mentioned I was interested in getting journalistic work in Ottawa.

She was obviously impressed by my ambition and enthusiasm because she invited me to join her and the new producer of the radio show she would be hosting in the fall for a drink in the stately old Chateau Laurier hotel.

Elizabeth had just finished a stint hosting a show called *Lady Is a Four-Letter Word.* She was an award-winning documentary maker and she was tough. She was also very convincing when she wanted something to happen.

John's move to Ottawa had had an interesting effect on my openness to relocating (yet again). If Toronto was the destination, then I had no desire to join him. But Ottawa was different. It was somehow like a Canadian embassy in Ontario, a place where I might live but still keep my western identity. I thought of it as the centre where the federal government lived and worked, rather than a city in its own right. And a place where the media were as crucial as the Houses of Parliament.

Elizabeth's new job was as host of the morning show at CBO, the CBC Radio outlet in Ottawa and that certainly was right in my line. After all, except for my brief time on-air, my broadcasting experience lay in morning programming. I had been the boss of the morning show, though with no one to boss but myself. If I got the job in Ottawa, I would be nominally moving down from producer back to story editor—but a story editor in the seat of government. Throw in the fact that John was there and it was an undeniably attractive proposition.

Elizabeth, her producer, Jack Fleischmann, and I convened in the second-floor bar at the Chateau Laurier, the large, turreted hotel on Wellington Street that looks, depending on one's mood and disposition, like either a castle or a fortress. CBC Radio has their studios and offices on upper floors of the building. The meeting left me feeling optimistic.

Jack seemed interested in having me on the program but made it clear that there were a lot of paper-covered hoops to jump through before such a thing might be accomplished. He suggested I go back to Regina, stay in touch, and he would work on trying to get me hired. I knew Elizabeth's interest in me was the strongest point in my favour. Jack obviously trusted her judgment and it was also clear that he, like just about everyone else who encountered her, was a bit afraid of her wrath.

I liked Jack. He could have passed for Billy Crystal's brother, but I didn't get much of a fix on him or his sense of humour at that meeting. He was young, slightly built, not much older than I was and obviously not a veteran like Elizabeth. She was only in her thirties but already had an extensive and enviable track record. Jack appeared reserved and quite matter-of-fact when he spoke. In retrospect, the presence of Elizabeth only accentuated those qualities.

Oddly, although it took years to develop, Jack has become one of the most important people in my professional life and a good friend. For quite a long time, however, we had what might be best described as an armed truce.

Like so much in my early career, it all fell into place exactly as I had hoped. Upon my return to Regina, true to his word, Jack set about trying to get me a position on *CBO Morning*. I like to think he saw something unique in me, recognized some latent talent that merely needed nurturing and developing. However, it's much more likely that Elizabeth saw me as an ally and bugged Jack until he had no choice but to acquiesce.

In the autumn of 1975 I packed all I could carry into suitcases and boxes, stored what I couldn't in my parents' basement in Wadena and moved yet again. This time the move took me across the country and into the next chapter of my life. There's an old saying that to make men out of boys and women out of girls, there is no place like home. The nation's capital was that new home.

4

The Hill

It is easy to learn something about everything but difficult
to learn everything about anything.

– UNKNOWN, but smart

OTHING in my early life could have prepared me for how I felt about Ottawa. For the political junkie, supposedly it's the ongoing debate that intrigues, but for me it was the trappings, rituals and landscape that overwhelmed me. Goose bumps would rise when I just looked at the Houses of Parliament. Every time I set foot in the buildings I felt a little like a pilgrim at a shrine. Hearing my footsteps echo on the marble floors gave depth and meaning to the expression I'd heard so many times before: the Corridors of Power. The possibility of social change, still the strongest motivation in my professional life, seemed to be housed inside those buttressed, Gothic Revival walls.

I joined the *CBO Morning* crew as a "story editor" and settled into my new routine. Compared with what I was used to, the CBO staff was enormous, maybe half a dozen people. There was actually a full-time researcher. It seemed lavish.

Elizabeth remembers that when I arrived for my first day on the job, the crusty, cynical and totally lovable Mac Atkinson, the CBC announcer on the program, dubbed me "Orange Blossom" because of my long strawberry-blond hair. My enthusiasm was boundless. I felt like a giant sponge ready and eager to soak up everything.

The stories we covered were of national importance—the crisis over bilingual air-traffic controllers became the symbol of Canada's dreams and fears. We followed postal strikes, the Tory leadership and the nationalism fuelled by the debate over the Canadian edition of *Time* magazine.

It was an activist phase in government in part because in 1972 the Liberals had been reduced to a minority and were forced to appease and please the NDP, which now held the balance of power. FIRA, the Foreign Investment Review Agency, was part of the price the NDP extracted for its support. The nation's capital was still a place that mattered, where decisions were made.

Now, nearly twenty-five years later, Ottawa is less relevant. It's a by-product of shifting economic power and a decade of politicians of all stripes making a compelling case for less government. And politicians command less respect. But back in the early seventies politics was a truly national sport. And in an unpredicted bonus, 1975 was also the year the NDP became the official Opposition in staid old Tory Ontario. We had stories galore.

One thing that became apparent to me was that I carried a certain cachet among other politically interested journalists because as a Saskatchewan expatriate I was associated with the province's radical image. When the NDP took over Manitoba in 1969 it was considered a breakthrough for the left. The moral victory in Ontario would be just as seismic. But in Saskatchewan it was neither new nor surprising when the NDP formed the government in 1971. The Co-operative Commonwealth Federation(CCF)—the forerunner to the supposedly new and improved NDP—had governed Saskatchewan from the mid-forties until the mid-sixties. The Liberal interregnum of Ross Thatcher was the exception to NDP rule. Medi-care, now frequently mentioned as one of Canada's defining and indispensable national characteristics, was born and raised in Saskatchewan.

One of the things that surprised me as I tried to adjust to life in the East was how much I missed the physical openness of Saskatchewan compared with the denseness of Ottawa. The trade-off was that I felt surrounded by experience and history.

John and I moved into a large bachelor suite in a rambling but now subdivided building that had been, in its salad days, a foreign embassy. I loved the fact that the buildings carried their years so well. At home, we called a building "old" when it had been around maybe fifty years and was beginning to look run-down. Sideboard and stucco, the staples of prairie architecture, get rattier with age. Ontario brick becomes statelier. Still, in Ottawa, it always felt as if everything was a bit too close together. And I'll say this and get it out of the way: to me the winters felt colder in Ottawa than in Saskatchewan. Ottawa always felt so damp, while on the prairies it's a dry cold. There.

But the characteristic of Ottawa that kept me feeling a bit like a country girl at court was that everywhere I went I kept bumping into the two kinds of people who interested me most: the powerful and the press. *CBO Morning* was, in theory, not much different from *Saskatchewan Today*. We did traffic, weather and local news. But just as the news in Regina frequently dealt with crucial local issues like agriculture, so the Ottawa local news always seemed to lead back to Parliament. Ottawa is a company town.

Government defines Ottawa as fields of grain define the prairies. For me it was a more than fair trade. The bonus—both professional and personal—was the opportunity to work with a host like Elizabeth Gray. I was constantly amazed at how she prepared for an interview.

First she would read and absorb whatever was available to her, often pages of densely printed material from newspaper clippings mixed with the producer's own research. Then, somehow keeping it all in her head, she would ask for the item producer's verbal input—kind of a pregame warm-up—which she would somehow, invisibly, integrate into the store of data already in her head. By the time she got to air she knew enough about her subject that not much could catch her by surprise. The result was that there was little for her producer to do but watch and admire. It seemed (at least to me) presumptuous to interrupt her in mid-stream to suggest a new line of questions.

I learned an essential lesson about the value of preparation that I've never forgotten and continue to emulate. When you're live on air, having the best available producer in the control room is comforting, but it can never take the place of having the facts and a three-dimensional picture in your head of your guest and their topic.

Elizabeth made another contribution to my new situation that was just as valuable: she took me under her wing. Very soon after I started work she invited me over for dinner, where I met her husband and three young children. John Gray was a journalist with *The Ottawa Journal* with a formidable reputation and resume, and he was one of the writers whose work I'd read and admired regularly. He is a warm, generous man and one of the few who even after all these years refuses to practise lazy man's journalism, the kind that feeds off cynicism, not curiosity.

My first dinner (in Wadena we called it supper) invitation was for a weeknight and, despite that, they served wine! They were, I thought, pulling out all the stops. I was to learn over the years that the Grays always serve wine at their evening meal. There was, however, a problem.

The meat was a little rare for my tastes and gave off an odd odour. This was not the smell of wild game like moose or elk, with which I was familiar. When your father hunts, you get used to the wild taste. As I pushed the food around on my plate, Elizabeth said she hoped I like lamb.

Well, being the well-mannered and slightly intimidated young woman that I was, I stifled a gag and choked down the rare lamb, even offering compliments to the chef. It was years before I finally confessed to Elizabeth that I had gone home that night and thrown up. My friends now all know that I would rather starve than eat those cuddly little critters whose mission in life is to provide sweaters, not dinner.

Elizabeth and John began to invite me along when they went out socially. Suddenly, along with a new city and a new job, I was thrust into the middle of a whole new way of life. Compared with the camaraderie around the kitchen table—the centre of social activity back home—the cocktail party was impressively genteel.

Through the autumn and winter I began to find myself, for instance, forking smoked salmon onto my plate in the dining rooms of power couples like the Ostrys or the Gotliebs or the Gwyns. At the time, Bernard and Sylvia Ostry were about the best-known power couple in the country, he as secretary-general of the National Museums of Canada, while she was the country's chief statistician (and, at her level of power, another example of a lone woman in a world of men).

Years later I found out that Bernard was actually from Wadena, but in those early days it wasn't a fact that ever came up in conversation.

My way of dealing with the sense that I was out of my element was to smile and charge forward confidently. I knew how to behave in front of adults. Fortunately, I was too honest to try to impress and, in retrospect, I think that's what got me through.

So with a drink in one hand and a cigarette in the other, I made a virtue out of a necessity. Intrigued, even mesmerized, by it all, I forgot about being nervous and simply struck up conversations with anyone within chatting distance. Even if the person I was arguing with was, like Allan Gotlieb, a Rhodes scholar.

Swimming in Elizabeth and John's wake led me into waters unfamiliar to a prairie girl. Then again, it would have been uncharted waters for any junior producer on a radio show who took the bus to work each morning in the dark.

Since Ottawa is a city made up largely of the powerful and the people who cover them, many of those who congregated at gatherings in the most important living rooms in the city were journalists. Before spring I had a passing acquaintance with many of the biggest "names" in the country, including most of the well-known wordsmiths of the working press. And, of course, my job itself was also a source of new friends and connections. I met Marjorie Nichols, for instance, because she was a regular commentator on our program and a friend of Elizabeth's. At the time Marjorie was a veteran Parliament Hill newspaper columnist, another example of a woman in a world of men. Sheila Moore had been one too when I'd met her. Marjorie, like Elizabeth and Sheila before her, wanted to make it a bit easier for me than it had been for her.

By reputation, Marjorie was a tough and honest reporter who'd taken on premiers and prime ministers. She had survived by being good at her job, by learning to drink hard with little noticeable effect and by using an extensive vocabulary that didn't appear in any newspaper. I found her more than a bit intimidating at first. She was tall and commanding. And what she saw in me was another tough young prairie girl who needed some guidance and instruction learning the ropes.

Marjorie hailed from Alberta and was as independent as they come. A free thinker with a generous heart. Her father had often told her she didn't have the looks so she would need to make her way in the world by using her brain. That she did. Good advice, even if given for the wrong reason.

Marjorie was witness to one of the moments of epiphany in my young life. In fact, she was the cause of it. One Friday afternoon she took me shopping with her on Sparks Street because we were going to the annual Press Gallery Dinner and she had, as the saying goes, nothing to wear. We went together to an upscale women's clothing store where she had obviously been before. We were cordially seated and the staff then began to display dresses for Marjorie's approval. She chose one, they went off to wrap it for her and she casually paid them a sum approximately equal to what I earned in a week of getting up before the roosters. What struck me most about the transaction wasn't how expensive the dress was, but how comfortable she was with it all. She had her own money and she made her own decisions. Suddenly I had a vision of the "independent woman," a vision I've never forgotten.

Marjorie presented me with a female model very different from Elizabeth's, who, alongside her work and feminist beliefs, had a husband, three kids and a fairly conventional family life. When I met Marjorie she was single—though she'd been married in her past—and she shared a house with a friend, columnist Hugh Winsor. Their place was known in certain circles as a drop-in centre. If you were looking for company or conversation, you could often find it at Marjorie and Hugh's house and you were as likely to find a cabinet minister there as a reporter. The partying and the drinking were legendary.

In later years Marjorie climbed on the wagon and stayed there, but she used to recount fondly that hundreds of the columns she had written back then were done under the influence. She would have to get up in the morning and read the paper to see what she'd said the day before and to find out whose career she might have altered. But she never wrote anything she didn't stand by.

She lived, worked and played hard. It was almost as if she were cramming. She was, as it turned out, closer to death than she should have been at her age. In 1991, at age forty-eight, Marjorie died of cancer.

It was Marjorie who first took me to the Friday luncheon at the National Press Club. Since Question Period in the Commons was held before noon on Friday—unlike Monday to Thursday, when it was scheduled for just after lunch—the end-of-week roast beef spread at the club was lavish. The assumption was clearly that there was nothing important to do after Friday lunch so why not eat, drink and stay well into the afternoon.

Our show was done by nine in the morning, without another until Monday, so I felt as free as the others in the room who'd filed their story for the day and were already feeling weekendish.

The afternoon was spent in relaxed talk, a good way for a rookie to meet other journalists and soak up the Hill folklore and custom that were part of our collective past. There was always gossip that certain reporters spent Friday afternoon cavorting with certain cabinet ministers' wives. I have to say the closest I ever got to verification of the stories was the bragging of those who claimed to be involved. Still, the rumours were always around and it was great fun to embellish them in the retelling.

In the Seventies there was a very different sense of what constituted publishable news. There was, for instance, constant talk among journalists about the then prime minister Pierre Trudeau's marriage, but among the Ottawa media, there was silence on the topic for publication purposes. It's interesting that the only Margaret Trudeau story that made headlines happened in Toronto— out of the ring of protection—where she had been spied hanging out with The Rolling Stones. The silence wasn't a partisan thing at all. It didn't matter if you were a Liberal, a Conservative, a New Democrat or a reporter; there was a very different sense than there is now of the privacy due to public people. And what could and couldn't be said was the subject of endless debate. Reporters would dissect Trudeau's answers in the Commons, mining each gesture or word for evidence that he was traumatized or angry or distracted. But little if any of this "context" was ever provided for listeners or readers.

Today the argument is that the public have a right to know intimate details about our leaders in order to evaluate the effect their private lives might have on their ability to govern. Twenty years ago the sense might have been that we should be equally aware of the pernicious effect unnecessary intimate disclosures might have on that same ability.

Another difference in journalistic sensibility between then and now is that though the Watergate disclosures of 1973–74 catapulted "investigative journalism" into the public consciousness, it still wasn't by any means the norm. To my knowledge, few Woodwards, Bernsteins or Deep Throats were hanging around the Press Club at the time. My young eye ascertained that the Ottawa media actually functioned as part of a system that on the one hand was designed to inform the citizenry about the government's antics but whose more pressing task seemed to be to get the government's message out.

Sometimes it seemed that, given the pressures of deadlines and budgets, we were like a glorified messenger service. Say, someone from the Finance Department was having a turf war with the prime minister's office. The former might drop a tidbit into the ear of a reporter, who would spin it into a story for the next day's paper, where the prime minister might see it. Message delivered. Response to follow.

It wasn't that different from what happened back in Regina when we forced the minister of health to do what he should have done anyway. The close association of the press with the people they covered seemed to be to everyone's advantage. The idea that we should be more Woodward and less Western Union was taking hold, but it would be several more years before it became standard practice.

The friendly relationship between the members of the working press and the subjects of their reporting didn't make anyone immune from honest, and sometimes brutal, criticism. It was understood and generally acknowledged as necessary that reporters might take shots at the person they'd shared a drink with the day before. Like two lawyers who fought each other strenuously in court and then picked up their amicable relationship when it was all over, we all knew it went with the territory.

It was also about that time that journalism school was becoming a more common route into the media than it had ever been before. The ultimate result of that evolution is that we're now producing considerably more J-school grads than there will ever be jobs for.

But my life in Ottawa wasn't just sprinting from one party to the next. John and I tried to settle into domestic normalcy. We moved from the old embassy, where our space was much too small for two energetic inhabitants, and found an apartment just down the street from the Grays and half a block from the famous Rideau Canal. The apartment had been recently vacated by Evelyn Gigantes, a journalist who later embraced her affection for politics by running—and winning a seat—as an NDP member of the Ontario provincial legislature. She was also a friend and colleague of Elizabeth's, which is how we heard about the vacant space in the first place. That apartment holds many memories. One night I sat alone in front of the TV watching the 1976 election in Quebec. The race was tight but the separatists had momentum. The tears streamed down my cheeks as the diminutive but passionate René Lévesque claimed victory and made history.

Over the years I had opportunity to interview Lévesque as he tried to make his brand of sovereignty association palatable to both Quebeckers and other Canadians. But after he left politics, I had a rare chance to share an evening and a stage with this compelling man. Such an unlikely duo to co-host a fundraiser for Rick Hansen, who had wheeled his way around the world and into people's hearts.

The gathering, the major social event of the season, was a roast. Tory cabinet minister John Crosbie was to be on the spit. Stand-up comedy was not my forte, but with the help of former broadcaster Rob Parker, who was organizing the event, we dreamed up some powerful potshots aimed at Crosbie, a man with a razor wit, but also at the self-important roasters, including Prime Minister Mulroney, lined up at the head table.

My first and most patient friend, Bubbles (1953).

LEFT: Mom and Dad as newlyweds (1947).
RIGHT: My sister Bonnie (age 7) and me (age 3).

Dad and me, Mom and Bonnie at home in Wadena.

Two remarkable women—Nan (Clare Howson), Mom's mom, on the left
and Grandma Piper (Edith Piper), Dad's mother, on the right—
all dressed up for my sister's wedding on October 11, 1969.

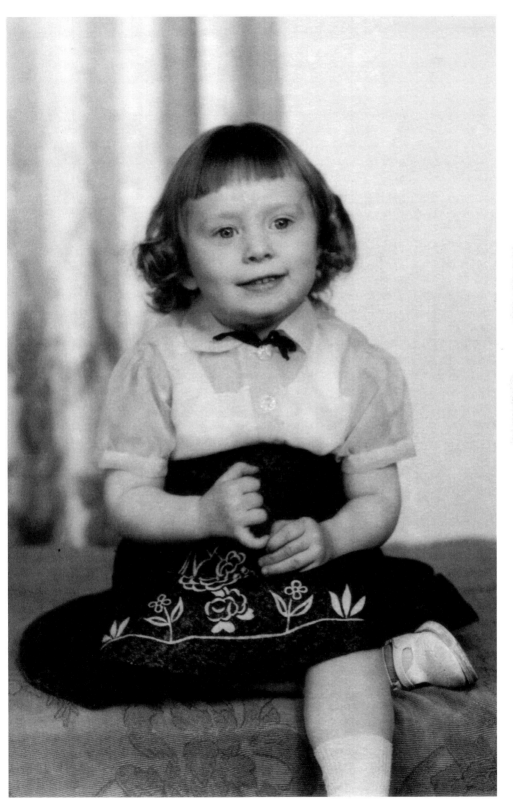

About age 4.

In front of the United Church on Main Street. I'm the one with the ringlets, and my best friend Shelley is to my right.

Test driving my 5th birthday present—a new blue bike.

A portrait of a budding feminist—at university in the early 70s—
it was a time of change, political awakenings and self-discovery.

The *As It Happens* cabal—that's me, third from the left.

The immediate family—my uncle Don (centre back row) and his family and the
Wallins, as well as Betty Ann, one of Bonnie's clients, and, of course,
my other sister "Honey Dog," Mom and Dad's beloved pet.

LEFT: Norm Perry and me in Tiananmen in January 1981, long before the tanks and the pro-democracy students changed the course of history.
RIGHT: The late Don Cameron—friend, mentor and boss.

Just talking hairdos and make-up with the Iron Lady, Margaret Thatcher, in Ottawa after her "victory" in the Falklands.

LEFT: John and Elizabeth Gray delivering the toast to the bride and groom (1987).
RIGHT: My lifelong friend Shelley, who has always been there for me.

With Mom and Dad on my 40th birthday at Splendido
restaurant in Toronto, April 10, 1993.

Ten years after I had watched him on television embracing his electoral win, there I was sitting in an Ottawa hotel room drinking coffee and smoking cigarettes with René Lévesque, at one time one of the great Quebec journalists.

This was a black-tie affair, but Lévesque was not one for such attire. He apologized to the event organizers but made it perfectly clear he was not willing to be decked out like the other penguins.

We rehearsed our lines and weighed just how far we could go without offending, and then took another verbal step over the line. Many of the politicians gathered in the room that night had been long time enemies of Lévesque's cause. From his perspective, some had willingly plunged the knife in his back with the signing of a constutitional deal that, as he saw it, left him and his people out. René Lévesque put his politics aside to support Rick Hansen's cause.

It was a measure of the man that Lévesque could recognize Rick's courage and dignity. This was a night to celebrate a Canadian hero who had remained undaunted in the face of a brutal twist of fate that had left him paralyzed.

Lévesque was small and self-effacing, and if you moved toward him and extended a hand, he always looked away, almost cowering. The fact was, Lévesque was a painfully shy man and I felt I had stolen a rare glimpse of a different side of this passionate politician and powerful orator. Over the years he was seldom seen without the trademark cigarette in hand. In fact, he refused interviews unless he could smoke throughout the exchange. As we prepared our patter, he was chain-smoking, revealing the nervousness that I felt too but refused to admit.

We were not George and Gracie, but we were, in the end, pretty funny that night. The politicans took as good as they gave. And I never confessed to René Lévesque about the tears I'd shed on the night he'd been elected.

The morning after that historic vote, I was anxious to get to work so I could exchange views with Elizabeth. By that time Elizabeth and John Gray were like family. Their kids, Colin, Rachel and Josh, filled the gap my lifestyle could not afford. (Colin is now a very talented reporter for CTV *News*, Rachel a multi-degreed mother and activist and Josh a budding filmmaker.)

When my mother and father came down east to Ottawa for a visit, the Grays embraced them warmly. To this day, all parties involved fondly recall the night my father took on several selected members of the Ottawa intelligentsia over the issue of gun control and, in full rhetorical flight, threatened to teach Warren Ally-mand (Allmand) a lesson or two at the point of a gun if he ever set foot on Wadena soil. Not much danger of that, given the realities of the electoral map, but the evening was filled with hilarity and maybe everybody understood the other's point of view just a little better. Politics is a passionate sport.

John was working with the militant and often newsworthy Canadian Union of Postal Workers at the time as communications director and we were both, by nature, most comfortable living life on the run. The cumulative effect of our frenetic schedules meant that between work and our respective circles of co-workers and friends, we didn't spend a great deal of time together. When we did, we went to movies or skated on the canal—often with one or more of the Gray kids in tow—and tried to carve out a life together. It would be some time before I recognized or least admitted that the relationship wasn't going to take hold.

At work Jack Fleischmann and Elizabeth were constantly at odds. Jack was very young, new to the business and quiet, while Elizabeth was none of those things. That disparity meant that though disagreements were frequent, they were thankfully brief.

If Jack was having trouble trying to be Elizabeth's boss before I joined the team, he had even less of a chance after my arrival, when I quickly fit into the position as her minion. If we had been cartoon characters I would have been the one standing a half step behind her adding "and that goes for me too" to whatever she threw at him.

Before the end of the first season with the show, Jack had had enough and left CBO completely. The good news is that Jack's best years as a producer were still ahead of him. Eventually he and I reconnected and now, twenty-odd years later, he is not only one of my best friends, he's also a business partner and I'm Auntie Pam to his younger son. In the spring of 1976, though, not even The Amazing Kreskin could have predicted that.

After Jack's departure the CBC, in its wisdom, decided that the local morning show should shift its focus from Parliament Hill back to the nuts and bolts of garbage collection, school-board rows and all the other mundane issues on the civic agenda. In preparation for the next season, they even asked Elizabeth to audition for her job, testing her skills by staging a telephone line going dead to see if she could handle a "crisis" in the middle of a live show. They concluded with luminous insight that she had the right stuff, but, in her own inimitable way, Elizabeth told them to stuff their myopic new morning show.

Although I had had experience as the boss of the morning show in Regina, was energetic and had a good head for politics, a new producer was brought in and I was "reassigned" temporarily to *Radio Noon.*

There was no pretence that this was a political show, and though I booked the required items, my heart was in Question Period and not at quilting bees in Carlton Place. It was politics, although not of the governmental sort, that saved me from this exile.

In the spring and summer of 1976, CBC Radio had undertaken a major reshuffling of the Sunday schedule that would ultimately turn it into *Sunday Morning,* and the man behind the new plan was Mark Starowicz, Barbara Frum's executive producer at the legendary *As It Happens.* Starowicz was known throughout the network headquarters in Toronto by his all-encompassing vision, the high standards he demanded from his staff and the three-piece suit he wore daily in a world where tie-dye was the norm.

The major problem with Starowicz's new plan, in terms of CBC politics, was that Ottawa would be losing the slot for its highly respected show on politics. The compromise was an Ottawa-produced segment that would be included in the new *Sunday Morning* as the program's third hour. Responsibility for that segment fell to Ottawa's network executive producer Nicole Bélanger. Patrick Watson and Laurier LaPierre were hired to do an in-depth interview and Nicole hired me to do the research.

It would be hard to name two better-known broadcasters in the country at that time than Watson and LaPierre. Their stint together at the provocative CBC television program *This Hour Has Seven Days* had cast them not only as respected journalists but as renegades against the forces that would be named "political correctness" only much later. The show had been cancelled in 1966 after only two seasons, despite its large and appreciative audience—on the indictment that it was sensationalist. What it was was controversial, cheeky and bold. No one, no matter how powerful or self important, was immune. And LaPierre was often emotional, in stark contrast to the staid presenters who were standard fare on the CBC. He stood accused of the crime of shedding tears on air in the middle of an emotional interview with the mother of Steven Truscott, the fourteen-year-old boy convicted of murder in 1959. But the show's defenders felt that it had been axed because it cut too close to some powerful bones.

Going to work alongside these two great journalistic giants was an extraordinary adventure. But going to work as their researcher was both salvation and a demotion. I had, after all, actually run a couple of programs at that point. Still, the stature of the people involved made this a larger-than-life opportunity.

The depth and precision of Watson's and LaPierre's interviewing and the standards they demanded provided an invaluable opportunity to learn and to shape what I'd gleaned about the business over the previous few years. I also needed a job badly so it was a perfect place for me to be. It would be a humbling experience.

Once a week in a radio studio Watson and LaPierre would, like a tag team, interview a single newsmaker for the entire hour. Guests ranged from Liberal cabinet minister Donald Macdonald to George Ball, the former U.S. under-secretary of state, to Quentin Crisp, the flamboyant author of the groundbreaking gay memoir *The Naked Civil Servant.* The research Watson and LaPierre demanded and needed in advance of the piece had to be insightful and thorough. Every week I spent days poring over newspaper clippings and transcripts of previous interviews, condensing my findings into several pages of notes that would also suggest possible lines of inquiry. When I look back on those days I am always reminded of a line from Linda Ellerbee, a candid and controversial TV journalist south of the border: "Steal from one person, it's plagiarism. Steal from more than one, it's research. I research." I too researched.

But most weeks the response to my labours would be the same, some variation on "What could we possibly ask based on this?" My youth was often the cause of my obvious inadequacies—I didn't know who half of these interview subjects were so I could hardly provide the nuance and detail I now know is the magic of these staged encounters. Watson and LaPierre meant no disrespect; it was just that my insights seldom enhanced their own knowledge. Another lesson learned, but one that didn't become clear to me until I was on the other side of the studio glass.

At the time, the response to my efforts seemed harsh, but now, when I quiz my own producers in a similar way or make impossible requests for information, I realize that the demands on me were never meant to be insulting. It was teaching.

In the end, there are an infinite number of ways to do almost any interview. The way the producer has envisioned the give-and-take of the conversation may be as effective as the way the host has in mind, but there's always a tug and pull over whose approach will prevail.

After an interview was over we would sometimes go out for a drink together, though the talk was always of the post-mortem variety rather than anything very personal. It's to Laurier's and Patrick's credit that they always treated me graciously. They still do, and I've had the pleasure in recent years of interviewing these two Canadian icons, as well as the true privilege of counting them both as friends. Ingrid Bergman once said of her crazed and controversial life: "Happiness is good health and a bad memory." I'm happy and relieved to say that Patrick's and Laurier's memories of that time are long on warmth and short on details.

I suspect Nicole Bélanger believed, although she never said it in so many words, that I was probably not destined for a career in journalism. Still, I'm thankful for her patience and high standards. It made me stretch, intellectually. And again I learned by watching.

In addition to the care and feeding of the "talent," it was Nicole's job to take the taped talk and spend hours carefully paring it down to fit the time slot. I'd had a little experience with editing, but most of my radio life had been spent in live situations, so watching Nicole's scrupulous concern with maintaining the integrity of the piece in spite of the power of the blade gave me a new way of seeing the possibilities of radio. She was a deft surgeon who could move whole ideas around virtually at will with a grease pencil and a razor blade.

Editing done judiciously and with skill, guided by an adherence to what had been intended, could turn a rambling conversation into a pointed, illuminating encounter. Others I would meet along the way would use their skills for lesser purposes.

When I encountered "unfaithful editing," editing that places things out of context rather than in one , it raised a whole new set of concerns for me about the world of journalistic ethics. But that disillusionment was still in the future.

Working with Patrick and Laurier sharpened every instinct I'd developed (and some I didn't know I had) since I'd fallen into the business. But before too long, as CBC Toronto consolidated its control over the *Sunday Morning* time slot, the Watson and LaPierre segment was condensed further and further, until they decided they didn't have enough room to do what they had signed on for. Politics giveth and politics taketh away. By Christmas of 1976 I was out of work again and about to do the previously unthinkable—move to Toronto.

In retrospect it's hard to believe that less than two years had passed since I'd left Saskatchewan and settled in Ottawa. In that time I'd had a front-row seat as some of the best interviewers in the country worked their magic. (Did you know, by the way, that Patrick Watson is a very talented amateur magician?) I'd learned that it's not always what you know or who you know. It's who knows you when it comes to the world of work. I'd also accepted that the life of the journalist must include a willingness to incorporate the habits of the nomad. And I'd discovered that there was at least as much politics in a large news organization as there was in the "real" world it covered.

And, though it's harder to explain, there was something else I learned too as my first tour of duty in the nation's capital was about to end. I learned to trust my instincts.

5

As It Happens

Hitch your wagon to a star.
— RALPH WALDO EMERSON

IT WAS AN ABERRANT, eccentric but remarkable place. And we were a twisted but talented cabal, motivated and on a mission to do what no one else could—to find people no else could find, to make the mute speak and the cocky contrite. And we wanted to do it first.

It required a willingness to say, do or promise anything to complete strangers, but the work was its own reward.

This was a time before CNN was sending instant pictures from around the globe to television sets across the continent. At *As It Happens* we used the only technology available that could reach anywhere anytime: the telephone. The pictures came out of the listener's mind, aided by Barbara Frum's evocative interviewing style and her ability to get guests to paint verbal pictures.

If you wanted a career in radio journalism, then Toronto was where you had to be. To many aspiring radio broadcasters, the old Radio Building was like Canterbury to Chaucer's crew of pilgrims. To my eye it was a run-down, barely functional assortment of rabbit warren offices connected by dark, uneven hallways. But there was no denying that what went on in those cluttered dens was nothing short of magic.

My own history didn't include a reverence for the Corporation that the lifers shared. I have no warm childhood memories of sitting around the radio on cold winter nights feeling connected to far-flung corners of the country. But the CBC, in addition to giving me the start down the journalistic path, was once again dangling a new enticement. It produced the best radio current affairs program in the country, perhaps the world.

As It Happens came out of the CBC's realization in the late sixties and early seventies that TV was here to stay and that radio had better adapt or go the way of the gramophone. An extensive study of the future of radio in a television world completed in 1970 set the tone. On the basis of the report the CBC shifted money and resources around to try to catch radio audiences in those time periods when they weren't sitting in front of the TV set. *As It Happens* played from 6:30 to 8:00 (half an hour later in Newfoundland) in the evening, just before the prime time television fare turned listeners into viewers.

The program was hosted by the most recognizable voice on public radio at the time, Barbara Frum, and steered to greatness by Mark Starowicz, the politically obsessed, creative dynamo who eventually left the show to execute the advent of *Sunday Morning* (and later, TV's *The Journal*). I knew that in the radio world *AIH* was the place for me.

I made a long-distance application, went to Toronto to be scrutinized and returned home to Ottawa to await my judgment. Ultimately it was proposed that if I did a stint at Radio Syndication, I'd be next in line for a spot on *As It Happens*. Since *AIH* had a reputation as a program with a predictable burnout rate, I guessed it wouldn't be too long before a spot came up.

I had grown to love Ottawa. I had a place to call home and a circle of friends there, and I'd never lost the excitement I felt around Parliament and the Press Club and all they represented.

As a journalist I felt I belonged as near as possible to the very centre of federal power, but radio, at that point, was the only kind of journalism I knew, and the best venue in the country to do my kind of political radio was, ironically, in Toronto. In January of 1977 I made the move that only three years before had seemed unthinkable.

Though we probably should have figured out by then that we were in trouble, John and I bought a house together in the city's east end. He had a wandering eye, and I attempted more salvage efforts than any self-respecting feminist could imagine. We finally called it off. John had been a part of my life for many years and the parting was painful. But no more so than the relationship had been.

For a while, I moved in with a friend, Anita Gordon, then the producer of CBC Radio's *Quirks and Quarks* and now a key advisor at the World Bank in Washington, D.C. But fortunately for me, I was soon to be part of the almost cult-like *As It Happens* community, which would more than fill the hole in my heart.

From Anita's I moved to the twenty-third floor of a high-rise apartment in the busiest section of the city, near Spadina and Bloor, and became a single woman again for the first time since university—in a sense for the first time in my adult life. In my new neighbourhood the streets were alive twenty-four hours a day. It was nirvana for the insomniac. I could shop at two in the morning. I was starting to feel the draw of the city I had so long resisted.

A strange and unexpected thing occurred in that apartment and I felt it from the moment I walked in the door. The apartment faced west and, from my vantage above the city, I could actually watch the sun as it sank below the horizon. I stood there on my balcony, remembering every evening how my father would stand at the window above the kitchen sink at home and watch the sun set, as if it were a show just for his appreciation. Mother Nature was now performing just for me. For the first time since I'd left the prairies I felt at peace, albeit twenty-three stories up.

My short shift at Radio Syndication was uneventful, but it gave me a chance to get the lay of the land. The Radio Building is still there on Toronto's less-than-posh Jarvis Street, but these days it stands empty. Built as a swanky girls' school late last century, when Jarvis was a genteel, tree-lined avenue, it became the centre of the CBC Radio network when the girls were done with it. Since then the Corporation has consolidated its numerous radio and TV locations into the new, airless and antiseptic office tower they call the Broadcasting Centre on Front Street in Toronto.

The purpose of the Syndication department was to commission short scripted pieces on current issues from freelancers across the country, to record the finished pieces on tape and to then feed them electronically to every CBC location for use in their local programs. In smaller centres with limited resources, syndicated pieces were the lifeblood of their broadcasts, giving even the most isolated and understaffed a national presence and access to some of the best minds in the country. It was necessary work, but after the constant whirl of Ottawa I found it mildly tedious. It wasn't long, however, before my promised position became open and I moved into the unique world of *As It Happens*.

Life at *AIH* felt almost mythical. I had never been in the middle of such a bizarre collection of smart, young, dedicated and competent people. *AIH* was a magnet tuned to draw in a particular type of journalist from clear across the land. There was no one there to whom the adjective "quirky" didn't apply. In some cases the quirkiness was subtle; in others you couldn't miss it. Though we were all generalists, everyone seemed to have a particular passion.

Alison Gordon ultimately became a baseball reporter for *The Toronto Star* and now, as a mystery writer, she has created a character called Kate Henry who is, not surprisingly, a baseball writer. The twist is Kate comes from Saskatchewan, so Alison still calls me to consult on crucial issues like "dinner" vs. "supper." Al Mendelsohn looked like a young Stalin, and had a brilliant mind and a penchant for taking out his frustrations on a typewriter or the punching bag that hung from the rafters (our low-tech anger management system). George Jamieson had the quickest quips in the room and was then and is again responsible for those signature one-liners that still introduce the show each night. Patti Habib, the production assistant and story editor, eventually went off and opened one of the most successful restaurant and dance spots in Toronto, The Bamboo Club. And the intrepid Linda McQuaig, whose particular passion, like mine, was national politics, has become a writer and leftist icon and is still intrepid. Michael Finlay, a reporter from the West Coast, was my best pal and there wasn't anything we couldn't spend at least a couple of hours fighting over provided a bottle of wine was involved. Others too numerous to name were also part of this disproportionately intelligent group. And most have moved on, successfully, in the world of journalism.

I was a natural for the Ottawa "beat." For each Friday night's show I would set up a discussion about the week's happenings on and around the Hill.

I never had a shortage of old friends and contacts in the Ottawa journalistic community to mine for on-air gold. It hardly seemed like work to spend hours talking politics with friends and former colleagues. In the *AIH* tradition I would always try to find at least one contributor who was in an odd location, at the scene of some drama or perhaps travelling to or from a hot spot, to speak to us from a phone booth near the action. The uniform around the office was jeans and attitude—and depending on whether you were inside looking out or outside looking in—that attitude was either proud and confident or annoyingly arrogant.

We saw ourselves as a band of self-proclaimed rebels, not only against the "system" but even against the Corporation, which paid our salaries.

We constantly ridiculed management, who seemed more concerned with whether we had a receipt for the quarter we'd dropped in a newspaper box than with the glories of investigating, reporting and analyzing the news of the world. We kept our own pinball machine in the hallway outside the main offices for tension relief. We climbed the old metal fire escape up the side of the building to the roof for a smoke break, even though it was forbidden—to use the roof, that is. Smoking was still considered normal and acceptable in those days, even in studios and control rooms. And we worked astonishingly hard to maintain our vision. When we weren't working together we were often playing together. It was a heady mix of ambition, energy and camaraderie, with a chaser of that feeling of family.

AIH was also a group with another difference, at least in my experience: its staff was almost evenly divided between men and women. In fact, CBC network radio generally was notable in that respect. Had I joined a short while earlier than I did, the head of Radio Current Affairs—the department responsible for *As It Happens*, *Morningside* and David Suzuki's *Quirks and Quarks*, among many other programs—would have been Margaret Lyons. *Morningside*, whose offices were just down the hall from ours, was run by Anne Gibson, Krista Maeots and then Nicole Bélanger, who brought Peter Gzowski back to radio. Barbara Frum, our host, was one of the highest profile broadcasters in the country.

The most memorable thing about the way we worked at *AIH* was the perfect blend of competitiveness and co-operativeness. It was a model I've tried to emulate in other workplaces. Our common cause was to produce the most electric current affairs radio show we could, and though we were a room full of talent and ego, it was always aimed together and outward rather than toward one another.

At the morning meetings the producers (there were usually at least eight or ten of us, depending on comings and goings) would fight for the right to put their items on the air. It was a ninety-minute show made up of about a dozen and a half items and there were always more ideas than there was room in the line-up. Every producer had a chance to "sell" the others on the importance of his or her proposed stories and then promise the most high-profile and to-date unreachable guest who would give the story voice. No shrinking violets allowed.

The discussions were always vibrant and intelligent, and the combativeness of the selling never carried over into the rest of the day. If someone else got the spot you'd wanted you felt no animosity toward the person but blamed yourself for not being prepared or persuasive enough. If you didn't average two stories a day, you definitely felt less than adequate, that you were letting the program— and the listeners—down.

Some days a producer might find herself, despite valiant efforts, with nothing on that evening's show. Then, like the haircutter who sweeps the hair from the floor of the whole shop because she's got no one in her chair at the moment, she would offer to help others out by making phone calls or editing tape. Another way to use time when you weren't working directly on an item (or waiting for the inevitable call-backs) was to try again, perhaps for the fiftieth time, to make a connection with a newsmaker whose private number had been laboriously uncovered or wheedled from somewhere or other. I chased Indira Gandhi, the on-again/off-again prime minister of India, for three solid months. I had cajoled, begged and pleaded to get her secret number from a foreign reporter (promising in return, I think, my first-born). One afternoon with a few minutes to spare between other tasks, I tried yet again and finally I heard her voice on the other end of the telephone. No one was more surprised than I. A quick warning by phone from the desk to the control room and Barbara and a dash down two flights of stairs to the studio and we had her. It was a bit of a coup and a moment of sweet satisfaction.

We did the program, like all network shows, live Atlantic time. Since *As It Happens* was on the radio at 6:30 P.M. in each time zone, we started our live broadcast in the Toronto studio at 5:30 local time when it was 6:30 in the Atlantic region (and, needless to say, half an hour later in Newfoundland). The broadcast would be taped in

Toronto's Master Control—the electronic brain of the network—
and replayed an hour later in Toronto, then bicycled again with an
hour's delay for each time zone west.

But if a story was in the process of changing, as many did when
they were unfolding half a world away, we often had to update the
show for the broadcast in our own time zone, perhaps again when
we played to points west. Many nights we were still sitting around
the office at eight or nine, gossiping and waiting for the latest word
on a breaking story.

Then there were days like the one in August of 1977. Pat Noble
ripped the story off the newswire and let out a yelp. The King was dead.

Elvis Presley was an idol for many people, as well as representing
a complex cultural phenomenon. It was our kind of story. We got
the news, as I remember, mere minutes before airtime. We knew
that meant a "remake," as we called it. Translation: throw out the
existing show and start from scratch. What happened next could
have been the pilot for *Mission: Impossible.*

We immediately sprang into action like a troop of trained com-
mandos, individual egos on hold as each of us volunteered what we
knew, suggested possible contacts and were assigned our tasks. A
producer's entire day's work on another story would be lost as
that item was shelved and replaced by an Elvis item. We managed
to have the story together as we hit the airwaves in the Maritimes.

We were proud and irreverent. Irreverence was the common
currency behind our own closed doors, though we would never
trivialize the tragedy of such an event on air. The King had croaked
and we'd beat everyone to air with the story! We'd hold a wake later
in the bar, but there was still work to be done.

As the program was repeated across the zones we continued to
add and update, making our coverage broader and deeper. I don't
think a single listener anywhere in the country could have known
just how little time we'd had to think of all the angles, find the
King's friends, enemies and fans, some of whom were already being

inundated with calls, and convince them ours was the call to heed. Research was done on the fly and raced to the studio, and all the while we never lost sight of our stock in trade—finding a balance between news and perspective, balancing the hero worship of millions with the reality of the situation, the surprise death of the most famous entertainer in the world.

Exhausted, we staggered out when it was over, feeling satisfied we'd done our best. We knew that when the papers hit the street their "news" would be many hours old and there would be little to add to what we'd already presented.

The centrepiece of *As It Happens* was, of course, host Barbara Frum. When I began to work at *AIH* I knew her only the way her listeners did, as an intelligent, engaging and often tenacious interviewer, with a charming laugh and a range of interest that ran easily from the political machinations in Ottawa to wars in Africa to parrots that sang and dogs that danced. We would interview people in phone booths in Northern Ireland or the Middle East with gunshots barking in the background. There was a chilling interview with Joshua Nkomo, at the time one of the factional leaders in warring Rhodesia, as he ate his dinner, the audible clinking of bones on his plate conjuring up a mixture of dispassion and death. We brought an immediacy to current events that was unrivalled anywhere. Our humour was black. One man's pain is a another's lead story.

Barbara had a genuine interest in everything around her, and she could tease fascinating talk out of just about anyone, but was especially adept with eccentrics. Which was a good thing, since the program, when it wasn't doing hard news, positively revelled in the eccentric. Barbara was a consummate interviewer and arguably the biggest factor in the program's enormous success. She didn't directly participate in the editorial meetings, although her views and wishes had a way of being conveyed and heeded.

And though she did do live interviews, often with little time to prepare, much of her work was prerecorded, then heavily edited before program time. Barbara was considered the "talent." In those days and in that medium the label still carried some respect, though I would find out later that in TV land, it was often a deprecating term used by producers to describe a mere performer, the person who presents the journalistic work rather than doing it.

Alan Maitland, the announcer of the program, was also considered "talent," but he liked it that way. He took great pride in communicating the *AIH* aesthetic—arch, intelligent, a deep concern for truth mixed with unsinkable gallows humour—in every word he spoke. He was very talented talent.

No doubt Barbara wielded considerable influence whether she attended meetings or not. Every producer knew that Barbara's off-hand comments were invaluable and therefore persuasive. If she noted in passing to a producer that a certain story idea was "interesting," then it was sure to be raised at the meeting. And in the course of doing an interview, Barbara always mixed her own approach in along with the producer's, though she had no control over a tape's final edited form.

If a story was live she enjoyed the prerogative of the person at the microphone and frequently followed her own direction. Meeting or no meeting, her journalistic instincts were always good. The complex truth is that Barbara had to work as much around her strictures as within them.

It's hard to say why this conceptual division between talent and producer existed. In part, I suppose that in smaller centres, producers were sometimes dealing with on-air talent that had little, so the producers were there to be or impose some quality control. In other words, the job of producer was being ventriloquist for whatever dummy was at the microphone. That was obviously not the case at *AIH*.

Within days of joining the program, I was to learn of *AIH*'s worst kept secret—Barbara had a fatal disease. The leukemia to which she finally succumbed in 1992 at age 54 was an open secret throughout much of the building but, as far as I know, not outside it, and it had its own effects on the workings of the office.

We didn't, for example, do cancer stories. It was never really articulated, but every new staffer discovered it soon enough. I found out early on that the editorial meeting would quickly dismiss a story on cancer death rates but would just as quickly agree to do something on a new treatment for Parkinson's. We had to keep Barbara's personal situation constantly in mind, but not because she ever made a big deal out of it.

Quite the contrary. She always played it down and we all knew that we were expected to do likewise. It was clear that Barbara wanted no inkling of accusation to arise that she couldn't do her job. Worse yet, being seen as vulnerable or an object of sympathy would have undermined her ability to be the tough, I'll-ask-anything interviewer she was.

But regardless of what Barbara would have preferred in the way of ignoring her condition, we couldn't. By the time I left the program in 1979, two seasons after I'd arrived, we were doing more and more prerecording of items to accommodate her schedule and more and longer documentaries that didn't require or involve her.

On rare occasions we, as producers, might even conduct the interview, then splice in her re-asks afterward, though it's a practice considered unacceptable by most journalistic standards. I would fight the practice on several occasions years later when I was back at the CBC. In retrospect, however, at *As It Happens* it was a small compromise for a woman whose own standards were high, who was fighting for her dignity and who was breaking trail for a whole generation of us.

There was another incident that has been given some perspective by hindsight and maturity—though back then it was an issue that young, bright purists on a journalistic mission would have debated for hours.

One summer evening Barbara had the *AIH* staff over to her lavish and, by the apartment-dwelling standards of the staff, enormous-looking home. We had a barbecue in the large, treed backyard while Barbara also prepared for a dinner party she was holding later that night. The guest list, we wagered, would include the kind of person we so often interviewed on the program. My Ottawa experience had made me understand that a reporter might socialize with a cabinet minister and still write an indictment of his work the next day. But from our vantage point, as blue-jeaned, transient story producers, Barbara didn't just associate with the ruling class. She was of them.

In the studio I would sometimes quiver with frustration when she would refuse to be damning of an interviewee in a situation where my suggested line of questioning was the equivalent of a table-banging demand for his immediate resignation from the government. I attributed it to her being too soft on her own. Now that I have experience on both sides of the mike I understand precisely what she had long since learned: that angry denunciation doesn't achieve much except elusive denial. I learned a lot from her.

There's no question in my mind that Barbara deserved all the acclaim she achieved. As I've said, she helped change the rules for women in broadcasting by proving that at the first sign of a wrinkle or grey hair women need not be tossed off the air. For decades a woman's "best before date" always came up first, while aging, paunchy, greying men simply became experienced and distinguished.

But others too helped make change. Anyone remember Gail Scott? She was another woman who broke ground in the broadcasting world by being one of the few women on Parliament Hill and as a pioneering host of CTV's *Canada AM*. So I wonder if Barbara would have been accorded her rightful place in the country's journalistic pantheon if she'd worked for a private network.

There is inside the CBC a perception that it, and no other, is the journalistic paragon that provides the news of record and creates the reporters of repute. Yet the track record contradicts the thesis. I say this provoked by dozens of conversations and interviews with people who got their start at the CBC but never finished there. A long list of those who gave many years of dedication and work to the CBC, only to be ousted unceremoniously, have felt that sting, from Tommy Hunter and the *Front Page Challenge* veterans to international successes like Norman Jewison and Saul Rubinek. Some of the news rejects have gone on to fame and fortune in the States, but there are also many news people who were discarded and whose legacy lives on only in the archives.

Am I being too cynical to suggest, knowing the fickle nature of the business, that the same organization that named the Atrium of the CBC Broadcasting Centre for Barbara would have just as easily shunted her into unwanted retirement if she'd ever come to be considered a liability?

Eventually, though life at *AIH* was in many ways as good as work gets, I began to grow restless. After two years of developing stories and booking the relevant guests, doing the research, writing the scripts and suggesting possible lines of inquiry to someone else over the talkback, I began to feel more like I was committing journalism vicariously. Increasingly, I felt the need to spread my own journalistic wings.

Two unrelated developments finally pushed me out the door of the Radio Building and back to Ottawa. I was assigned to travel on a campaign plane for several days during the 1979 federal election, and my colleague Alison Gordon left radio to become a newspaper writer.

In the spring of 1979 Joe Clark ran in his first national election as the leader of the federal Progressive Conservative Party. Standard procedure was that each party would calculate the costs of operating their campaign plane and then sell seats to interested news outlets to help defray expenses. *AIH* bought a seat on Clark's campaign plane and I, as the in-house Ottawa expert, was assigned to travel with him for a week, gather material and produce a documentary when it was all over. The show's sense, and certainly mine, was that

Clark could win the election and become the next prime minister, the first (and only) person ever to beat Trudeau for the job. That such a possibility existed made the work even more engaging. Trudeau had been the only prime minister I was ever consciously aware of in my lifetime.

Travelling on the campaign plane was a process that sounds more romantic than it was. Flying from place to place, you lived out of a suitcase, stayed in cheap airport hotels and listened, until your mind was numb, to similar speeches in similar halls. During flights, to pass the time, we smoked, ate, drank and schmoozed. With one another, that is. Joe sat up at the front among his handlers and, by edict, we mostly left him alone. The experience crystallized my thinking. I wanted to be a real reporter.

A few months earlier, Alison Gordon, a producer I'd worked with my entire time at *As It Happens*, had decided she needed a career change. Alison was a baseball nut and she wanted to devote her energies entirely to covering the game. There was no place on the radio for that kind of specialization, but in the newspaper world it wasn't uncommon. What was uncommon was that a woman should be doing it. The *Toronto Star* decided it was time to change that tradition and Alison traded in her *As It Happens* electronic family for the world of ink.

When I saw that she was happier for the change, I began to seriously consider that if I was going to get to where I wanted to be in the journalistic world—back to the front lines and back to the Hill—perhaps Alison had just provided me with a game plan of how to do it.

Though I liked the *AIH* unit and had formed some close relationships in the office, I had no romantic tugs or strong ties to Toronto except that great view of the sunsets. In Ottawa I still had friends and colleagues with whom I'd stayed in touch both personally and through work. So there it was. Having contrived less than three years before to get from Ottawa to Toronto, I now felt I needed a way to get back. I was twenty-six years old and still had put down no roots. The only constant in my life was that I knew I wanted to practise the craft of reporting—political reporting.

I was no longer a rookie at the journalism game and had become convinced that my instincts in that direction had always been pretty good. I had lost any feeling of being a child banging on doors in the adult world, asking to be admitted (though, to be honest, I'd never had too much of that). I felt like a professional—not a veteran, certainly—but a professional. It was time to choose my professional way with intention, rather than following an accidental path set years before by a sick host at Regina's *Radio Noon*. It wasn't radio I was drawn to. It was news and federal politics.

Following Alison's lead, I brazenly called *The Toronto Star* to ask them to send me to their Ottawa bureau. Can you imagine? That was the prestige bureau and one usually *earned* the right of the posting. I actually managed to get Lou Clancy, the national editor, on the phone, who of course had never heard of me. Once he recovered from his shock at my audacity—my entire print experience was two or three book reviews I'd sold to small magazines to make a few extra dollars back in Ottawa—he agreed to meet and talk to me. I'm sure it was mostly to satisfy his curiosity.

As It Happens gave me much to consider, and all these years later I still mull it over. Having spent much of the last fifteen years as a "host" myself, I think back on the kind of journalism Barbara Frum practised and the power she wielded from her seat in the radio studio. That power came from her ability to ask the right questions.

On the other hand, as the acclaimed queen of the airwaves and the leading expert of the art of the interview, so much of what she did was edited into a form that satisfied the producer of the piece or the program. Although I didn't realize it then, this approach to journalism began shaping my views about the deprecating characterization of ability as "talent" and the importance of the live, unedited encounter. It was one of the reasons I enjoyed my years at *Canada AM* so much. And why I love my current program.

The downside is obvious. Working live means flaws and idiosyncrasies and ill-formed questions are there for all to see. But it also levels the playing field and allows for a fairer and freer exchange of ideas.

Over the years of editing people's comments and thoughts into ten-second sound bites or reducing complex political stories to a simplistic exchange between black hats and white hats for TV news items, the process, and often the result, began to become distasteful. But I had a lot of work to do and mistakes to make before that journalistic penny dropped.

6

Byline

I ain't no lady. I'm a newspaperwoman.

— HAZEL BRANNON SMITH

I MET Lou Clancy, national editor of *The Toronto Star*, in a trendy bar in the basement of a bank not far from the Radio Building. Lou was a beer drinker, and while I like wine, I didn't much like the hanging plants and suited patrons. We trashed wine bars and those who frequent them and the ice was broken. I'd heard good things about Lou, not only from Alison Gordon but from everyone I called to get a fix on him. I knew that he'd been in the newspaper business since he was knee-high to a grasshopper, working his way up from copy boy to national editor. But how would he react, I wondered, to someone who thought she could just jump right into the middle of the line?

I knew there must be dozens, maybe hundreds, of bright, young, energetic people who would love the job as much as I knew I would. And any one of them would have more print experience than I did. A day spent hanging around any paper's water cooler outdid me in that department. But that didn't stop me.

In my initial phone call to Lou I had referred to myself as the national editor at *As It Happens*. I deliberately dropped the names of several respectable journalists I'd worked with so as to suggest—not too subtly—that I had at least the right friends and backers, if not the credentials or newspaper experience. In the end, I'm sure the reason he agreed to meet with me was that he could tell I wasn't about to stop pestering him until he did.

From my perspective, a face-to-face meeting was crucial if I was to convince him that I was right for the job. Getting up and walking away from a human being is far more difficult than ending a phone conversation. In spite of the fact that I was begging for work as a writer, no letter would do, particularly when I had no other samples of my writing to send along. With time and tenacity, I was pretty sure I could talk him into giving me a chance. That confidence to convince or cajole on a world-class level was partly a result of my *As It Happens* experience. It was one of the primary tools of the trade, as in "Yes, I understand that he's just had both kidneys and his heart replaced, but if you could just press the receiver into the pillow next to his head, this will only take a minute and it would mean so much to the lovely people from coast to coast who have been praying for his recovery since the operation."

The *Star* was my objective for two important reasons. One was that Alison Gordon offered me very practical advice: "This is who you call and this is what you tell them." The other was that I felt a certain editorial comfort level with the *Star*. And while I may have disagreed with their apparent opinion that a story's relative importance rises in direct proportion to its proximity to or connection with Toronto ("31 Killed in Riot in Algeria: 2 Had Cousins in Metro"), I felt they were more likely to take a chance on me.

I had arrived at the meeting in the *AIH* uniform—blue jeans— and immediately was pleased to see Lou was also dressed for a newsroom rather than a boardroom. So far so good. He had longish hair, a beard and seemed a little nervous, too. I made my pitch. I loved the news, I said, and I wanted to go to Ottawa to be near the news I best understood. I dodged direct references to my typing and spelling abilities, instead stressing my experience as the *AIH* Ottawa specialist and my earlier stint in the nation's capital, convinced it would carry some heft.

Lou, as I would come to learn, was a man of few words. He sat with his shoulders forward, his hands clasped in front of him and his eyes down, glancing up only when I would make some enthusiastic claim about my potential that even I knew wasn't remotely credible. Though he tried again, and again, I persistently brushed aside his obvious questions about my newspaper-writing experience or lack thereof.

I finally conceded that I had none. But what the heck, I said, it's a skill like any other and that meant I could learn it, didn't it? He finally cracked a smile and his eyes flashed a hint that we were now getting somewhere.

But he couldn't help remarking that the Hill beat was a much-sought-after plum usually reserved for those who'd "paid their dues" out in the boondocks.

I confidently responded that I had paid dues, just different ones, and that with my Ottawa experience it was a job I knew I could learn to do well. More important, I argued, it was a job I wanted with an intensity he'd have trouble finding in anyone, anywhere in the country. He certainly knew by then that if I took the same determined approach to a news story as I had to this job interview, I'd at least get the story—even if I couldn't write it.

I don't know what tipped the balance in my favour (I know we didn't drink that much). Maybe it was my obvious passion for the work I was asking him to give me. Maybe it was what I'd accomplished in radio mixed with my grasp of the Ottawa political scene. Maybe it was that I was a woman at a time when many large organizations were just beginning to find that an attractive attribute, partly as a public relations manoeuvre and partly because they were actually discovering that women offered something valuable and unique in a predominantly monosexual working environment.

My guess is it was all those things. Not to mention the fact that he could tell I wasn't going to leave him alone for a minute until he gave me what I wanted. Tenacity, as I've often said, is a journalist's best friend.

Dubious to the last, at least Lou hadn't dismissed me as delusional. And before we parted that evening he decided to give me the chance I wanted. He probably figured that if I couldn't cut it in Ottawa we'd both know soon enough.

But before we settled anything he wanted to see a sample of my writing, and since all I had were the brief introductions to *As It Happens* interviews and a few book reviews, he told me to take a story from the newswire and rewrite it as if it were going into tomorrow's *Star*.

Back at the office the next day I enlisted the aid of Lesley Krueger and Michael Finlay, two of my *As It Happens* colleagues who had some newspaper experience, and together they gave me the shortest-ever course on the art of newspaper writing. We ripped a story from the wire and the two of them showed me the crucial rules of writing for the eye rather than for the ear. Alison aided and abetted by telephone.

I can't remember what the story was, but the truth is, my doctored submissions were hardly great prose, and despite the diligent efforts of some of the best reporters and editors in the world of print, I still write for the ear. But I now know how to fashion a grabby lead when I have to.

Lou accepted my homework, and though he was clearly not as impressed as I might have hoped, we struck a deal. Lou suggested it might be a good idea if I learned a little something about the newspaper business before I went off to join the crew on the Hill. He assigned me to spend a few months on the overnight news desk in Toronto, a job I reluctantly accepted because I thought I was just marking time. But he was right, of course. I learned a lot and in the end it wasn't too bad a set of hoops to jump through in order to get where I was going.

As I thought about moving back to Ottawa from Toronto I could not have guessed that I was about to begin the biggest adventure of my life. Having shifted locations six times since leaving Wadena as a teenager, this move held no particular portent.

My professional goals had changed several times in the few years since I'd started university, and my decision to be a social worker, like my plan to teach French, had been made by a very different person. But though each movement, each shifting of objectives, had led to another far more congenial to my growing sense of self, my brief stint on the radio had left me with no particular desire to be an on-air broadcaster. My passion was for gathering and reporting news, parliamentary news in particular. Winding up on television, which was to be the ultimate result of the move back to the Hill, was the furthest thing from my mind.

I left the very self-sufficient world of *As It Happens* knowing that I would stay in touch with many of my ex-colleagues and friends, just as I had with the people I was returning to in Ottawa.

But first, there was my initiation into the world of print, conducted in the high-rise headquarters of *The Toronto Star*. I found the pace at four in the morning in the *Star* newsroom quite different from *As It Happens* at four in the afternoon, but it was hard work nevertheless. There were only about half a dozen of us on the overnight shift, tearing copy from the wires and preparing it for the next day's edition. The senior editors rewrote stories and dreamed up outrageous headlines, most of which never made it to print (but should have because they often portrayed the story more accurately than the acceptable ones did). We talked to reporters about what they'd filed (you can call a reporter at one in the morning and get away with it) and updated breaking stories.

The collegial feeling was there, though very different than at *AIH*, but it was enhanced by the eerie feeling often shared among nightshifters that we were the only people on the planet awake at such an unnatural hour.

I learned an astonishing amount in a short time about the workings of a newspaper. I was, after all, starting from scratch—making learning both easy and essential.

What was most useful to me later in my move to Ottawa was to have experienced, first-hand, what the editors in Toronto had to say about what they received from their colleagues in the field. It was both humbling and, in a way that had nothing to do with style, exceedingly useful. Let me explain.

When you're in the field it's possible to think of your dispatches back to headquarters as being invariably earth-shattering both in their import and in their panache. It can be discomforting to have your flawless prose tightened, refocused or just chopped away like dead wood. And it can be jarring to see your piece on a mild disagreement between parliamentarians headlined as "MPs' Battle Gets Bloody," especially when your name is so prominently displayed just under the headline.

It's a profound education to see up close how your stories are viewed—and, shockingly, sometimes even improved—by the editor who receives them. That's the humbling part.

As for the useful part: when the subject of your report complains to you about how the final product displeased him or told an inaccurate story, it's invaluable to be able to reply, "Sorry, but it's those jerks in Toronto." My guess is that in every field there's some comparable group to "those jerks in Toronto." They're a mixed but necessary blessing.

Thankfully, that part of my apprenticeship was brief, and I gladly prepared to return to Ottawa, in the shadow of Parliament Hill. My capabilities had increased immensely since I'd left, even though I'd been gone only a couple of years.

I had moved to Toronto as a young radio story editor looking for work, but I was returning as a reporter in the Ottawa bureau of the largest circulation newspaper in the country. As I unpacked my few belongings and prepared myself for yet another job among yet another officeful of colleagues, there was no thought that the next time I travelled that road—back yet again to Toronto—it would be as a television reporter on my way to becoming a household name across the entire country. But if someone had predicted that particular future, I'm sure I would have said it was highly unlikely. Still, I've always felt that much more is possible in our lives than our imaginings can conjure. I was taught that from birth.

I managed to find a quite wonderful apartment across from the National Museum of Man (later renamed the Canadian Museum of Civilization) on Argyle Street. Large, bright and cheap it had a great story attached to it. In 1916, the original centre block of the Parliament Buildings (built in the 1860s) was savaged by a spectacular fire. Parliament was moved into the building that housed the museum, and my building, directly across the street, became a temporary home to several displaced members of Parliament. In addition to the sun porch, the enormous living room, dining room and kitchen and the two bedrooms, I loved the fact that the apartment had a dumbwaiter. MPs had to have their food delivered directly to their rooms, after all.

As I recall, the whole thing cost me under $300 per month, no more than I'd spent in Toronto for my box-like aerie. I missed the twenty-third-floor sunsets but had less need of them. I felt home again.

As it turned out, I still had a marvellous view to enjoy daily. The *Star* had their offices on the seventh floor of the nine-storey National Press Building on Wellington Street, and though I didn't have a window myself, the larger space looked out directly onto Parliament Hill. I couldn't think of a view that could fill me more with a sense of purpose and connection. It all felt so perfectly right.

And it was a building filled to the roof with people just like me. With the exception of Canadian Press, which had its own building, almost every major news-gathering organization in the country had offices in the Press Building.

The place was bursting with Hill watchers, and if you didn't run into some lively talk in the corridors or the elevators, the National

Press Club had its home on the second floor. The expression "felt like I'd died and gone to heaven" springs easily to mind.

During my settling-in period I managed to reconnect with many of my old friends and made some new ones. Like the *As It Happens* crew, the *Star* gang often travelled in a pack and in many ways how we spent our off-time was reminiscent of my university days. We liked to talk, often late into the night, sometimes late into the morning. It was work in as much as we were always debating the current conspiracy theories or possible scenarios, but it was also a kind of connection that makes friends out of colleagues.

I knew Southam reporter Bill Fox because we had used his services on many occasions for the *AIH* political panel. But we'd only known each other by telephone and through his byline until we'd finally met when I'd been assigned to the Clark campaign plane for *As It Happens*. I remember walking over to introduce myself and him just throwing his arms around me. It was friends forever at first sight. He was a big bear of a guy, funny, with a hearty and infectious laugh. At some undeclared point in his Irish-Catholic upbringing in the Northern Ontario mining town of Timmins it had been decided that Bill would become a priest. Now, let me be clear about my friend Bill. He is a kind, generous and loving soul, but the Pope, if not the Almighty himself, would have intervened to change the course of history if Bill hadn't. Lucky for the news junkies of the world that wine, women and sports nudged Bill away from the higher calling and toward a journalistic one. He was a great reporter and now he was coming to work at the *Star*. I watched and worked alongside him as he meticulously covered, or should I say uncovered, the unfolding constitutional story.

The intergovernmental strategies, the Machiavellian machinations of the federal brain trust, separatist threats and the internecine legal and political warfare dominated the nation's agenda. And Bill could make it all read like a suspense thriller.

It helped that the personalities involved were colourful. The flamboyant and talkative New Brunswick premier Richard Hatfield leaked like a sieve, British Columbia's Social Credit premier Bill Bennett, son of Wacky Bennett, often said what he meant even when he didn't mean to and, of course, there was Pierre "Just Watch Me" Trudeau. There was also the coterie of federal backroom boys like Tom Axworthy, Jim Coutts and Michael Kirby, and from the provinces, bright young minds like Hugh Segal and a young Manitoban named Michael Decter, now my partner in life, who swears we met at some late-night dinner where journalists and sources talked off the record and actually kept the official spin to a minimum.

I watched Bill work, filed my sidebar pieces and then tried to keep pace at the bar. Bill, my girlfriend Terry Keleher and I spent many an evening helping the owner of Don Alphonso's restaurant pay his mortgage. Bill is a gentle, softspoken man, but occasionally his Irish temper would flare. He was my friend, my teacher and my protector.

One night at a cocktail party after the annual Press Gallery Dinner, a fellow reporter made an untoward gesture toward me. Bill quietly came between us, threatening to put the man and his ego through the nearest wall if he ever stepped out of line again. To say Bill is loyal just leaves too much unsaid.

Bill always called me, and sometimes still does, the Queen of Wadena. Jock Osler, a Calgary businessman who was then working in Joe Clark's office, may have actually coined the phrase, reflecting my constant references to home and to the judgments of those who lived there on the goings-on in Ottawa. It was, from Bill, a term of endearment.

I also had a circle of smart and creative women friends, which made the period of adjustment back into Ottawa pass by all the more quickly and pleasurably. Elizabeth Gray, Terry Keleher, Mary Janigan, Carol Goar, writer Charlotte Gray, Stevie Cameron, Sandra Gwyn—whose husband, Richard, I worked with at the *Star*—

and Sondra Gotlieb all contributed companionship both emotional and intellectual. There were regular lunchtime gabfests that included mostly writers. We read one another's work and always had something to offer in the way of support or useful criticism. And of course we gossiped, the main currency of the nation's capital.

Then there were the larger "gatherings of the girls" at my place, which we dubbed Broads Canada, always full of laughter and talk of the sort you rarely get to enjoy after leaving the confines of campus.

Though it may seem obvious, I loved parties and threw a few. Food was always an important part of it all and I took great delight in cooking. To me, it is a gesture of love and respect to prepare good food for good friends. Richard and Sandra Gwyn always made good-natured fun of the ever-present jellied salad that in my books was a staple of any decent buffet table. Yes, I know it's a shocking culinary faux pas, but brightly coloured Jello adorned with marshmallows or laced with shredded carrots was always on the menu.

At the time, the *Star* crew was composed of Bill Fox, Richard Gwyn, Carol Goar, Dave Blaikie, Andy Szende, Bob Hepburn and bureau chief Ian Urqhuart, as formidable a group of Hill watchers as you could hope to learn from. Bill Fox eventually became bureau chief after John Honderich, son of *Star* chairman and publisher Beland Honderich, had taken his turn at the helm. John was touted to follow his father to the head of the *Star* organization, and his stop in the Ottawa bureau was a necessary part of the grooming for succession. He was a good reporter who worked hard to overcome the snide comments of those who had a less obvious and predictable future.

Beland was known as a man who was both socially conscious and who adhered to A.J. Liebling's dictum that "Freedom of the press is limited to those who own one." The senior Honderich's own obsessions and the paper's were largely indistinguishable. It was to all our benefits that politics and parliamentary news were something he cared about.

Byline

There's a story repeated about Beland Honderich when journalists gather around the proverbial campfire, which, even if apocryphal, contains an element of truth. Honderich, the story goes, once rode the subway downtown to the *Star* building one morning when a blizzard made navigating the streets of snow-scared Toronto impossible. Upon his arrival at the office he commented on the experience. Without ever a directive or a memo in sight, the entire newsroom was spontaneously seized with a passion to do an in-depth series on public transit and road repair. The point is, if the editors thought it interested Honderich, it all of a sudden became news, and if it didn't, well, it could go in someone else's newspaper.

Each morning the Ottawa bureau would receive their assignments for the day. Journalists had a gallery in the Commons right above the Speaker's chair and from that perch we could watch the proceedings, always with an eye on the particular story or individual we were there to cover. Frequently the object of our interest was a minister from Toronto just because he was. TV had been permitted in the Commons in October of 1977 as an experiment, but attendance in person was still the journalistic norm. Increasingly, though, reporters had taken to watching the proceedings on TV, then scurrying up to the Hill for the post-Question Period combat.

In reality there wasn't room for everyone. Membership in the Parliamentary Press Gallery was expanding and more than doubled between 1975 (158 members) and 1995 (340). At 3:00 P.M. media scrums took place outside the chamber, during which time whatever members were at the centre of that day's drama were swarmed by reporters pushing microphones into their faces while lights and boom mikes on high poles surrounded the scene like a fence. Soon after the media scrum dissolved there would be a frantic rush back to the typewriters to turn the day's developments into fast-paced, hopefully enlightening, prose for the next morning's paper. And there in ink for all to see, between the headline (added by those jerks in Toronto) and the story itself, was my byline.

No more the intermediary as I was as an *AIH* producer, I was now the direct route, the conduit, between news and the reader.

Only once was I assigned to cover a funeral, that of a child—an event with absolutely no party-political overtones—and to try to get some gripping photos of the grieving family or their child. I rebelled, suggesting that my beat didn't include the cemetery, but was summarily informed that that particular decision was certainly not mine to make. I did as I was ordered but personally drew the line at begging for photos from the distraught family, because I couldn't bring myself to impose on a truly private moment and because I really didn't see the need to have the loved ones sobbing out of the newspaper pages to convince readers that families are emotional when a member dies.

Having already discovered the power of rebellion (nil), I tried a new tack: I lied. When I reported back with my story I related how, unfortunately, my request for a photo opportunity had been refused. It was my last funeral story.

Stories were assigned to whichever staff member had particular expertise in the topic at hand or, failing that, on the basis of which of us was available. I remember the first story I wrote that made the front page. It was not some earth-shattering scoop by me. No, it was history in the making.

In April 1980, Jeanne Sauvé became the first female Speaker of the House of Commons and I was assigned to do the interview, I suppose because a woman's byline would look good on this story. That's not a complaint, just an observation. The story was also, as they say, a no-brainer. Even a novice couldn't miss the import of this one.

Being a woman, I quickly discovered, was frequently a great asset in an environment where the title "reporter" usually implied male. So if I called a minister to suggest that we grab a coffee and have a chat, I was often treated as a potential date rather than a possible troublemaker, and invited instead to dinner. I never refused and I never misled anyone about my intentions. But as a result I often got more of a story than a male colleague might have. Dinner would actually let you and the minister explore the issue at hand and probe a little deeper into the political imperatives of a policy or a piece of legislation.

And I have come to believe that both men and women often find women easier to open up to. Tina Brown, former editor of *The New Yorker*, says that men talk about what happened, while women talk about what really happened. In other words, we are more sensitive to subtext.

I dislike sweeping gender stereotypes, but other substantive research into gender and communication makes supporting points. For example, Deborah Tannen writes that women tend to understand conversation intuitively and consider it an opportunity to make contact with others, so they respect and nurture those connections. I think our "subjects" sense that and respond. Tannen quite eloquently described the process this way: conversations are "negotiations for closeness." It has proved true for me both professionally and personally.

But what was perhaps more valuable at the *Star* than my gender was that I spoke fluent western Canadian. For that reason alone I drew the Peter Lougheed mission I mentioned earlier. It was a truly satisfying and successful personal moment in my career.

I hadn't been in the Ottawa bureau very long when, in October 1980, after regaining power following less than a year in exile, the Liberal Party under Pierre Trudeau introduced the National Energy Program in their first post-election budget. World oil prices had risen dramatically in the previous year or so and the NEP was the federal government's way of attempting to deal with a growing crisis of both economics and anxiety, especially in the energy-needy industrial centre of Canada, Southern Ontario. It was also heavy-handed power politics. The stated intention of the act was to ensure Canadian self-sufficiency and oil-price stability, both noble sentiments.

But the act was based, unfortunately, on two problematic premises.

The first was that world oil prices would continue to rise forever. They didn't. The second more serious problem with the NEP was that the federal government's stance toward oil-producing Alberta was a firm "like it or lump it." Westerners became incensed at what they saw as yet another example of eastern Canada's treatment of the West as a junior partner in Confederation, or as just another cow to be milked. Peter Lougheed wanted ownership, control and a fair price for Alberta's precious oil.

The bottom line for westerners was that the federal government was essentially taking control of provincial assets. But there was little political risk for the federal Liberals because the West was, politically speaking, a wasteland. The government's power base was energy-hungry Central Canada, which wanted oil at bargain prices. By 1980 Lougheed had been premier of Alberta for almost a decade and he was very popular, not least because of his dedication to ensuring that Albertans received fair returns on their own natural resources.

His institution in 1976 of The Alberta Heritage Savings Trust Fund from oil revenues was prescient and unanimously cheered throughout the province. This event verified him as a man who, unlike too many politicians, had an attention span of more than four years. To Albertans in general, and to Lougheed in particular, Ottawa's plan was somewhere between an insult and an assault.

Lougheed held a press conference in Edmonton to express outrage at what he and his province believed was eastern disregard. I was assigned to attend as the representative of the most Toronto-centric publication in the country, with the possible exception of a chamber of commerce brochure. It's not much of an under-statement to say eastern journalists were considered very much like KKK-ers at a civil rights meeting.

Lougheed had a reputation for accidentally on purpose ignoring representatives of newspapers whose editorial views seemed to show blatant disregard and misunderstanding of westerners' viewpoint.

I had attempted in advance to arrange an interview with Lougheed. My request was neither refused nor granted: it was simply disregarded. So here I was at the press conference to make my queries. The room filled with reporters as the premier's press secretary, in a style generally associated with similar gatherings south of the border, stood beside Lougheed and selected which representatives of the press would be permitted to address him.

Finally I was acknowledged and I put forth my question as well as identifying which paper I represented. The answer from Peter the Leader was patronizing, to say the least. The clear insinuation was that I, an easterner, could have no possible understanding of the implications, economic or emotional, of what was making westerners so furious. Well, I became as angry at Lougheed's treatment of me as he was of Trudeau's handling of the situation. And, like Lougheed, I wasn't about to stand for it.

I stood my ground. My credentials as someone who understands the feelings of the West, I told him from the middle of the crowded room, were unassailable. Heard of Saskatchewan? The province next door? The one that's about two thousand miles west of Ottawa? I was born there. I care about the West and furthermore I understand it. Who would you rather have explain your anger to Toronto? But birthplace, I also knew was beside the point. A question asked should be answered.

Lougheed's manner changed noticeably and he responded respectfully and fully. When the press conference was over he sent word that he would meet with me one on one. What he had seen in me was exactly the person I had always hoped to be as a journalist: a fair interlocutor whose objective was to ease communication between those who wielded power and those who bore the consequences of it.

I knew, and so, evidently, did Lougheed, that I would take some pride in presenting a reasonable case to the East, even though the vehicle was the dreaded *Toronto Star*. What he couldn't have known was that, ironically, I was often in the position of interpreting the West to my superiors at the *Star*.

The interview was a bit of a coup and would be played prominently in the paper. I used a tape recorder during our talk and a transcript of the interview ran under a banner headline. Except for battling with Toronto about how the interview would be edited ("Edit? But every word's gold!"), the whole affair was among the great moments of my career to that point, both professionally and personally. It helped establish my credentials as a reporter who could be taken seriously, even by those who were initially doubtful. I had stood my ground in hostile territory.

Peter Lougheed and I eventually became friends, though not at that first meeting when we were still, as representatives of our separate constituencies, doing our work. But over time I have come to think of Peter as someone I can call just to talk over the politics of the day. It was on the occasion of his receiving an honorary degree in Toronto recently that we were reminiscing about that first meeting. It would be difficult for me to think of anyone in public life who more deserves to be honoured for his dedication to public service.

Here's one additional (and short) Lougheed story that I think makes the reasons for my esteem clear. A couple of years ago Peter learned a library in Jerusalem was to be named after him. It was proposed that the occasion be marked by a fancy black-tie dinner so that the man who had earned the honour could bask in its glory. Peter's response? Nobody needs another black-tie dinner. Put the money into a one-day seminar on the future of Canada and invite the best minds from across the country to attend.

I was pleased to be asked to moderate the session that brought westerners and Quebeckers and native leaders together for some frank and full exchanges. And we came dressed for comfort and not for style.

I was happy in my work at the *Star* and the social life was always interesting (and exhausting), but events were about to occur that would change my life, and my career, yet again.

Perhaps all the teasing I took from my colleagues about being a better talker than writer foreshadowed events. You see, my time at the *Star* was in the precomputer era, but that didn't stop me using what is now the "cut and paste" function on any computer. I would type up my stories, then haul out the Scotch tape and scissors to reorder the paragraphs for better effect and style. I sometimes even cut out individual sentences and pasted them in new locations. To my mind, it was efficient and saved all the unnecessary retyping. It seems even then I had a short attention span when it came to the mundane details of actually filing a story. Getting the story was far more interesting. But the cut and paste would always provoke howls of laughter from my bureau mates and a few caustic comments from Lou Clancy, as he could trace the tape and scissor lines on the pages that I sent down the line to Toronto. Still, I was making progress on the wordsmithing.

It's true I was a very verbal person. How's that for a euphemism! As my early report cards from school attested, this had been a long-standing tendency and I'm sure my colleagues would support my teacher's claims. But I hadn't even considered the logical conclusion that maybe I should hang up my scissors and talk for a living.

The notion may have escaped my attention but not that of Bruce Philips, the CTV News Ottawa bureau chief. Bruce was also the moderator of *Question Period*, a half-hour television program on CTV that dealt, as few Canadian television shows did at the time, with the nuts and bolts of national politics. The format was always the same. Bruce presided over a meeting that included the guest of the week and three invited journalists or panelists covering the story to lob shells at the person in the hot seat. Of course, they also had to be at ease in front of a TV camera, which many people are not.

At some point during my initial time back in Ottawa I received my first invitation to appear as a panelist on *Question Period*. Looking back now, it seems ironic that I left radio to go to print and I wound up on TV instead.

But in a way my career mirrors the change in focus in the world of journalism. Today, most people say they rely on television as their primary source of information. And not just in urban North America. Even in remote villages in the mountains of Guatemala or scattered across the hillside slums of São Paulo, you can see the blue flicker of TV screens. It's a powerful and pervasive force.

The former president of NBC, Robert Sarnoff, described this new emerging medium back in 1962:

> For centuries, he said, man has dreamed of a universal language to bridge the linguistic gaps between nations. Man will find his true universal language in television, which combines the incomparable eloquence of the moving image—instantly transmitted—with the flexibility of ready adaptation to all tongues. It speaks to all nations, and in a world where millions are still illiterate, it speaks as clearly to all people.

Pretty heady stuff. Perhaps today it seems naive and idealistic in view of all the fuss over violence on TV and the cult of the talk show where too many make public what should be private. But Mr. Sarnoff was also prescient. Television is ubiquitous.

Still, it's fair to note that nearly four decades since those words were uttered, the printed page survives. It is no longer the only real journalism, but it has the merit of being tangible in a world of fleeting images. Today's clinical, cubicled, computerized newsrooms don't have the appeal of those long immortalized in great old black-and-white films like *The Front Page* and *His Girl Friday*, where fedoras, cigarettes, tough talk and a jaded world-weariness were trademarks.

Byline

The ink-stained wretches, always unlucky at life and love, would heed the call to become the truth-seeking sifters of evidence. And even though the pay was lousy and the respect hard to command, it was an exclusive club of front-line warriors out to defend the public's right to know.

And if that cloth or fedora didn't fit, well then there was always the more exclusive world of words, where the intelligentsia traded witticisms and carved character assassination into an art form—a world inhabited by Dorothy Parker and pals, whose Round Table luncheons at the famous Algonquin Hotel in New York were legendary. The first time I ever travelled to New York City, covering Trudeau, I made a special trip across town just to look inside the Algonquin, but my search for the round tables was in vain.

I find it reassuring today that, despite all the Cassandra cries that radio, TV or the Internet will render the printed page obsolete, predictions of the industry's demise seem premature. In a recent and rare interview with Canadian media mogul Conrad Black, I could still sense the seductiveness of that ink-stained world in his eyes and words as we wrestled about the future of his newspaper empire, the power of those who run one and the importance of ideas.

Soon the convergence of television, computer and the Internet technologies will render our old debates about form redundant. But with any luck, we will turn our attention to content and to the capability of technology to help sort through the veritable flood of facts and information that wash over us each and every day.

Did you know that the total of all information available to us today—all that fills every brain, every library and every computer chip—represents just one percent of what we will have access to in our own lifetime?

It's a stunning statistic.

My hope is that despite the increasingly isolated and individualistic approach to consuming news that technology affords, there will still be a role for the journalist to keep sifting and seeking truth.

I don't mean people should forfeit their responsibility or the right to stay and be informed. But perhaps we will come to see the modern journalist as a live search engine who will continue to help sort through and determine what is most important to know out of all that we might know.

But if that is to happen, journalists must become more than the "merchandisers of polarity," a phrase coined by Hugh Segal in his book *Beyond Greed* to describe the simplistic good guys–bad guys approach to news and politics. And we must give up on the all-too-easy resort to the "politics of solutionism," where we, even though we know better, expect that all problems could be solved by politicians if only they were smart enough to devise those politically correct, legally defensible and fiscally responsible miracles on the spot.

Edward R. Murrow, the late great journalistic icon who eventually moved from print to the world of TV, was a source of inspiration then and now, with insights such as "It takes two to tell the truth— one to speak it, one to hear it."

It has always been the responsibility of journalists to see that wrongs are, if not righted, at least exposed for the world to see and pass judgment on. But it is also true that the readers and the viewers must take the time to listen, to hear and to decide for themselves whether they will be willing participants in or passive spectators of our democracy on parade.

7

Lights, Camera, Make-up

Instant gratification takes too long.

— CARRIE FISHER, actor and author

You're probably reading this book because you know me from television. You've seen me looking back at you either from behind a studio desk or perhaps from some foreign capital or hot spot.

TV makes whatever—or whomever—you see on it larger than life. I mean this quite literally. People frequently stop me to point out, depending on their degree of sensitivity, that I am either so much taller on TV or so much shorter in real life.

Since I first appeared on television in 1980 much has changed, both for television and for me. I had been at the *Star*'s Ottawa bureau for less than a year when CTV called and asked if I'd appear on that week's *Question Period* as a panelist. I saw this opportunity as yet another positive result of being one of the few women in the journalistic pool. Qualified journalists in skirts were harder to come by than ones in suits and the need to have a woman on the set was beginning to be seen as more important than it had been even two or three years before. I didn't hesitate about accepting the invitation. I was a reporter and this was a program for Canadian reporters, probably the best.

The American versions of the program, shows like *Meet the Press*, have long and proud traditions, but Americans always cover politics as sport and therefore their programs have always appeared less substantive to me. Then again, that's my perpetual bias about differences in news and current affairs journalism on opposite sides of the 49th parallel.

I don't remember whom we grilled that day, but I do remember exactly what happened after we were off the air. The host of the program, Bruce Philips, a man whom I had respected by reputation long before I had the opportunity to verify personally how much he deserved it, remarked how noticeably without fear I had seemed in front of both the camera and the cabinet minister.

It hadn't really occurred to me to be nervous, I replied. I'd done my homework, was prepared to engage in pointed exchanges with the guest and had merely, in fact, been practising my craft as a journalist. That a camera—with hundreds of thousands of sets of eyes behind it—had been watching us wasn't a big issue for me. That, he said, was exactly his point.

Maybe it was that Bruce, despite his many years as a newspaperman, had a more prescient sense of the growing power of this relatively new medium than those of us who still considered TV a thin companion to print when it came to political analysis, but he told me to consider my responsibilities. Many can report the news but few, he said, can do it so comfortably in front of the demanding eye of the camera. It was a gift, he said, and not one to be taken lightly.

Bruce understood how to use the TV camera better than almost anyone I know. It is an intimate medium and he used it instinctively. He never bothered with the big booming anchor voice—

instead he would tell his stories in a quiet tone that would actually make you stop and pay attention.

Few words are allowed in TV because of the relentless ticking clock, so each must be carefully chosen for maximum impact. Bruce taught me that TV is both art and craft. It's about nuance and tiny wry smiles, sweaty brows and shifting eyes. And it's about telling a story.

In the early eighties, *Question Period* was must-watch viewing for the politicos. Bruce had been a newsman long enough to be a real "veteran." More than anyone else, he started me thinking of the word *veteran* in a very new way—not as meaning ancient but as having been around long enough to know that news is cyclical. Bruce had perspective.

His "Brucegrounders," which he delivered at the end of the CTV national news, always contained an angle on the events of the day that made you understand that while time never stops flowing in one direction, most things that concern us deeply have happened before, even if they were dressed differently.

And if what goes around comes around in politics, then it is surely true in life, as well. It's time now to go back to the National Press Club and re-introduce Jack Fleischmann.

Jack, you may recall, had been my boss at my first Ottawa job as a story editor on *CBO Morning* with Elizabeth Gray. You may also recall that between Elizabeth and me, Jack had run screaming for the exit and had actually left radio entirely after a year of working with us.

It's fair to say that Jack and I had not parted as friends. Instead, we had parted with a mutual feeling that if we ever met again one of us might feign a heart attack as an excuse to exit the room. Well, we did meet again and it was at the Press Club. Given our history, things were a little tense. I had come down from the *Star* office several flights up for a moment or two of quiet thought over a ginger ale. I was standing at the bar and there was only one other person doing likewise.

When I realized it was Jack I found myself wishing my ginger ale were a vodka. It was impossible not to acknowledge each other. We did and began, tentatively, to talk. He was now the news producer in the CTV Ottawa bureau. And we were both a little older and wiser. As we parted this time to return to work, we left, if not as friends, then at least with the possibility of becoming so. It's funny now to think how uncomfortable the two of us were, but that accidental and serendipitous meeting marked the beginning of years of friendship and association.

I had been appearing on *Question Period* fairly regularly and that sparked some tentative interest from both CBC and CTV. The CBC was talking about offering me work in one of its western bureaus. But I had just made it back to the Hill and I wasn't about to be seduced away again.

CTV's offer was too vague to consider seriously, so for several months I quite happily continued my double life of print reporter for the *Star* and regular television contributor. *Question Period* was recorded live to tape (no editing) on Friday afternoons and shown on the CTV network on Sundays. Because there were so few political forums on Canadian TV the program always attracted the biggest newsmakers and what was said often made news of its own.

Bruce, with little ego and the confidence that experience brings, was the type of moderator who felt his job was to get the topic rolling and perhaps to direct traffic, but the actual ankle-biting was left to us terriers on the panel.

There's a special responsibility that comes with facing a subject in front of a live camera and it was even more so when politicians' private lives were still considered by the press to be worth publicizing only if we could establish some real relevancy to their public duties.

One ministerial guest was known to insiders to be both married and involved in an intimate relationship with his press secretary. Before heading off to the studio, I wrestled with the issue with some of my *Star* colleagues to decide if it was fair game to raise a question about the relationship. We all knew that the press secretary jealously guarded access to her boss and her reluctance to make him available did constitute interference in the natural process of press accessibility. But was that serious enough to make it an issue of some national importance? In the end we concluded that although the situation was a bit of a pain in reportorial circles, it didn't justify asking the minister about it on national television since it seemed to have no serious effects on his work.

So I didn't ask the question, and I still think it was the correct decision. And just as a postscript, the minister eventually left his wife and he and his former press secretary now have their own family.

Usually on *Question Period* I asked whatever was on my mind and often, it seemed, it was the only venue in which I would get a spontaneous and heartfelt response. One such encounter involved Peter Lougheed. It may have been our first "on-air" meeting since our brief skirmish and resulting truce in Alberta.

In between our two meetings—in November of 1981—the federal forces of Pierre Trudeau and the premiers had forged an agreement to amend the Canadian Constitution, which excluded the province of Quebec. It was the so-called patriation battle and it caused a wound in the national body that has yet to be healed.

René Lévesque, the premier of Quebec and a separatist (his provincial referendum on separation the previous year had been soundly defeated), and Peter Lougheed, premier of Alberta, had an affinity of sorts, based on their common feeling of being "outsiders," though for very different reasons.

Without reviewing reams of history, much of which is still to be written, at the eleventh hour an agreement was hammered out by the key players including federal attorney-general Jean Chrétien, Saskatchewan's attorney-general Roy Romanow and Ontario's attorney-general Roy McMurtry and their backroom boys, supposedly in a kitchen.

All the premiers except Lévesque (and Manitoba's Sterling Lyon, who was absent) were informed and approved of the agreement, and the "kitchen compromise" was redrafted to form the final accord. When it was sprung on Lévesque the next morning, predictably he refused to sign it and the province of Quebec was separated from the rest of the country almost as significantly as any referendum might have done. It was in the days following this historic clash that Lougheed was a guest on QP. My question to Premier Lougheed was: If anyone might have convinced Lévesque to understand the consequences of his refusal to join the rest of the country in a process that had eluded solution for a century, it was Lougheed. Shouldn't he have gone to Lévesque to make one final appeal? Would the entire course of Canadian history be different if he had at least tried to prevent Lévesque's being cast so obviously as odd man out?

All Lougheed could say was that he honestly didn't know for sure. And here's where TV becomes so powerful. Because it's not just what you say or don't say. It's how you look when you do so. In print, the question would have been almost not worth asking, because the answer was not in his words but in his eyes. Live on television, you couldn't help but notice the thoughtful look of a man who has, as well as a long list of accomplishments, another list of "what-ifs."

My TV encounters were a very different experience for me from doing interviews captured on a tape recorder or jotted down in a notebook and then used piecemeal in news stories. But both TV and print were aspects of the same process for me: opening up the world of national politics for those people whose only access to political information was through the media.

Though I wasn't making a point of being in front of a television set myself when a program aired on Sunday afternoons, I certainly made a point of letting my parents know that I would be on. One of the bonuses of working on TV is that it gives you contact with far-flung family and friends. Colleagues noticed my frequent appearances and always had a comment or a bit of advice.

Sometimes even people I met on the street would remark that they'd seen me on TV. The instant gratification of someone responding to my work was great. In newspapers, reporters are often invisible to the reading public and the feedback comes mainly from your editors. Slowly I began to reform my ill-founded bias against the "two-ton pencil"—a slight on the cumbersome nature of TV and all its technology and toys.

Bruce was generous with his encouragements, even though a look back at some of those early tapes suggests just how much polishing I needed, despite the lack of self-consciousness.

To me there wasn't much difference between scrumming in the foyer of Commons and doing the same thing on national television. I liked to ask questions and get answers, and I felt it was important work. Where and how I did it were less important to me.

It was in this context—as I gained a new appreciation of the power of television to reveal what the printed page couldn't—that I became much more receptive to the first serious offer from CTV.

The network was prepared to create an entirely new position that would allay my fears about leaving Ottawa. I was to become, if I went for it, the Ottawa-based co-host of CTV's national morning program, *Canada AM*. I could stay in the familiar embrace of the Hill and do exactly the kind of stories that were my reason for wanting to be there in the first place. The catch was that the show went on the air at 6:30 A.M. and I would have to appear live. It wasn't an easy decision for me to make. I was, after all, just settling into the world of newspapers and I liked it there.

On the positive side, at least Jack and I had made up, so that would make it possible to work in the bureau. And Bruce was the most important teacher and ally you could have. But, among other concerns, I am, by nature, a night person. And I had vowed I'd never do another morning shift again. So I wavered.

Don Cameron, CTV's vice-president of news and a man who would have a important influence on my life, came from Toronto to make a pitch. Don was a feisty old-school reporter and he regaled me with stories about the wonders of live TV. As the evening wore on he became more and more convincing. I didn't sleep for the next few nights.

And for the new few days I grappled with my doubts. I talked it over with Lou Clancy, my boss at *The Toronto Star* and Bill Fox, my friend and colleague at the bureau. Terry Keleher, a civil servant who had become my close friend, listened patiently for hours as I weighed the pros and cons. They all said the same thing: go for it, that if it didn't work out I could always come back to print with no face lost. Lou Clancy has never really admitted whether he meant it or not. Fortunately for him, and maybe for me, he was never put to the test. The support and encouragement that I received from my friends and colleagues were gratifying and, in the end, made the decision less onerous. Except for Hubie Bauch, a friend, a brilliant writer and a reporter at the Ottawa bureau of the *Montreal Gazette,* who warned me solemnly that the killer TV would sap the blood from my journalistic veins. We've kept in touch over the years and when he agreed several years back to do a regular television "gig," he called to ask me if I had any words of advice or warning. We had a good laugh.

Along with their best wishes, my colleagues at the *Star* presented me with a copy of a recent bestseller, *I'm Dancing As Fast As I Can*. It was the true life story of the very successful and influential producer and filmmaker Barbara Gordon, who, overwhelmed by the anxiety and pressures of her high-stress, high-profile job, gets hooked on Valium and spirals into a massive depression. Those of us in the news business have a macabre sense of humour. But kidding aside, there was a gentle message there. Be careful and keep what's about to happen in perspective.

My emotions ran the gamut as I reluctantly agreed to leave the

Star and, with the enthusiasm of the naive, set out to become a full-time broadcast journalist.

Television technology, always both the advantage and the impediment to news gathering and reporting, was evolving at a staggering pace—along with the technology to transmit the voices and pictures the camera could capture. Newer cameras were lighter, less cumbersome and more portable. CNN, the fledgling cable news network, was to change the face of television news by doing with pictures what *As It Happens* had done with voices on the telephone. The place of television in journalism was rapidly expanding. Though I still felt that print was, in many ways, the real thing, I was excited by the sense that I was moving into a new and expanding field. I have never regretted the choice.

I worked incredibly hard, even in comparison with other jobs about which I might have said the same thing.

The day's assignments would be planned in conjunction with the powers in Toronto and with Fiona Conway, *Canada AM*'s Ottawa producer (now the senior producer in New York at ABC's morning show, *Good Morning America*), and we would set about lining up a guest or guests for me to interview.

Since stories and priorities changed all day long, the work never ended. I would do very much what I was used to doing when covering a story—phone calls, research, meeting with contacts. The homework was the same, but with the added complications that come with the necessities of the world the critics call light, bright and trite, everything from make-up and hairspray to having the right pictures to help tell the story. But there was also a kicker: as I said, I am not a morning person but I had to be in the studio looking and acting awake and alert while most self-respecting roosters were just rolling over for another hour's sleep.

My days often started before dawn and usually didn't end until late in the evening. In addition, I eagerly accepted other duties, a first ministers' meeting, for example, that might have me reporting or co-hosting with Bruce Philips on location while Lloyd Robertson, CTV's main man on mike for such events, ran the show from the Toronto anchor desk.

But my first obligation was *Canada AM*. The show had two able on-air hosts, Norm Perry and Gail Scott. At some prearranged point in the morning's show I would be introduced from Ottawa and do my segments, always handing back to Gail and Norm. At nine I'd begin the rest of my day's work.

It was in those very first days as a regular on-air contributor that I had one of those experiences that is the stuff of nightmares for the broadcaster. But it left me with some very important lessons, and it shows a very human side of the business. I certainly wouldn't choose to do it again—though I may well.

I had been assigned to cover the G-7 economic summit at Montebello, Quebec (a Wadena-sized village), an hour or so outside Ottawa. It's a place for conferences and retreats and summits. We had taken our cameras on location to record as many interviews as we could. The logistics of booking these world leaders was a nightmare in itself, but we had managed to nail down a couple of the biggies.

We were coming up to a commercial break with maybe a minute to go and I was proudly announcing the roster of guests that viewers could look forward to hearing in the next hour of the program.

"British prime minister Margaret Thatcher will be with us," I said with some excitement, "and so will chancellor of West Germany Helmut Shit."

I heard the words at exactly the same moment as everyone else and their effect on me was nothing short of terror. The moment is etched indelibly on my mind. I had two thoughts: first, I was actually afraid that I might have set off an international diplomatic incident (though it probably wasn't the first time Mr. Schmidt had heard the mispronunciation); second, it was clear my brief career was over. And, to make the situation as awful as it could possibly be, the unblinking camera was still staring at me, waiting to be satisfied for another three-quarters of a minute.

By that time the cameraman was on the floor in fits of laughter. But I continued to talk—though, to be honest, I can't begin to remember about what. Finally I handed back to Norm, and the commercial break. As CTV sold some Remington shavers, I collapsed into a quivering mess. For the first time in my memory, I was literally speechless.

I felt a sense of almost quiet relief knowing that my brief career was about to end, because even if I wasn't summarily fired I knew that I could never and would never show my face in public ever again. At that moment Bruce Philips strode into the office, laughing, and opened with "It was bound to happen. It's happened to all of us."

Though I knew he was probably telling me the truth, it still wasn't comforting enough to turn what felt like a globally witnessed humiliation into just another fluffed line. What he said next, however, while not saving the day, did provide a valuable lesson. "You'll see," he said, "that no one will believe that you really said it on television." I was astonished to discover that he was right. Of course I pulled myself together and continued through my day. And to my amazement—and relief—anyone who mentioned the event offered some variation on "You know, I thought I heard you say something really rude on the air this morning, but it was so early and I hadn't had any coffee yet so it must have been me. But I could have almost sworn you said . . ." I must confess that I didn't rush to correct the record.

What I learned from the incident had nothing to do with the fact that I could make embarrassing mistakes. I already knew that, and, as Bruce reminded me, it happens to everyone. What I learned was much more important. I learned that I could keep going in the face of a crisis, that I could continue to talk coherently and professionally to the camera and the audience behind it even when my own mind was momentarily paralyzed. And I learned just how much power is bestowed by the television universe on those of us who inhabit it. People actually disbelieved their ears and gave me the benefit of the doubt. They just didn't think I would do it so they were convinced I hadn't.

It is that power to convince, that armour of credibility that our medium gives us, that we, as journalists, mustn't ever misuse. To be blasé or cynical about what we say is to undermine our implicit contract with viewers. Slips of the tongue are one thing, but the ease with which ill-chosen words can have an impact on the lives of those we cover, or those who watch, is just an example of the many ethical and moral dilemmas that we must weigh and balance each time we open our mouths. There's not a day goes by that I don't feel the burden of this responsibility.

Just a final thought about those of us who live in the ultimate glass house. I believe we owe it to those who put their trust in us to examine our own actions, be they individual or collective, to determine whether we could withstand the same scrutiny we expect others to withstand. In a world where a free press is a freedom we have come to take for granted, media accountability is a concept that deserves more attention.

While we're on the topic of how TV journalists are perceived by their audience, I'd like to take a brief, unscheduled detour here and say a word or two about make-up.

Getting up for work before the dawn had even begun to wash the sky was not a new experience for me when I began *Canada AM*. I had done morning radio in both Regina and Ottawa and in both cases had reported for work about the same time as the milkmen. But the only people who saw me were the few other red-eyed folk who worked on the same killer shift. Not so on *Canada AM*, where several hundred thousand people had the daily opportunity to pass judgment not only on my work, but on the outfit I'd chosen from my dark closet before my eyes had really opened.

Lights, Camera, Make-up

When I was at university I wore almost no make-up. It was a political statement made at a time in my life when it cost me nothing to make it. I was a teenager and, like most if not all young women, I didn't really need make-up unless I was aiming for an intentionally dramatic effect. In other words, I didn't need to use anything to camouflage the passage of time or the effects of little sleep.

And in the world of radio, glamour is not a prerequisite for its producers, because the telephone, like its progeny the Internet, permits one the advantage of being unobserved. So my no make-up policy, though it mutated slightly to become an *almost* no make-up policy, remained largely intact.

At the *Star*, my duties were out in the real world, in the public sphere, so I was much more conscious than I had ever been in radio of presenting myself publicly in the way a professional journalist is supposed to look. And for my brief appearances on *Question Period* a professional make-up artist did what was needed.

For a woman in any occupation where she meets and greets the public, there were the mandatory prescribed facial additives, but I always wore the absolute minimum I could get away with. However, when I became a television journalist all the rules changed. Television tolerates few compromises and there was continual input over how much and what colour.

Suddenly, besides getting the story or the interview or the tape, besides waking up in the middle of the night so I could get to the studio on time, ingesting enough caffeine somewhere along the way to pass as conscious and sounding both knowledgeable and friendly when I appeared on camera, now I had to look a particular way.

It was the thing I disliked most about the entire television experience and I raise it now because it was only going to get worse. At that point I could still handle the what-shall-I do-with-my-hair issue by tying it back in a ponytail so that it hung almost unnoticed behind me—but that was about to change too. Though it may seem like a small thing compared with the hard work that television's sleight-of-hand requires, it continued to raise questions for me about the synthetic, staged nature of so much that occurs on TV.

Just for the record, I currently wear make-up regularly and even more of it on TV. And anyone who has looked at herself under harsh lights and on camera without the benefit of appropriate make-up knows the reason any professional puts it on. So many people think this is vanity. It is quite emphatically a necessity.

I was amazed at the rather catty observation made by a feature writer who came to interview me at the CBC when I worked at *Prime Time*. When the article appeared he wrote that I had to come to my office (the same place as our studio) with make-up on! For me, that's getting ready for work, not primping for a reporter.

Then again, going without make-up on Saturday mornings to the grocery store is also a depressing experience. Viewers come up to me to comment on the program but invariably also comment on my looks. Usually these comments are generous and kind. Some say I look younger in person, but then there are those faces fill with disappointment at the first sign of recognition. "You look so much different on TV," they say, when most of the time they really mean better!

With the move from the *Star* to CTV and the change in lifestyle, the last year had been dizzying, aided and abetted by my insomnia, which allowed for both late dinners and early shifts. Suddenly things got complicated again. Don Cameron, the vice-president of CTV News who had convinced me to try the remote-host trick, buzzed into town, took me to dinner in Hull and asked me to move to Toronto to take over Gail Scott's chair at action central.

I quickly calculated that if I said yes I would be facing my eighth move since leaving Wadena, and then surprised myself by not immediately refusing to leave, yet again, the closest thing I'd had to a home since childhood.

It was actually a terribly difficult decision for me to make and I told Don so. I didn't much like the very idea of being one step removed from the story. But as a graduate of *As It Happens* I had a very high respect for the power of the interview and the role of the interviewer. And I knew that CTV, considerably more than the CBC, gave on-air journalists a freer hand to do their work. Lloyd Robertson had jumped networks for that very reason.

Cameron left me to consider his offer. On one hand, I didn't want to leave Ottawa. On the other, being the co-host of one of Canada's foremost news and current affairs television programs—many called it the best job of its kind in the country—was seductive.

Ottawa had always been a comfort zone for me. I had good friends and good memories. Playing croquet dressed all in white on the grassy grounds of the Supreme Court Building was a July 1 custom among tongue-in-cheeky journalists. Broads Canada gatherings helped me keep perspective in the middle of a life that otherwise could seem a bit frenetic. I still hung out and carried on with my friends from the *Star*. And, of course, there was only one Parliament Hill.

I called my parents to let them in on Don Cameron's offer. They were proud and said I should follow my heart, but not before first listening to my head. They would be happy as long as I was with whatever decision I made.

So here I was again at decision time, and as I always do I canvassed my friends and advisors and most told me I'd be foolish to refuse.

I knew from the last time I'd done this shuffle that I wouldn't lose touch with people because the combination of technology and the work we were all in assured that we'd be bumping into each other whatever address was on our driver's licence. And over and over I heard what an opportunity this was and what regrets I might have if I passed it up. There is that wonderful quote, and I can't remember who said it, but it goes like this: "Regret for the things we did can be tempered by time. It is regret for the things we did not do that is inconsolable."

Still, I tried to have my cake and eat it too. I proposed that they let me co-host from Ottawa, and when Don quickly refused that option as being impossibly expensive and forbiddingly difficult, I agreed to take the job. Move number eight was under way.

I took my new position on *Canada AM* on December 7, 1981, the anniversary of the bombing of Pearl Harbor. My very first morning as co-host on *Canada AM* I had an allergic response to the make-up. My eyes turned bright red and swelled, until I looked like I'd been in a bar fight the night before. There was nothing the make-up artist could do but camouflage. So I made my television debut that morning knowing that I must appear to be in the midst of some tearful personal crisis. There was no opportunity to explain and I could make no reference to my appearance. That was the least of my problems as things turned out.

I had no idea at the time—no one except the odd South American general could have—that I would barely have a chance to warm the seat beside Norm Perry before my life would absorb another dramatic shudder.

By April of 1982 there was a war in the Falklands. The fighting lasted about two months and I was stationed in Buenos Aires during most of it. Before that war ended I had a new respect for television, and a husband in the making.

8

War!

Fools rush in where angels fear to tread.
—ALEXANDER POPE

HERE WAS A COMBINATION
of factors that kept me unset-
tled for a while after my ar-
rival back in Toronto as co-host of *Canada AM*. The short version is
that while I could tell what a cabinet minister was thinking at fifty
paces, I was not as attuned to the new office politics. I had taken a
high-profile and much-desired job and it came in a package that
contained a lot of other people and their ambitions too.

I was staying in a hotel and trying to find a place to live and adjust to an even earlier wake-up call in the middle of the night. And I
was leaping on planes between Toronto and Ottawa to cover events in
the lead-up to the official signing of the new Constitution of Canada.

It was in the midst of this crazy time that I accidentally received
a very special honour. It wasn't that it was an accidental honour; it's
just that I almost missed receiving it.

Pierre Trudeau had invited the Queen to Ottawa to proclaim
Canada's patriated Constitution. By that time, so much horse trading had gone on in order to bring the Constitution home and for

Trudeau to have his much-cherished Charter of Rights attached to it that no one, not even the new fathers of Confederation, was clamouring to claim it as their own.

Terry Mosher, the cartoonist known as Aislin, had captured the moment: the Queen is sitting in the Speaker's chair in the House of Commons, holding out a tattered and torn document to anyone who will accept it. All she says is "Here."

I was in Ottawa for the signing and there was to be a state dinner that night in honour of the Queen, during which she was to bestow some honours herself. It was April 17, 1982, and I had just celebrated my twenty-ninth birthday. As was common, some members of the press corps were invited as guests and not just as on-the-job reporters covering the event. And I was fortunate enough to be an invitee.

I had planned to attend the dinner, but as the day progressed it wasn't looking as if I would be able to make it. We had a crisis with the guests for *Canada AM* the next morning so I was working late to smooth things over.

Finally, an aide from the prime minister's office called to check on whether I would be attending. I said I'd try but that the show came first. She strongly urged me to attend, which I found a little odd. In the end I showed up, took my place at the assigned table, only to discover that I, along with a group of others, was about to be named by the Queen as a Young Canadian Achiever!

Even though I was neither prepared nor dressed for the occasion, and despite my embarrassment, it was still a wonderful, albeit surprising, honour. The accidental achiever.

I flew back to Toronto after the show the next morning, but within days I was back in the air, this time headed due south. Argentine forces had invaded and claimed a small group of British islands several hundred miles off the South American coast and set off a war with Britain that was to produce global anxiety, much destruction and a thousand young dead. It would also change my life forever.

The Falkland Islands have a population of about two thousand people and they mostly raise sheep. Even a curious Charles Darwin had ignored the Falklands, sailing past what he described as "miserable" little islands, which were basically used as a penal colony.

The islands had been a dependency of Britain since early last century, but the Argentine government had been arguing for control of them for most of that time. On March 19, 1982, Argentine soldiers posing as scrap-metal dealers raised their country's flag on what they call the Islas Malvinas. By April 2, while talks were still going on over the future of the islands, Argentine forces overran the place, many claim because the generals who ruled the country ruthlessly at the time needed to distract the population from the brutality of their regime and bolster their image across the country.

Margaret Thatcher, then prime minister of Britain, had her own image to protect and an election to win and so responded quickly and forcefully. It was all-out war.

CTV, like every news-gathering organization on the planet, immediately sent in its own troops. Craig Oliver was CTV's man in Washington and he and his crew of two (camera and sound) were on assignment in Central America, where there was continuing conflict between American-backed forces and several local governments or rebel forces. The three of them had been surrounded by fighting for close to two months with no break, but since they were the closest CTV crew to Buenos Aires they were inducted into the Falklands War, media division. Craig, feeling the effects of being away from home for much too long, asked Don Cameron to arrange for some relief. Don obliged by sending in an Ottawa-based reporter, Peter Lloyd, though Craig stayed on briefly to help him get settled.

The problem there was that Peter's Canadian passport showed that he was British-born and he felt especially vulnerable in a city that was bubbling with anti-British sentiment and that had a reputation long before the outbreak of the dispute as a terrifying place run by military forces with no regard for personal rights.

Just days before Peter's arrival, a British journalist had been found in the middle of an Argentine highway, beaten, stripped naked and left for dead. After three or four days, during which time he stayed close to his Buenos Aires hotel room, Peter finally headed for home. Not surprisingly, that didn't sit well with Don, a veteran reporter from the Vietnam days. Peter's argument—that he had been hired to cover politics not wars—fell on deaf ears. His television career would be shortlived.

So the problem of who would pinch-hit for Craig Oliver was still unresolved. It hadn't occurred to me that I might be the lucky one. I was, after all, the new host of the morning program, not a roving reporter and, though Ann Medina was a familiar face reporting from the Middle East (always a war zone of some description), front-line war duty was still generally not considered a job for women.

Don Cameron reminded me of that when he called me in to give me my assignment. "Screw this up," he said (or words to that effect) "and you'll ruin it for all women who want to be war correspondents."

Don was also nervous about whether this situation would prove too dangerous. CTV had recently lost reporter Clark Todd in the Middle East, and his bloody death had raised many questions about whether the network had put him in harm's way. Without the knowledge of the CTV assignment desk, Todd and his cameraman had headed into dangerous turf and had come under artillery fire in the Shouf mountains in Lebanon. Todd was shot and bled to death. Don Cameron and Tim Kotcheff, who was second in command in the news department, risked their own lives going into the combat zone to retrieve his body. The network certainly didn't want to have to go through that again, particularly if a woman was the victim.

Besides having the fate of all female reporters on my shoulders, I also felt the pressure of the more obvious problems: covering a war in a strange country, the ruthless military dictatorship, my inability to speak the country's language and the general local antagonism toward English speakers and media people in particular, just to name a few.

The truth is, I was thrilled to go, but I never completely shook the feeling that Don was boneshakingly right. If I did this badly it would not be good for women who felt, as I did, as capable and deserving as any man in the profession of any assignment in the world.

Once I had absorbed the news that I would be, in a matter of hours, on the next flight out, I was quite exhilarated. I knew I would be flying headlong into danger but that the actual war was far away from the capital, in the waters off the coast or on the islands themselves.

Being in Buenos Aires had its own dangers, but most of the excitement came from being part of the biggest story of the day. This was the first time an actual war had broken out since television technology had advanced enough to cover it almost in real time.

We all remembered the images from Vietnam, but in those days the film still had to be carried out of the war zone by hand. Sometimes the reports and pictures were days old before they reached viewers. But this time from Buenos Aires the media could show all of Canada what was going on and try to make sense of it as it happened.

I left almost immediately, prepared for a three- or four-day stint that would permit Craig to return briefly to Washington where he was posted as the CTV bureau chief. As things turned out, Craig never did come back and I remained in Buenos Aires for almost two months—because that's how long it took for the fighting to end.

Every day of those two months was filled with all the drama and satisfaction I could have imagined—and considerably more.

I had no realistic idea of what to expect when I arrived since there wasn't much time to do research on the country or its people. I had never been to South America and adobe huts were what I had visualized during the endless flight. As it turned out, Paris would have been more a appropriate image.

Argentina's population is mostly of Spanish and Italian descent and Buenos Aires compares in modernity and stylishness with any of the most striking cities of Europe.

I was travelling with producer Barry Barnett , and we were met at the airport by an interpreter and whisked to the Buenos Aires Sheraton, where I met up with the CTV crew in the lobby just as they were on their way out to dinner.

Craig Oliver was still there, waiting to get me settled into my new duties so he could finally get out and home. The soundman was Peter Arciuch, about whom I knew only one thing: he was very good at his job. The cameraman was Malcolm Fox, about whom I knew two things: he was very good at his job and, as Don Cameron had specifically warned me, he had a reputation as a ladies' man. Don's advice was to stay clear and stick to business. I have never been good at following advice. The trio gave me just enough time to throw my bags into my room before we were off. That evening, though it might have been the next, Malcolm and I started to fall in love.

My time in Buenos Aires was intoxicating. It's a perverse irony that has escaped no working journalist that we thrive on tragedy. I don't enjoy the misfortunes of others. If there are journalists who hope for war or disaster, then I've never met them. But journalists and the organizations we work for too often reach our highest level of achievement and garner our greatest professional rewards under the most terrible of circumstances. For two months I covered an event that killed a thousand men and raised the tension level on the planet a few notches. And I watched and worked from the capital city of a country already bowed in sadness and fear from years under the oppression of its military government.

I'd had just a day or two on the ground to settle in when Pope John Paul II arrived for a visit planned long before the outbreak of hostilities. Hundreds of thousands gathered to catch a glimpse of the pontiff and I had only one chance to prove to my new colleagues that I was up to the job. Malcolm set up the shot and explained that at the very instant the Popemobile passed by on the street behind I was to do my stand-up. I'd have somewhere between eight and fifteen seconds to say my bit and sign off with the Pope as my backdrop. There was only one chance. I rehearsed, quietly knowing it would be a great shot if I could do it. It would also buy the novice reporter some goodwill with the seasoned veterans. I did it and the smile on Malcolm's face was my reward.

The Buenos Aires Sheraton looked like the command centre for D-Day, but considerably more advanced. The American networks had whole floors booked to accommodate their manpower and technology. ABC, for instance, seemed to have more electronics strewn throughout the hotel than CTV had in their entire network. We made a deal with them to piggyback on their studio and satellite facilities for the morning show and to pool tape and crews for news purposes, which was both convenient and cheaper for us. The trade-off was that we had no bully power.

Because CTV could not afford the costs of being a full satellite partner, we were always low man on the totem pole and therefore generally the last to feed out our reports. But doing more with less was a credo at CTV and the arrangement meant that we were able to do live hits into *Canada AM* early in the morning, the late-night national news and just about anywhere in between if there was anything worth reporting. I was sending back, in addition to news reports, several voice reports every day to update news bulletins. We always felt a certain pride that our work, in terms of content, was always just as respectable as anything an American network produced with tenfold the resources and manpower.

Because the time difference between Toronto and Buenos Aires is small—Argentina is located just under our Maritime provinces—our day started much as it might have at home. I began with a live segment for *Canada AM* just as I had when I'd been the Ottawa-based host. I even tried to look the part, dressed for the studio not the streets. Then we went to work. By the time I was feeding into the national news late at night I looked like . . . well, like I'd been in a war zone.

I didn't know it at the time, but television being what it is, the variation of "looks" actually helped to enhance my reputation as a reporter with range.

Malcolm, Peter, our interpreter and I spent our days covering the press conferences, the diplomatic comings and goings and scouting out material that would help explain the nationalism fuelling this war and the puzzling willingness of Argentines to support the ruthless regime that was making people's lives hell even when there wasn't a war. Our job was to give this confrontation a face, whether it was soldiers on board ships facing battle, frightened citizens waiting for word of loved ones or intransigent rulers watching their own fortunes rise and fall with the fortunes of war.

I said my time in Buenos Aires was exciting but it was also fearful and sad. Every street corner had armed soldiers. These recruits, some perhaps as young as twelve or thirteen, were left to patrol the streets while their elders were fighting at sea. Then there was the ongoing story of the "disappeared."

Over the preceding years, hundreds of young men and women had simply vanished, disappearing into the back of the Ford Falcons used by the secret police. You could tell it was secret police because the licence plates were tipped forward so no one could read the numbers and try to trace them as the police whisked some poor young citizen to a shallow grave.

We went to talk with the mothers of the "disappeared" one morning while they paraded, as they did daily, around and around the Plaza de Mayo, their deep eyes a mixture of sorrow and anger. Each carried a photograph of a loved one about whose fate they knew absolutely nothing except that he or she had gone missing, not in battle but into the grim clutches of the shadowy authorities who tolerated neither dissent nor criticism. This was a dictatorship, not a democracy.

It was moments like this that the girl from the prairies would silently pray to whatever higher being exists out there and give thanks that I had a predictable and peaceable country to call home and to go back to.

One afternoon when the four of us were driving around the city, we were stopped and taken in by uniformed, gun-toting authorities. We had been warned this might happen. You never really knew whether these people were legitimate police, secret forces or military personnel. They took us to a place that bore no official signs and looked more like a vacant commercial building commandeered for their private use.

Our interpreter was immediately separated from us. I believe he was taken away so that they could exert extra pressure on him by playing on his vulnerability as a local citizen, and one with identity papers that showed his mother to be British. But I also sensed it was so that they might claim—if they needed to—that there had been a miscommunication between them and us. Without our interpreter there was no way to make our case.

It added to the tension—I guess that was part of the intent—wondering what kind of danger our interpreter might be in for merely being found in our company. As it turned out, whoever they were, they seemed to want little from us except to scare us for their own perverse entertainment. But we also knew that freelance thugs roamed the city and took people at will and so we couldn't underestimate the potential risk.

I was somewhere between anxious and frightened, but I had two things in my mind that kept my confidence secure during the ordeal. One was the power of publicity. I felt, perhaps naively, that we were protected because we were being watched—metaphorically, at least—by the world. Oddly enough, Canadians weren't, at least not then, held in as much contempt by the Argentines as Americans, because even though we were seen as more closely connected with Britain, the Yanks had openly sided with the British position, while Canada had been considerably less vocal in its support.

The second source of comfort was Malcolm. By the time of our arrest he and I were more than colleagues. I knew instinctively that Malcolm was trying to protect me from them and maybe even from myself. He had spent much of his career in and out of war zones and had faced this type of intimidation before. He was absolutely cool and he'd warned us from the outset to remain polite and non-committal.

Like animals, bullies smell fear, and Malcolm didn't want to give them the satisfaction of knowing we were frightened. I, on the other hand, was thinking that a brazen demand for answers and explanations would show them we were not afraid. But I bowed to Malcolm's experience and the reality that my demands could only be made in English, a language they probably didn't understand. After an hour or so, we were released unharmed.

Since our first meeting in the lobby of the Buenos Aires Sheraton, there had been an instant attraction between Malcolm and me. In the beginning, when I was expecting a stay of less than a week followed by a return to my usual life, I had taken a devil-may-care attitude toward any relationship with Malcolm, and he, my guess is, had felt the same.

But as my stay was extended one day at a time our relationship grew. And though Malcolm and Pamela might not have the same resonance as Rick and Ilsa, there's no denying that living that close to the shadow of war breeds a very poignant sense of mortality, the shortness of time and a we-all-could-die-tomorrow feeling about life, though probably more so for me, the war-zone novice. It wasn't long before our feelings had become as intense as our situation.

The "war zone" romance is heady, intense and surreal. There is a bonding that occurs, even if love doesn't, that ties you to someone forever. That Malcolm would actually save my hide if not my life in the midst of a brutal mob scene sealed our fate.

It's odd what sticks in your mind, but two lovely memories stay with me from our first days together. One occurred on my second night in Buenos Aires, when Malcolm came knocking on my hotel room door at the end of a day's work with a bottle of water in his hand. He'd come to warn me that I shouldn't drink the local water, not even from the hotel's own faucets.

I was touched by his concern, though I have to confess, I knew my health was not his only motive. I invited him in. Several weeks later Malcolm gave me a beautiful antique ring set with black stones, which he'd picked up for me in the city's old market. Since Buenos Aires was on a wartime footing, many stores and cultural attractions like the opera were closed. But on Sundays, in one of the city's oldest sections, it was possible to poke about in small shops and discover some lovely antique pieces that had been brought in by the earliest Europeans, many of them British. Again I was touched by Malcolm's gesture, this time with no reservations.

I loved watching Malcolm work. A good cameraman is a pleasure to see in action. The eye behind the lens has to have as good an editorial sense as the on-air reporter because the visuals can either enhance the viewer's engagement or obstruct it. Malcolm knew what shots were needed to tell the story. I learned more about television from him than I might have in years of sitting in a studio or a journalism class.

On one of my first days in Buenos Aires, we were shooting a stand-up outside the hotel where a beautiful old clock tower presided over the square. I knew the location shouted "I'm in Buenos Aires!" and I asked Malcolm to try to put both me and tower in the shot. He lined up the camera and then told me to change places with him, to look through the lens and see what the shot I had asked for would look like to viewers. I'd never tried that before and was startled at what I saw: a man with a clock tower rising out of the top of his head like a light pole. To get the clock in the shot meant the reporter would be the size of a bug on the screen. If I'd been watching at home I would have been calling the family to come see the absurdity on television and I wouldn't have heard a word of the report. Point made, point taken.

We tried to keep our personal feelings private, which involved more clandestine room-to-room dashes than a French farce, because we didn't want to raise any accusations of dereliction of duty. The opposite was in fact true. Our desire to share our mutual passion for our work only made being on the job the best way to spend time together and the longer the hours the better. I also suspected that Don might intervene the moment he received more news than he'd bargained for.

On April 30, 1982, the u.s. sided vocally with Britain. For a short while Canadian stock went up because we weren't American. On May 3, the Argentine cruiser *The Belgrano* was torpedoed, resulting in almost four hundred missing sailors. Sea battles raged all through May with loss of life on both sides and still I stayed on. That journalists thrive amid the tragedy of individuals and whole nations was never more clear to me than during my time in Buenos Aires. And the intensity of the work and the new relationship combined to make me feel I was living, as Marshall McLuhan said of the young, "mythically and in depth." But we never forgot that we were surrounded by a brutal regime, frightened citizens, pervasive antagonism and constant casualty reports.

By the beginning of June, the Argentine forces were clearly beaten. Although the outcome had been determined, the issue for the military junta was now how to cast blame. From the balcony of the Pink Palace in Buenos Aires, a locale most associated with Evita Peron, General Leopoldo Galtieri, president of Argentina, was to speak to an enormous crowd of people clamouring for some defiant response.

We showed up. He didn't. And all hell was about to break loose. Since the war had been an attempt to mobilize national feeling, to have lost the fight was more devastating than if it had been merely for profit or even principle. It was a national affront. And that the man who had led them into this battle was too gutless to show provoked some anger. The crowd began jeering and shouting something that could be roughly translated as "son of a bitch" about the absent leader. Then the crowd turned on those who would have to now shoulder the blame for their loss and humiliation. Inevitably the journalists were seen as the proxies for those evil, imperialistic forces.

It was evident that hostility toward us, and anyone else who was obviously from the outside (a TV camera is a dead giveaway), was about to erupt. We continued to record what we were seeing, even as the crowd began to turn on us. The police responded by lobbing tear gas into the square, but made no move to protect us from the angry mass. We began to weigh our options. That's always the journalistic dilemma. Is this worth it? Are these pictures necessary? How great is the risk to life and limb?

But fear can be intoxicating too, and adrenalin, if not brains, keeps you going. My shoes were off by that time so I could run more quickly. Then someone knocked me down. Malcolm helped me up and told me to stay close, to hold on to his jacket so we would not be separated. But eventually his helping me was restricting his ability to manoeuvre and protect himself while he captured the ugliness on videotape. He told me to stay down as he pushed me behind the protection of a parked car so he could go back into the fray for some final shots.

We were approaching deadline by that point and had to get back to the hotel to write, cut and edit our piece to make the eleven o'clock deadline. I did my report for that night's national news with barely time to catch my breath, explaining the pictures that showed the mayhem from the vantage of the eye of the storm. I concluded the report with the simple assessment "It's over" because it was obvious that this war was. I was struck by how the U.S. reporters couldn't quite say it. For them it "seemed" to be over, or "appeared" to be over, or was "apparently" over.

The Americans saw my simple statement of the obvious as "hard-hitting." A couple of u.s. network producers said that if I wanted to work stateside I should call them after this was all said and done. Of course I was tempted.

But I had a new job to go home to, and with the benefit of such proximity, I also saw first-hand how American reporters worked. It was clear to me that if I moved south I would have lost some of the very freedom to speak so plainly that had attracted their attention in the first place.

I was always surprised to hear u.s. reporters arguing with the desk editors in New York about adjectives and the tone of a story they were covering. No such nitpicking happened at cTV. In fairness, editorial freedom at cTV was more often by default than design. There are benefits to having fewer managerial eyes watching your every move, even if it's only because the outfit you work for can't afford any more. But there was also a trust in those of us who were on the scene to report events as we saw them. The u.s. media, as representatives of a superpower, always had to keep in mind the greater good of their empire.

I left Buenos Aires for home with so much more than I'd come with, both personally and professionally. I was absolutely captured by the medium of television. I had seen a bit of what TV could do before this experience, but after the Falklands War I knew without a doubt that television was adding something to news coverage that would irreversibly change how people saw their world. And I wanted to be part of it.

My print colleagues would file their reports and twelve or fourteen hours later Canadians would read news that was by that time outdated.

The new technologies were extending (just to go back to McLuhan for a moment) our senses. People in Canada could now look through a window in their den and see right into the streets and squares of Buenos Aires. But someone had to carry the electronic eyeball. And part of what the electronic eye saw was the reporter whose job it was to condense the enormous range of human sight to fit the electronic medium's requirements.

I had discovered the essential core of the medium: immediacy. Before Buenos Aires I had harboured a secret fear that when I found the central concept of the television experience I'd discover it was to do with hairstyles, make-up and whether the blouse matched the skirt. Thankfully, I was wrong. Hairdos and make-up may be tools of the trade, but the mission is so much more important. We see history on the run and the journalist's job is, to paraphrase a greater mind than mine, to be the writers of the rough draft of history. It's no less a task for those of us carrying the two-ton pencil.

When I returned to Toronto, Malcolm came with me for a week or two before heading back to Washington, where he was based. We had talked about future plans, perhaps someday working as a team, an itinerant pair of journalists, our lances free, but we put the idea away for now.

It was June of 1982, and as I returned to an early summer in Toronto I was feeling content with the hand fate had dealt me. I was glad to be home, even though I was uncertain about what this experience would mean for me. However, one of the things I discovered was that while I wasn't looking, I had become somewhat of a celebrity and, this time, for all the right reasons.

9

The Dawn to Midnight Shift

To love what you do and feel that it matters—
how could anything be more fun?
—KATHERINE GRAHAM, publisher

I WAS TAKEN ABACK to discover that my Argentine assignment had become newsworthy back home. "Courage Under Fire" or "Women In War Zones" were the angles. Though I'd been the subject of some interested ink when I took up my *Canada AM* duties, my hiring was considered "entertainment" news. This new attention was very different, since the questioning related directly to the actual work I'd done as a journalist. Still, it felt a little odd to be on the other side of the microphone.

Actor Alan Thicke was host of an afternoon talk show based in Vancouver and I was flown out to appear as a guest. Like movie stars who always bring along a clip of their current movie, I was asked to bring along the footage of the riot in the streets of Buenos Aires. There I was talking about my near-death experience, only to be followed moments later by comedian Howie Mandel doing a stand-up routine. Television makes for strange bedfellows.

Being interviewed wasn't unpleasant, because the emphasis was on my experience in the war zone. There was no controversy in the story that time out and my days of feeling misquoted and misrepresented were still in the future. In fact, I was actually pleased at the attention, in part because of Don's admonition about the fate of women reporters if I failed to perform and also because I believed that women need all the publicity they can get when another stereotype has been shattered. I might not have produced award-winning journalism in Argentina, but what I had achieved had been frank, direct and at least as good, if not better, than some of my American cousins.

CTV, specifically Don Cameron, had given me, and by extension other women, a real opportunity. I have never been in favour of a quota system that dictates what number of women (or any other group) must get what number of jobs. No one is served if the less-than-the-best person gets a position just to meet a target or to assuage some guilt quotient at head office. This problem is much greater in large, more bureaucratic operations. But at CTV there wasn't money or much room for dead wood or token appointments. With Don, if you showed him you took your work seriously, he took you seriously. That's all we ask in the end. Just let us rise or fall on merit.

As glad as I was to come home, it was difficult to settle back into the relative tameness of a studio setting after two months on the loose. But while *Canada AM* was not a war zone, it sometimes felt like one.

Two and a half hours of live TV every day is very much a by-the-seat-of-your-pants operation. Guests don't show up, lines go down and news happens at all hours all over the world. And I was still learning the ropes and running on adrenalin.

The verbal sparring with the likes of the precise and brilliant Marc Lalonde or John Crosbie, one of the most literate parliamentarians ever to grace the Chamber, and doing this knowing my facts had to be absolutely right because it was happening live for the country, my journalistic colleagues included, was exhilarating. On the personal front, I of course missed Malcolm, though we were staying in close touch by phone and regular visits.

In the interviews I gave I had talked about our teamwork, which is the essence of TV, and about how my cameraman had come to my aid in the melee in the square among other times, but I gave nothing away about our personal feelings. I didn't want our work in Argentina to suddenly be cast in a nudge-nudge way and, to be honest, I really didn't have much faith in long-distance relationships. Many romances, forged in the line of fire or in the heat of war-zone reporting, are short-lived.

I wanted this one to last, but it's tough to be an optimist in the face of so much evidence to the contrary. Still, I could not keep my news from friends, and before I'd had a chance to confess, Elizabeth Gray confronted me immediately upon my return to ask for details. I was astonished that she knew anything about my romance and demanded to know who'd tipped her off. It had been, she said, her housekeeper, Adelene, who had watched my Buenos Aires reports religiously and had, at one point, declared to Elizabeth that something wonderful had happened to Pamela. "You can see," she said, "that Pamela's very happy." She was right. Adelene was one of those women with highly honed powers of intuition. When I heard the story, I was reminded immediately of Nan's ring and the special knowledge that some women possess, and I had to smile.

As I settled into my chair as co-host of *Canada AM*, I discovered that some of the issues that had occupied me before my sudden departure for Buenos Aires were still hanging around like ghosts in the attic and still needed to be confronted.

There were the usual tensions and battles that go along with high-stress jobs. Sleep deprivation, for one, which even for an insomniac takes its toll. But some of the battles were more difficult to handle because I felt they involved my integrity in a quite personal way. Some of the battles were over content, what stories to cover and how. And the question of my on-air appearance, the continuing saga of hair and make-up, had once again reared its unsightly head.

CTV had hired me, they said, because I had a brain. Now increasing attention was being focused on what was wrapped around it. With the help of some generous make-up artists I learned how to do my own face. It ensured a consistent look and I wasn't left in the lurch by having to do my make-up and Norm's if someone failed to show up for work. I kept my long hair tamed in a ponytail or a chignon. In Argentina, I had been at the mercy of the circumstances, but with the aid of hot rollers I was always neat and tidy.

It was only when I had returned to home base that small incursions began to intrude upon my cosmetic independence. Don Cameron's assistant took me in hand because the network, she assured me, wanted my look to match my position. I was a representative of CTV, I was told, and had responsibilities beyond mere journalistic standards. What I wore on camera was now a collective concern.

This seemed reasonable, even helpful, and initially I decided that this was not a war worth fighting. In Argentina I had already come to the conclusion that make-up could be a good friend when the long hours started to show on air. But now I was being told to cut my long hair. "Too distracting for viewers. Make it simpler." Suddenly what had been an intrusion became an invasion. I resented that how I looked should, in the eyes of my employer, overshadow the work I was doing. CTV's argument was that my appearance was part of the work I was doing and had a major impact on the success or failure of it.

They were right, but again I began to wonder whether trying to practise journalism on television might require trading the content of reporting for the requirements of the camera. I felt silly even trying to assess whether the length of my hair—and who got to decide it—was a quitting issue. It wasn't.

So, in the end I gave in, but I was almost in tears when I used the hairdresser's phone to call for help. Once again, my white knights rode to the rescue.

Lou Clancy, the man who had hired me at the *Star*, and Bill Fox, my former *Star* colleague from my Ottawa days, are two very special people in my life. Both are loyal mentors and friends. I trust their judgment implicitly and their advice has always been impeccable. I asked them to meet me for a drink at a downtown bar. With a certain amount of melodrama, I confessed that despite how silly it sounded I was afraid I was losing my soul to television. Bill and Lou were both patient and supportive and if they rolled their eyes over the hair and make-up histrionics they never let me see it. And, as with most crises, in the end I had to work it out myself. And what I eventually worked out was that the network was actually right.

Here's how, after many uncomfortable hours and days, it fell into place for me. The unique value of television lies in its ability to allow you to communicate one on one with as few distractions as possible. The look in a cabinet minister's eyes when she's answering a question adds an irreplaceable dimension to her answer. And though these days media training may have diminished the weight of this fact somewhat as public figures are taught to betray as little as possible in either their words or their faces when in front of the camera, it's still true that anything that detracts from the viewer's ability to watch what's on the screen will diminish the effectiveness of the broadcast.

A quirky mannerism, a gawdy pair of big earrings or a blindingly pink blouse all serve to distract. So I concluded this was not some plot to put me in the television blender and pour me out as predictable mush. Ironically, despite all my hand-wringing, what I came to understand was that the journalistic characteristics I wanted to be known for were actually being enhanced by the requested changes.

CTV wasn't trying to play up my appearance; it was trying to de-emphasize it to clear the path for content. Sort of like not doing a stand-up with a clock tower growing from my head. It was with a great sense of relief that I came to understand that make-up, hair and on-air clothing were tools of the television trade no less than cameras and lights or typewriters and paper are for the scribes.

When I had accepted the offer from Don Cameron to move to Toronto to co-host *Canada AM*, the executive producer of the show had been Howard Bernstein, a well-respected newsman with a long and successful history in the business. By the time I had joined the program, however, Howard had moved on. Here I had packed up my life and moved down the road yet again on the assumption and the promise that there would be an experienced professional at the helm to help me through these uncharted waters.

I knew (or at least believed) it still wasn't too late to retrace my steps if I had to. I could be taken back into the *Star* fold, for instance, but I had to act quickly to keep that option alive. Before Argentina, I wasn't really committed to television.

My first priority was the content of what I was applying my journalistic skills to, not the medium I was doing it in. On the other hand, I had invested a lot of effort, energy and hope in a new position that I'd barely begun to explore and I hated to give up without some attempt to set things right.

I had been to see Don Cameron about this issue before he sent me off to cover the Falkland Islands War.

I told him the absolute truth. I didn't want to work under the present circumstances and would rather return to my old life than try to continue. I needed a strong producer who shared a vision of the program and what it could be. From my perspective this was not an ultimatum, merely a statement of fact, but in retrospect it put Don in an awkward position. He asked me who I thought I could work with who might produce the kind of program I wanted. My first choice was his Ottawa bureau producer, Jack Fleischmann.

Watching Jack work in the Ottawa bureau showed me he was a journalist with a clear and strong sense of what television could do and what it could do better than any other means of communication. He was also a newsman at heart and a political observer who understood the nuances of life on Parliament Hill. We knew each other's temperaments. To me it seemed like a good fit. Apparently Don thought so too. Jack was in the control room when I returned from Argentina, and under his unique and often annoying leadership *Canada AM* became a powerhouse.

The transitional crises having passed, the road, in spite of the need to get rolling daily at about three-fifteen in the morning, was straight ahead.

So began my decade with CTV. Was I settled for a while? Not quite. My CTV life was a ten-year period that involved changing jobs and cities with the same frequency I had become accustomed to. Within three years I was back in Ottawa. Then, a few years later, back again in Toronto. In between I shared *Canada AM* with at least three different co-hosts during my several stints on the show, was Ottawa bureau chief for the network, hosted *Question Period*, the show that first put me in front of a camera, nursed my dear friend Marjorie Nichols as she confronted death, and got married and divorced. All that really remained constant for that decade was the name of my employer.

The *Canada AM* years were some of the most exciting and adventurous of my career. Within a very short while we were the program that guests wanted most to appear on and, consequently, we were the show that Canadians were choosing to wake up to.

I met and interviewed the rich and famous, the powerful and influential. We talked with Canadians whose lives were affected by the news. We talked with those who made it. And on occasion we made a little news ourselves.

Sometimes we did it by asking the right questions. Sometimes we took to the road to discover it—like the time Jack, Norm Perry and I and a handful of producers and technical people made TV history in Beijing.

Because of the lifelong contacts Don Cameron had made in his reporting days and as an executive at an American network, CTV, where he now reigned as news czar, was the first network to open a bureau in the forbidden land. Trudeau had officially recognized the Chinese government and their old ties to Canadian Dr. Norman Bethune—a hero there, if not here. So before the CBC or any American network could, we took our program to China in early 1983.

We might just as well have landed on Mars. And the Chinese would have had reason to believe that may well have been our point of origin. With strawberry-blond hair, a fur coat and red winter boots, I was a strange-looking creature to say the least. Even at just five feet one-and-a-half inches tall, I towered over many Chinese. Doing stand-ups attracted enormous crowds.

Most Chinese did not know what these odd contraptions with lights atop were. Television was almost unheard of and there had been only rare sightings of foreigners. We caused chaos when we set up our cameras in the middle of streets that were massive seas of bicycles. And roaming through Department Store Number One, so named because the Chinese bureaucracy that runs all state enterprise didn't grasp the concept of marketing, caused people to grab their children and keep their backs to the wall.

To try to apply or judge what we saw by Western standards was one of the first biases we had to shake. But try as we might we always see the world through our own prism. Marketing didn't make much sense because there wasn't much to buy in the stores anyway and most had no money for much beyond basic necessities. Communism had spread poverty equally—except of course for the party brass who lived very well.

Other scenes provoked a peculiar combination of the absurdity of our system superimposed on a society with totally different values. Watching Chinese women curiously prodding packages of make-up designed for white Western faces and trying to apply it made me cringe with guilt. Our great Western corporate ethic of dumping unnecessary and stale-dated goods on an unsuspecting nation and enticing people to spend what little they had seemed shameful.

Business hoped that China would be, when and if its doors were ever pried open, a financial bonanza. A billion people had spent a lifetime in the consumer equivalent of a sensory-deprivation chamber. Western governments hoped that the prying eye of the TV cameras might inch the Chinese toward democracy, though it still hasn't happened.

We all stayed in the newer of the two hotels open to foreigners. It was a bleak, ice-cold January. Norm changed his room three times seeking warmth, before a frustrated desk clerk called Jack and me in desperation. We sat, bundled in our coats, drinking a little vodka to keep the cold at bay, trying to explain to Norm the harsh reality of the week to come in a hotel and in a country where the heat, or lack thereof, would be the least of our problems.

One evening we did a shoot at a restaurant where the chefs performed some amazing culinary stunts—but eating in the cold and with spittoons at the side of each table curbed my appetite somewhat. So too was my hunger checked at the official banquet when our Chinese hosts offered a traditional Peking duck feast complete with stuffed duck head and webbed-foot soup. I took an unscheduled tour of the kitchen, feigning great interest in the chef's workplace to avoid offending our hosts. In China, refusing food is the ultimate insult.

It was a tremendous experience, a look at a culture caught in a time warp. We visited schools and communal apartments and were under the watchful eye of Communist Party spies at every turn. I went back again later, following Brian Mulroney on his Asia tour. In less than three years China had changed radically. It was progress, I suppose, but more consumer goods and more foreign investors do not a democracy make.

The foreign jaunts and domestic trips helped balance the relentless nature of the studio work, and Norm Perry was the perfect person for me to have at my side as I tried to adapt to the requirements of my new position.

First of all, he was consummately professional, easy to work with, kind, although a little eccentric, and was never impatient with the new kid. Second, we had a perfect distribution of interests. Norm's passion was international news and mine was national. The only problem we had was in deciding who would handle the stories that were in neither of our camps, specifically entertainment. Far from fighting for the right to talk to the biggest names from Hollywood, our division of labours ran more toward "I did the rock singer last time. You do the actor."

I remember a battle royale about who would have to interview an up-and-coming young Canadian comic. I lost the toss but afterward declared defiantly that he wasn't at all funny and shouldn't have been booked in the first place and, most important, that Norm owed me one. That young man's name was Jim Carrey. Oh, well.

I suppose I resisted doing the entertainers because they required a different style from the one I was used to. I'd been hired in part because of my willingness to question aggressively. But that wasn't always appropriate on a program of *Canada AM*'s wide range. Jack had a chance to drive that fact home to me soon after we began working together.

A guest had come on the show to talk about the newly "discovered" G-spot, a place in the female anatomy alleged to be a new and definitive pleasure centre for womankind, though it was also reputed to be difficult to find even with a roadmap. My opening to our guest? "Thanks a lot. Something else for women to feel guilty about when we can't find it."

I heard Jack's voice through my earpiece, calm but with an unmistakable edge, "Loosen up. We're not talking about the budget here. Can't you just have fun with the story?"

It was an actual moment of learning. Being new at the game I thought that stern signalled professional, so that sternness, more often than not, was my *modus operandi*. I needed to allow my own natural sense of humour to emerge, because not every story needs the Parliament Hill approach.

Over the years Jack has always used humour, saying all manner of rude, disgusting and outrageous things in my ear while I was trying to conduct a serious interview. He says he was just trying to help me keep it in perspective. This is, after all, only TV, not brain surgery. But when Jack gets totally out of line, I have the last laugh. I can always just turn down the volume, and often have!

Jack and I developed the secret language that producer and interviewer use. A subtle head movement or a shrug can speak volumes when no verbal communication is possible. That shorthand helped produce one of my most satisfying and personally memorable interviews of those early days. It was with a performer, exactly the type of thing I might have previously tried to foist off on Norm, and I loved every minute of it.

Liv Ullmann, the Norwegian stage and screen actor (who was actually born in Japan), was stopping in Montreal for a few days on a cross-continent tour in support of her humanitarian cause. She was known professionally for her work in Ingmar Bergman's brooding films and had a reputation for being unusually thoughtful. She had no plans to come to Toronto so Jack and I took a day trip to Montreal to do a piece with her.

We set up in her hotel room with a crew borrowed from the CTV's Montreal affiliate—we always had to do everything with one eye on economy even as the other was on standards—and I began to do the usual eight or ten minutes with her.

Before we were finished we'd done an hour of tape and we could have gone on for another hour. She was absolutely fascinating. I was totally engaged in our conversation, but I kept looking at Jack for some sign that he'd had enough. I didn't know how we could even use the piece, since our program format didn't allow for the luxury of such length. He kept assuring me, with gestures since silence was mandatory during the taping, that he was as riveted as I was.

Back in Toronto the next day we broke all *Canada AM* rules by dividing the edited interview into two parts, which we placed on either side of a newscast.

This only happened for prime ministers or major breaking news. But Liv Ullmann was compelling TV. In total we ran a piece of almost twenty minutes and, as unlikely as it might have seemed to me beforehand, with an *actor*, not a politician. I think of that conversation often, now that I have the perfect venue for long and introspective talk. It may be that the seed of the kind of program I do today was planted in that Montreal hotel room.

There is an invisible thread that ties the on-air person to the producer. Just as every writer needs an editor, every interviewer needs a producer. It's easy, as a naturally curious person, to get caught up in a conversation because of personal interests and to forget that the point of the interview is to satisfy and enlighten the viewer, not the interviewer. If your guest is talking about computers and you happen to be a computer fan, it's possible to think that everyone who's watching will be as enthralled as you are when he goes on about mega-this and giga-that. Your producer, however, may and should tell you otherwise.

And the reverse is also true. If you're having too good a time, as I was listening to Liv Ullmann's considered opinions on everything from the symbolic order in Bergman's films to the international politics of famine, you can override your natural curiosity and cut the piece short from a fear that you've lost touch with what the viewers might want from it.

It's your producer's job to tell you "This is working, keep going," or "You may find this fascinating, but you've lost me and ninety percent of the country."

It's this other ear that can be so valuable—especially when you're live on air—but only so long as you trust the head it's attached to. And Jack Fleischmann, in my opinion, has one of the best ears in the business.

This was reinforced very recently when Prime Minister Jean Chrétien was on *Pamela Wallin*. Before the broadcast I reminded myself that this was not to be a typical go-for-the-throat interview. There are plenty of news venues for that. My objective was to offer a glimpse of the man inside the prime minister's body.

We started off on his childhood and his family—things about the private man that I'd seldom heard him talk about before—but I began to wonder, is this too soft? Am I missing a chance to pin him to the studio wall over something he's said, over some of his government's flip-flops? But I also knew that his willingness to reveal such a personal side provided a rare perspective.

We were several minutes into the interview, with me trying to choose between my two impulses, when I heard Jack's reassuring voice in my earpiece saying, "This stuff is great." That was all I needed. He had confirmed my instinct to reach for the personal, not the political (although everything is when a prime minister's in the chair) so I stayed with it.

Jack and I are a good team. It was with Jack at the helm, for instance, that we put together our first political panel on *Canada AM*. Every Thursday morning we convened a partisan threesome that included, over the years, New Democrats Stephen Lewis, Roy Romanow and Gerry Caplan; Progressive Conservatives Hugh Segal, John Tory and Bill Fox; and Liberals Tom Axworthy and Michael Kirby. It was one of the liveliest and most insightful political free-for-alls anywhere in the country.

These were men who were as close to the centre of political power as anyone can be, who were thoughtful and intelligent, who respected one another and the audience and who loved (as I do) a good tussle. It gave viewers access, overtly and subtly, to what was on the minds of the powerful. These were all men with an insider's view, but none of them was just a party mouthpiece. Eventually, as our panel morphed over the years, our regulars became Kirby, Caplan and Segal.

Hugh Segal, one of the country's great and compassionate minds, had as a young lad written inquiring letters to all three federal political leaders. The only reply came from John Diefenbaker, so Hugh became a Tory (of the red variety) and has been close to, or inside of, his party's backrooms ever since. He sought the Tory leadership when Jean Charest was drafted by Quebec Liberals to unseat the separatists.

Michael Kirby was one of the ingenious strategists of the Liberal Party and is one of the few senators who deserve the sinecure because he takes the responsibility seriously.

And Gerry Caplan was a longtime socialist whose intelligence and passion always informed the outrage he aimed at Segal and Kirby.

I looked forward to our weekly meetings and was never disappointed. From the response we received at the show it was apparent that we were dishing up just the kind of meaty political stew that viewers liked with breakfast. It always made Thursday mornings a must-view.

I'm sure it's obvious, but I considered this the best job in the world. I was using my brain, honing my skills and having a great time. And there is no better crash course than the real thing. Live TV is the real thing.

In Argentina I had learned much about the needs, limitations and possibilities of the technology we worked with. The dynamics in the controlled environment of a studio where a specialist does a single job are very different. But one rule remains constant. And as Bruce Philips had explained, television is about direct contact, about looking straight into the eyes of each and every one of our viewers and talking to them individually.

I was trying to practise what Bruce had so eloquently preached. And I was frustrated when things got in the way of that connection with the audience. Any time the director in the control room, the person who picks which camera shots and angles, used an over-my-shoulder shot during the show I would object, saying that I didn't like having my back to the audience. In my books, it was just plain rude.

This may have branded me a bit of a troublemaker on the set, but the come-from-behind shots stopped. It was the need for unencumbered communication with the audience that had reconciled me to the loss of my hair and my cosmetic and sartorial independence. I certainly wasn't going to forfeit the lessons of that battle for a wide shot designed just to show off the set. It's the people that matter.

Learning the necessary skills of brevity and direction in questioning is also crucial on a live show. In newspaper reporting you can ask what you like, go on long mining expeditions hoping to uncover a nugget no one else had even been searching for, then cover your tracks before press time. On live television you have to know where you're heading with an interview because you don't have the time to work out a directional plan while you're in the middle of it. That also means restricting the opportunity of a guest to filibuster or fill the time with a prepared statement rather than the answers to your questions.

Years later at the CBC, I was sent to a so-called training session on how to conduct an interview; you can imagine my reluctance. To add insult to injury, they brought in a print reporter to enlighten us. His theories were great if you had unlimited time—a luxury only our print colleagues enjoy—and could choose, after the fact, the pithy and insightful comments to quote. But that's not how live, unedited TV conversations happen. You don't ask a politician to "tell us what your party is doing about x," because you'll hear the predictable party line and valuable and fleeting time will be eaten up before you know it.

At *Canada AM*, Jack matched my penchant and passion for hard work. The program went on the air at 6:30 A.M. and ran until 9:00.

Jack and I were often still at work well into the evening preparing for the next morning's show. Then I was up again early the next morning. It was a time in my life when I benefited most from my need for little sleep.

Crucial to coping with the hours was having time in the morning to digest research and read all the morning papers and catch up on overnight developments. The ride to the studio was valuable working time and I could always get my voice in working order by engaging the crusty and reliable cab driver in conversation. I would settle into the backseat with my papers spread around me for the half-hour drive. I would always comment aloud on the news I was reading. "Jesus Murphy," I would declare. "Can you believe this?" It was several weeks before I learned that his name was Murphy, and all along he thought I'd been cursing him! When that was settled, he bought me a beautiful outside light for my home so that I wouldn't stumble and kill myself as I made my way to his car in the dead of night.

Adrianna was the next steady driver, a feisty Chilean who was intent on making a business out of the daily drive that brought us all to work. She was a wonder, helping out with the extras that I never seemed to have time to do. She'd pick up dry cleaning, deliver research and could even give a great massage.

She eventually became the official greeter for *Canada AM* and is still there, smiling with coffee in hand, awaiting the guests who arrive in various states of consciousness for their fifteen minutes of fame.

Then along came "the Boys" and the start of what is still today a very special relationship. Bill Milley and his young son Al took turns taking me to work in their Co-op cab. We clicked immediately. And before too long , father and son decided to go into business on their own. They bought a sedan limousine and I was now being ferried to work in the lap of luxury. They arrived each morning with fresh coffee, and as they ran me around town and to and from the airport we became friends. In fact, I guess they are the brothers I never had.

When I was first divorced Bill would dispatch Al to help me out with chores. They'd even babysit the adorable but very needy Kitty. Once, when I was out of the country, Bill called Mom and Dad in Wadena to read them a flattering article that had been written about me in a Toronto paper. As a parent, he knew they needed to know. And whenever Mom and Dad come to visit, they treat them like royalty.

In fact, there isn't much the boys won't do or put up with. Dorato Gambacorta, also one of the boys, has often had to turn a blind eye while I changed for work in the back of his car, and when I was working nearly around the clock during the Gulf War coverage, Dorato would take me for dinner at one in the morning because he knew I needed something to eat before heading home for a quick shower and back to the studio. We even call one another on Christmas morning and my family always asks about the boys in my frequent conversations home.

Today they are still very much a part of my family. We know more about one another's private thoughts than we'd ever admit and they are kind and generous friends. I think this closeness began as a result of shift work. It was true in the car and it was true in the makeup room and the newsroom.

At *Canada AM* there was a coterie of sleep-deprived news junkies. Our manner of communication may have surprised or even shocked anyone who didn't know us. We all talked about sex, or the lack thereof, confessed sins and inadequacies and reached out to one another in a way that can only be described as intimate. We knew one another at our most vulnerable moments, through lousy lows and hysterical highs.

Jack and I formed a pattern of communicating then that we often resort to today. We have spent much of the last twenty-five years denouncing each other, often quite vigorously but always good-naturedly. Partly it's a defense mechanism because saying tough stuff to a friend and colleague can be difficult, so exaggerated rhetoric allows a more subtle point to be made and received without insult or pain.

To be able to respond honestly with your gut feelings to the people you work with is crucial. Jack and I have couched much of our professional interaction in personal insult as a way to underline that it's not. Between Jack and me an insult is a mark of affection. It also helps to keep you humble when someone you trust and count on reminds you how stupid you can be sometimes. And that would be a comment of the milder variety. Most of our exchanges would be unprintable.

When I did research for Laurier LaPierre and Patrick Watson I took their less than enthusiastic response to my work quite personally. What I didn't know then, and what I was beginning to appreciate the more as I worked in the business, especially on air, was that there was no personal attack implied by a negative comment on an idea. To say to a co-worker "That idea is stupid" does not say anything about the person who had it. It is merely a response to the content of the suggestion. It's possible, of course, to be more diplomatic than that, but there's often no time for niceties and in the hothouse atmosphere of a newsroom or a live program you need the freedom to react without the fear that you've sent a thin-skinned colleague into therapy.

I'll probably never know how much trouble I've gotten myself into over the years by saying what I mean. But compared with Don Cameron ranting in the middle of the newsroom when a story had been missed I would have been nominated for Miss Congeniality.

Speaking my mind openly about story ideas or the technical execution of the program comes from the same place as the aggressiveness that I need to do my job. Apparently writer Margaret Laurence had the same habit. I am going to steal her defence.

"I was tactless," she said, describing how she always spoke her mind even if it gave offence. "But I was tactless because I always believed profoundly in what I was saying."

But there was another habit of mine that often had a unfortunate effect on colleagues too. It was saying, "I'll do it myself." It was always meant to be expedient, certainly never as a putdown. By the time I was hosting *Canada AM* I had been making journalistic contacts for almost a decade. I'd also been a reporter, a researcher and a producer. I knew how to find a person or a fact quickly, often considerably more so than if I described to people what I needed and how I thought they could most easily get it. I could get a phone call returned by many simply because my name and job were known to them.

So, for the record, for all those I have offended with these three idiosyncrasies—"That's a stupid idea," "I don't like that camera shot" and "I'll do it myself"—I'm sorry. But I can't help but add, "It's not personal." See my problem?

This frankness was especially problematic during my tenure at *Prime Time News*, where the CBC's corporate culture demanded considerably more obfuscating language and political correctness than at the much freer CTV. That said, I know I have always rubbed some people the wrong way with the kind of aggressiveness that can make for good interviews but bad feelings.

Still, my relationships with the people I shared on-air duties with at *Canada AM* were, in my opinion, always fair and honest. You don't have to like people to work with them, but it sure helps. I've already mentioned Norm Perry, who had to get used to his new co-host and help me find my TV legs, and who did both those things with patience and pure professionalism.

Then there's Lloyd Robertson, one of the people I recall with the greatest affection and respect. Lloyd had anchored the CBC's national news from 1970 until 1976, when he joined CTV in protest against CBC's rigid job divisions. He wanted to be more of a newsman, to be able to write or change copy without violating some jurisdictional parameter—in other words he wanted to be more than just "talent," which was all he could be at the Corp.

It's hard to explain, but the cultures of CBC and CTV are radically different. There's something about limited money and resources and a small staff that keep you honest and focused on the task at hand. In a large bureaucracy, in any industry, television included, in-house politics and the power of cliques can overshadow, even stifle, creativity, talent and efficiency.

But it's not just a question of size. It's also a reflection of the leadership. In large bureaucracies, managers are sometimes too far removed from the process of creating the actual TV product—the programs. An open, responsive and accessible leadership creates an open and responsive workplace, but that's certainly easier in a smaller operation.

Lloyd and I worked together under two very different kinds of circumstances. The more common situation was that I would do a report for the newscast he was anchoring. On those occasions we had minimal interaction beyond "And now here's Pamela with a report from . . ." although from time to time there would be a live Q and A at the end that was seldom more than the predictable "so what happens next?" kind of exchange.

But we also did specials together and it was then, when we were essentially in his comfort zone more than mine, that I discovered what a truly generous man he was both personally and professionally. I remember early on, for instance, a royal visit to Victoria during which I was to share duties with Lloyd on a *CTV News* special in addition to doing *Canada AM*. Lloyd is a royal watcher and has a feeling for the monarchy and all that it represents. I'm not against the monarchy by any means, but it's not a topic that's high on my list of personal interests. I don't know what Lloyd must have thought when he was paired up with me—new kid and not a royal watcher—but he made sure we both looked good, and that we delivered a good show.

That day Lloyd did the running commentary—the part that needed some real factual information—and I did colour, the part

The night Argentina lost the war—Malcolm and me
knocked down in the melee that followed.

LEFT: Laine Drewery and Alan Fryer, drinking champagne out of my shoes!
RIGHT: Me and the CTV crew on the Great Wall of China—
the one Mila thought would be bigger!

Prime Minister Brian Mulroney, Marjorie Nichols, Malcolm Fox, Carol Goar
and me at 24 Sussex, as Marjorie began her battle with cancer.

Election night, with Fiona Conway and Lloyd Robertson.

Ottawa, October 26, 1986—a rare pair. Co-hosting with René Lévesque to raise money for Rick Hansen's Man in Motion tour.

The Thursday Morning "Boys"—Hugh Segal, Senator Michael Kirby and Gerry Caplan are three of the best minds in the country.

Prime Minister Jean Chrétien—a rare conversation about his family. October 16, 1997.

Interview with Pierre Elliott Trudeau in Montreal, for CTV.

LEFT: Our beauty parlour on Wadena's Main Street—my first entrepreneurial project.
RIGHT: Lynne Delfs and me on Pamela Wallin Drive in Wadena.

Me with Air Farce's Luba Goy, playing me! They had the props department do a special set of P.W. hair care products, which are now on display at the Spa in Wadena.

LEFT: My last day at CTV with co-host Keith Morrison. Dan Matheson is now the host and Thalia Assuras had gone on to a career stateside. RIGHT: Bruce Philips and Victoria Terry. Bruce was not just a mentor, but a visionary when it came to television.

The most amazing group of friends. Back row (left to right): Michael Decter, Rick Muller, Bonnie Brownlee, Bill Fox, Jack Fleischmann, Lou Clancy. Front row (left to right): Rhonda Clancy, Toni Stevens, me, Peggy Taylor.

LEFT: Me and Candice Bergen (a.k.a. Murphy Brown).
RIGHT: My sister Bonnie with (clockwise) husband Steve
and daughters Erin and Meaghan.

November 1997—*PW* team in Hong Kong.

LEFT: Michael Decter and me—Stockholm, December 1997, at the Nobel Prize ceremony.
RIGHT: The beautiful and talented "Kitty."

My friend and business partner Jack Fleischmann.
A gesture of affection or a cuff to the head?

that needs eyes and a mouth. He might offer the audience some interesting detail about the Queen or her family and then turn to me and say, "Quite a crowd here today, isn't there, Pamela?" All I had to do was add what I was seeing. It could as easily have been the Santa Claus Parade or a football game.

Lloyd knew my strengths and weaknesses and made sure we both played to strength. He gained my respect and I gained his trust. That was to prove very valuable on dozens of occasions such as election or referendum nights or the first Gulf crisis, when knowing glances and implicit trust get you through tough moments and gruelling hours.

In fact, I know Lloyd would have been just as understanding as Bruce Philips had been once when I said, while covering a first ministers' conference with him live on-air, "Well, they're down to the short strokes now." Bruce had waited for the commercial break and then suggested quietly that perhaps certain expressions that worked fine among friends had no place on television. It hadn't occurred to me that the expression had a blatantly sexual derivation.

"Think about what you're going to say before you open your mouth" was the implicit advice he gave me. I had learned that lesson (though I can't claim to have always followed it) by the time I began to share the microphone with Lloyd on major events.

The politician in me says that part of the reason Lloyd and I got along so well is that I was no threat to him. I wasn't after his job and he certainly didn't want mine. And I always tried to make him and the program look good. But it was more than that. Lloyd believed he had a responsibility to mentor and to help create a team.

Once, for reasons I have never been able to fathom, a producer told Lloyd, just before a broadcast we were to share, that I had been agitating to upstage him. The same producer then told me that Lloyd was intent on keeping me in my place and resented my delusions of equality. It sounded so out of character for Lloyd to say something like that, and it must have seemed as strange to Lloyd to hear such things attributed to me, that we sought each other out before air time. In minutes the fictional problem was defused. It's as close as we ever got to tension. There are some strange people in television.

I spent almost three years as the co-host of *Canada AM* and I have to say I had a wonderful time, though the workload was daunting. My work continued to use and reinforce my natural tendencies.

From Bruce Philips through Don Cameron, Malcolm, Jack, Norm and Lloyd the message was identical: be yourself. Very quickly I left behind my previous fears that television required inauthenticity and demanded compromises of a very personal and unacceptable nature.

My relationship with Malcolm was surviving both the distance and conflicting schedules and enough time had passed that I began to believe we were more than a war-zone affair. He stayed in Washington for most of the year after our return from Argentina, but we commuted as often as our two overloaded lives permitted. Most of my time at *Canada AM*—with the exception of specials and road trips—I was tied to the studio, though I logged a fair amount of plane time trying to carry on a personal life with Malcolm in Washington. All in all, I was very comfortable in my life, though a little self-conscious about the celebrity aspect of my job.

Don Cameron was a news junkie and liked to live vicariously through his younger protégés. Jack was forever being dispatched to some hot spot and in August of 1983 Don decided to put me back in the line of fire too.

The American government had grown increasingly hostile to the Nicaraguan Sandinista government throughout the early eighties. The Sandinistas were openly quite left in their politics and the u.s. was nervous about growing relationships between the Central American country's government and the Cubans and the Soviets. With u.s. money and support, a group of armed rebels—the Contras—were fighting the government with a great deal more than words.

Don Cameron decided that Jack Fleischmann and I should go down and take a look. For me it would be the first time since the Falklands that I would be in a country on a wartime footing. And this time I would be within earshot of the bullets. En route to Nicaragua, where a bloody civil war raged, we stopped in neighbouring El Salvador, also waging an internal war, to await visas and permission to go into Nicaragua.

Cameraman John Jackson and editor Chris Trudel were with us and we teamed up again with the ABC crew assigned to the region. With the help of fixers, locals who know the language and their way around, we found ourselves barrelling down unfamiliar roads in a van bearing the *prenza* (press) flag, in search of evidence of El Salvador's civil war.

You could, on almost any given day, decide whether you wanted to meet up with either government or rebel forces. The soldiers were so used to TV crews that it was completely normal for them to confront the enemy with TV cameras in tow. Civil wars are far riskier than country against country because the good guys and the bad guys are harder to tell apart. And the rebels were waging guerrilla war, which means the normal rules didn't necessarily apply. There is no front line. Killing simply erupts.

What we found in Central America was a universal truth: whoever is fighting, whatever the politics or the goals, it is the civilians whose lives are destroyed, literally and figuratively. The scene that remains most vivid in my mind from that assignment, and I'll never be free of it, is that of a refugee camp we visited on the border between Nicaragua and El Salvador. There we found hundreds of people with no homes to return to living in clearly subhuman conditions. Many of the refugees were children. Mostly I remember the stench. If death and disease and despair have a smell, that was it.

On subsequent trips to the Middle East, I again encountered those kinds of camps for Palestinian refugees. Gaza, the last time I was there, was a hellhole. And that same smell is always in the air.

Another thing I remember, though it can't compare with the camp for pure horror, left a bad memory of a different kind. It resulted from our working relationship with the crew from the American network. Our arrangement was that we would travel to different places and then, at day's end, we would share information and pool the results of our crews' collective efforts.

I had no objection to giving the reporter a briefing and our visuals of the camp since, in my opinion, the more viewers in their comfortable living rooms saw the terrible conditions of these unfortunate victims of politics and war, the more likely there might be some international push toward resolution. But I was appalled when I saw his final report.

He spoke as if he'd been to the camp himself, suggesting the stench had burned his nostrils—the exact phrase I used in describing the scene to him. While it's both common and necessary to use or voice-over pictures or events that may not have been personally witnessed, it's still bad form to pretend you were there.

I was still glad to have given the situation as much coverage as possible, but confrontations with television's power to tell little white lies, even in the name of truth, have always made me uncomfortable.

The reporter should have gone himself if he was going to say he had. And though he reported the smell, he couldn't have known its overwhelming power.

After ten days in Central America, mostly in El Salvador and Guatemala, we were denied travel permits for Nicaragua so Jack and I returned to Toronto. I was happy to be home. Again, as after my return from Buenos Aires, I could never take our endless Canadian sport of constitutional negotiations quite as seriously when I compared it with the life and death struggles that many people face without the luxury and comfort of democracy, as flawed as ours may be.

I suppose that's why I have over the years grown more and more impatient with Quebec's demands for independence and the ultimate clash that they might someday provoke. Looking at the realities of nations divided is not a pretty sight. Perhaps Lucien Bouchard should spend some time in a war zone.

No one seeks out pain and death and tragedy, but I can't deny the rush one gets from the dangers implicit in covering such stories. Yet there is also a satisfaction from just trying to demystify the circumstances that cause and prolong such suffering to those who have only the media to inform them.

Then again, there's no shortage of reporting and explaining to do with the stories that take place within our own borders, especially political ones. In September of 1984, Brian Mulroney's Conservatives won the federal election and formed the government. Though it certainly wasn't on the Conservative agenda, their landslide victory caused me to change jobs and homes yet again. When Mulroney offered Bruce Philips a spot in the Washington embassy under ambassador Allan Gotlieb, CTV needed an Ottawa bureau chief and, though my mother lamented the choice, I left my host's chair at *Canada AM* to go back to Parliament Hill. This time I would be running the CTV operation as well as reporting.

10

Two Deaths

We understand death for the first time when he
puts his hand upon one whom we love.

— MME DE STAËL

IT SOUNDS, even to me as I go back over the times I've already considered in these pages, as though I've made a point of leaving out the tough and unpleasant parts of the story. I've tried not to.

Of course there have been broken hearts and setbacks at work. And at the time these crises, personal or professional, always seemed like the Third World War. But one of the joys of being a journalist is that each day you can turn a new page. It's the way the business works and pretty soon it's how you begin to cope with your own life.

I was loving my work as CTV's Ottawa bureau chief. It was exactly the kind of job I had always aspired to—to be in a position to influence the actual day-to-day coverage and understanding of the world of federal politics. The new Mulroney government was a rich, deep vein and we mined it daily. I was surrounded by energetic colleagues and good friends. Then, in early 1987, Marjorie Nichols, my friend and often my inspiration, was diagnosed with terminal cancer. She was told to go home and settle her affairs because she probably had no more than a few months to live.

For the next while as I was, on one hand, enjoying the rewards of my professional success, I was also nursing Marjorie toward her death. My emotions ran the gamut—anger, sadness, fear. It wasn't the first time death had entered my life in such a direct way. Let me backtrack to explain.

One of the perqs of being at the *Star* had been that as the resident westerner I was first choice when someone was needed to cover a story west of the Lakehead. It was because of this mobility that I had reacquainted myself with my grandma Piper. We'd never really been out of communication, but it had been restricted mostly to being in the same place at Christmas or some family event. During my time at the *Star* I began to visit her whenever I was in British Columbia on assignment and we became friends again.

She and Archie, her second husband and the only one I'd known, had moved to White Rock, largely though not exclusively a retirement community about fifty kilometres from Vancouver. In the years after Archie died Grandma Piper remained active in many clubs and groups. She was a talented artist, and loved bowling and bus trips to Reno (to gamble, of course). Then she met and eventually married the man who had moved in next door to her.

It turned out badly—he was a charmer during courtship and a taskmaster as a husband. Albert Figg was mean-spirited, opinionated, domineering and a cheapskate. Grandma was none of those things. But, true to form, she outlasted him and, ultimately, sold the house and moved into an apartment close to her many friends.

Now when I visited, we were two adults enjoying each other's company. I always laughed wandering through Grandma's apartment. I'd find small notes taped or clothespinned to lamp shades or walls or mirrors that would say things like "Ask Pam about Trudeau and the PQ" or "Ask P. about budget."

She had always had an interest in the news and she now felt privileged to have a supposed insider to question. She was more than a slight sceptic and believed that now, for perhaps the first time in her life, she had access to more of the truth than she could get from the regular sources.

Grandma was still living in White Rock on her own when my father called to say that if I could I should make the trip if I wanted to say my goodbyes. She had had more than one brush with cancer and this time upon being put into the hospital she had announced, "This is it."

It wasn't a dramatic and fearful statement about her condition, simply a decision. She'd had enough and at eighty-three she was ready to go without more prolonged or painful medical heroics. I headed for B.C. immediately.

Her children—five of the six were still alive at the time—were also on their way, but so far only my father had made it.

Dad, despite his sensitivities, has never been one to show a great deal of emotion. As a kid, I had seen him cry only once, when our cocker spaniel, Bubbles, died and there was nothing he could do to ease the dog's pain or our loss. There would be nothing he could do this time either, except to grant his mother the right to make this choice and to resist his own urge to intervene and demand a miracle.

My grandmother's impending death seemed to contain more release than sorrow. That's certainly the way she presented it. She was very calm.

The problem was, Grandma was in a hospital room with several other sickly old women, one of whom appeared to be quite clearly off her rocker. During a nighttime ramble, this mentally unstable woman had pulled the IVs from the arms of other patients. I resolved not to leave my grandmother alone. The irony didn't escape me that I felt compelled to protect her from dying in any way except the way she intended.

My dad and I took shifts. Many of my views about important national issues like medicare and how or whether the system can accommodate the aging population are a product of these very personal moments.

For several days, while we waited for the family to gather, it was clear that Grandma Piper was staying alive for one reason only: so she could receive her children and bid each of them farewell.

I detected little sorrow or fear in her, only a kind of hurried patience. We spent much of our time just talking, though often she would be somewhere I couldn't join her, as she rolled in and out of lucidity. When she came back to me she would sometimes report on where she'd been. Sometimes she was in her own girlhood, reliving a memory three-quarters of a century old. Sometimes, out of nowhere, she might say, "I always loved that Elvis Presley." I would try to go to where she was.

The one kind of talk she absolutely forbade was of the "Don't worry, Grandma, it'll all be all right. You'll be well in no time" variety. She wanted none of it.

My father and I have always been close in a quiet way and we became even closer through the time we spent with Grandma before the rest of the family arrived. My grandmother had never been a word-mincer and the three of us had agreed to not hide the truth of the situation. I felt privileged to be permitted into my grandmother's most intimate experience, to be exposed to her ultimate vulnerability.

I remembered what my father had told me as a sobbing ten-year-old when Bubbles died: "This isn't about you. It's about her. You want her pain to end, don't you? Don't be sad." That sentiment was true this time too.

The family finally convened and my grandmother spent time with each of her children and grandchildren. I don't know what she told them, but I know it wasn't earth-shattering, merely personal. It was about closure.

But she did say one thing to me that caught me totally off guard. Amid all our talk at various times about my work I had told her that I did my own make-up when I was on television. As she was formulating the most final of her final wishes she said, "Fran [one of her daughters] knows what dress I want to be buried in. I want to look good for Archie and I want to be buried beside him. I want Barb [another granddaughter] to sing one of her own songs at the funeral—not a hymn, there'll be plenty of hymns. And I want you to do my make-up. You always look so pretty on television."

She had mentioned to me at one point that she'd been appalled at the look of a friend of hers whom she'd seen buried quite recently and she was not going off to meet her Maker or Archie looking a fright. The resolution of her request was not a task I relished, but we did it just as she asked.

My father had some convincing to do as he explained these deathbed requests to the funeral home. But there we were the day after she died, my father, my cousin Barb (a hairdresser as well as a singer/songwriter) and I. Barb did her hair and I did her make-up. And, since you'll likely never find out for yourself, let me tell you that doing a dead person's make-up is no cinch. I won't go into detail—just take my word.

And as bizarre as this may sound, the experience is one I will always cherish. Barb and I prepared our grandmother to meet Archie, while my father kept us company. The three of us grew progressively giddier as the task neared completion, almost as if there wasn't enough oxygen in the room. Grandma had given us a most precious gift—the gift of peace. She had shown us death in its most gentle form, made each of us aware that such a death existed.

Marjorie's death was very, very different. First of all, she was only forty-eight years old. And second, she didn't want to go. From the minute she received the terrible news she fought it. From the minute before, in fact. Marjorie and I were at the hospital where her friend and colleague Jack Webster, visiting from British Columbia, had taken her for tests when her lingering cough and congestion had become ominous.

Marjorie had been a fighter all of her life. As a young girl she was a competitive speedskater and the same drive and discipline shaped her journalistic style as well. She sought out stories and pursued sources relentlessly. When she was sure of her facts she stood her ground fearlessly, regardless of the consequences. She was intimidated by no one.

So, when the doctor who had come to deliver the verdict ordered me to leave the room Marjorie objected. "She stays," Marjorie insisted and the doctor seemed more put out at her rebelliousness than dismayed at the news he was delivering.

In what seemed a most heartless way, he told her she had just a matter of months to live. At that moment I hated him and loved her with an intensity I'd seldom felt. But the doctor's headline didn't begin to tell the story. It was not the end, but rather just the beginning of Marjorie's three-and-a-half-year battle with cancer. Sheer force of will would stay the execution.

Humans are ultimately selfish beings, and I have to confess that as I heard the news it was my life not hers that flashed before me. Marjorie had played, worked, drank, lived and smoked hard for many years and she was, it seemed, paying the price for it. I was just a younger, more moderate version. In a terrible vision my fate seemed inevitable as I looked at her in that metal stretcher they called a bed. It's strange that somehow we blame ourselves, and conclude we must deserve this fate because of how we lived life.

Marjorie tried everything and encouraged anyone who might possibly help her to do their damnedest. She offered herself as a guinea pig for any therapy the medical establishment might think provided even the slimmest hope, or for any medicine they might want to pump into her.

When the news came out that Marjorie was terminally sick there was a flurry of concern in the nation's capital and across the country. Prime ministers, past and present, visited. The flowers spilled out into the hallway, although Marjorie insisted they be distributed to other rooms. And her room was so busy that I became known as "the General" for my duties as gatekeeper and traffic director.

But as time wore on, things, as they always do, reverted to normal, though the stream of colleagues, protégés and politicians never completely dried up.

While others got on with their lives, Marjorie got on with fighting for hers. We researched and read and worked the phones on both sides of the border so she could go to every meeting with the doctors armed with the latest data. Predictably, Marjorie turned this into an exercise in investigative reporting.

She alternated between resignation and resolve. She complained about the unfairness of having to give up a second great pleasure, cigarettes, when she had already, several years before, voluntarily quit another, booze. She railed against medicine and its practitioners, while simultaneously thanking them and giving them rein over her body. When she was undergoing chemotherapy I would stay with her for great stretches of time because she seemed so vulnerable in the face of an apparent shortage of nursing staff.

Sometimes I just had to get out of the room and used, believe it or not, going outside for a cigarette as an excuse. At the beginning it was kind of a joke—"Come stand close to me," she would say when I returned from a nicotine break, "so I can inhale." After a while the smell just sickened her more and I actually quit, but only, I'm embarrassed to say, for her sake, not mine, and only for a short while.

She went into remission twice, but the cancer returned. And she always knew. We were in a budget lock-up together—that's when journalists are allowed an advance peek at the upcoming budget but are sequestered so they can't spill any beans. Marjorie shouldn't have been there, but her work was so much a part of her life she couldn't resist. And, as she had once admitted late at night, if she had known how short her life would be she would have worked even harder. There were so many stories and so little time.

That day, amid the mounds of budgetary documents, she simply said to me, "It's back." I asked her if she'd been to a doctor and she said no, she just knew. She was right. She had grown extremely sensitive to her body's messages.

Marjorie had made her reputation and her mark as an opinionated but always well-informed columnist who said what she meant. Despite her illness, she continued to write and became, if such a thing is possible, even more vituperative. She alienated many people. But strangely, some of the harshest criticism she bore during that period was for saying something nice. The problem was that she said it about someone who one got more points for attacking than defending, the prime minister.

Brian Mulroney had invited her to dinner at the prime ministerial retreat at Harrington Lake when word of her situation had spread. It was an act of affection and affirmation. "It was so I could be on the inside rather than the outside just once," Marjorie told me, and she was clearly moved by the gesture. We had all spent many hours standing and shivering on the road to Harrington in journalistic stake-outs, waiting for the first ministers to dot an "i" or cross a "t" on some accord and then pronounce upon it.

She wrote in her column that there was another side to the man about whom many journalists had no good words to say. The result was she was criticized harshly for letting her personal life interfere with her objectivity. It was an unfair shot at someone who, and she'd been that way all her life, was unafraid to break from the pack.

Sometimes Marjorie and I would try to be playful about her illness. During rounds of chemotherapy I would do her face with my TV make-up. She took to wearing colourful turbans over her baldness and they became her signature accessory. She continued to alternate between a fatigued giving up and a feisty, almost violent, fighting back.

Two Deaths

The chemotherapy made her nauseous and she would throw up so often I'd barely have time to rinse the pan and get it back under her chin. As she retched again, she'd miss the container and hit my arm instead. It felt like it would burn a hole in my skin. I'd feel the sting for hours. And for weeks I'd experience a phantom pain whenever I thought of her.

I could no more imagine what the treatment was doing to her body than I could imagine what the disease had done to her spirit. As I watched Marjorie, one of the most alive women I'd ever met, move inexorably toward her end, I knew I had decisions to make about my own life. Both my work—I was supposed to be running a news bureau—and my personal life sometimes seemed secondary to my sense of responsibility to Marjorie. This was life and death. TV was not.

My long-distance relationship with Malcolm was getting short shrift. I knew this couldn't go on much longer. With my friend as a human testament to the shortness of time and the surprise and suddenness with which it can end, I felt I couldn't any longer put off things of value. I was too afraid I might lose them.

Eventually I moved back to Toronto, but I was in Ottawa every week and I always spent time with her. She defied the doctor's verdict for nearly four years. Modern medicine marvelled at her capacity to withstand the assault of treatment and still work and live and sign on for more. At the end, Marjorie went back to Alberta, where her parents and family lived. I was home in Wadena for Christmas when I discovered there was no more time for Marjorie. We were in the middle of a prairie winter storm and I knew I couldn't possibly drive to Alberta safely or in time.

I tried to find someone with a plane. My uncle Don is a crop sprayer, but the bad conditions meant he couldn't fly into Wadena to get me. I tried an old school friend who lived just outside town who also had a plane. But the weather kept us grounded. I wasn't there when she died. I wish I could have been.

There's a journalism scholarship in Marjorie's name, but the young winners likely won't know who she is because you're only as good as your last story and it's been a while. They can check the morgue, as the newspapers call their library, because that's where she lives now. If they do check they'll find a rich deposit of her wicked wordsmithing.

Her funeral in Red Deer was a gathering of the journalistic clan, with everyone telling a favourite Marjorie episode, each one even more outrageous than the last. Marjorie's best friend, Allan Fotheringham, delivered a eulogy that had us all in tears of sorrow and joy. She was a legend.

Several weeks later we organized a memorial service on Parliament Hill and just about everyone in politics and the press was there to celebrate her life and mark its untimely end.

Marjorie Nichols was living, breathing evidence that a creature called the independent woman existed. But it was the way she faced her death that started me down the path to the kinder, gentler Pamela of today. She warned me to expect the criticism that can come when a reporter breaks ranks. She was right, as usual.

11

Prime Ministers
I Have Known

It is not easy to lead a cavalry if you think you look funny on a horse.

— ADLAI STEVENSON, U.S. presidential nominee

M Y STINT IN OTTAWA as bureau chief was bookended by
Brian Mulroney's first term
as prime minister. I took over the job just after his win in 1984 and
for the next four years I ran the bureau, was the host of *Question
Period,* did the Ottawa week in review every Friday morning on
Canada AM and was a reporter for the nightly national news. In
addition, I was still co-hosting special events with Lloyd Robertson
and, at year's end, there was the televised, hour-long one-on-one
with the prime minister of Canada.

I continued to commute back and forth to Toronto every week
to maintain some semblance of a personal life. *Busy* doesn't quite
capture the frantic pace. But after several years on the morning shift,
I couldn't quite break the habit of waking up in the middle of the
night. It made for long days, but then again, I accomplished a lot.

The major political preoccupation of the first Mulroney term can be summed up in two words: free trade. Although it was the 1988 election that was to be specifically fought on the plan for a trade agreement with the U.S., the Tories ran in 1984 on a platform of opening the country up to outside investment and cosying up to our oversized cousin across the border.

"Our message is clear," Mulroney said after his victory. "Canada is open for business again." Mulroney was true to his word and much of the next four years involved considerable travel to encourage that business. I followed him to, among other places, China, South Korea, Germany, Japan and of course the US.

I had met Mulroney briefly in 1976 at the Conservative leadership convention, where after a marathon day of voting he and a raft of others had been beaten out by Joe Clark. In 1983, when Mulroney was again a contender for the leadership, I was part of a group of journalists who questioned the leadership hopefuls on a televised all-candidates panel.

Mulroney was friendly to me, in part, I think, because we had a mutual friend, Bill Fox. Bill was a colleague from my days at the *Star*'s Ottawa bureau and would soon be working for Mulroney, so he had probably put in a good word for me. It didn't last.

Before too long Mulroney and I found ourselves on very opposite sides of things. That's not a political analysis but a professional one. He became prime minister of Canada and I became Ottawa bureau chief for CTV. My job was to examine everything the government did and report on whatever looked questionable. Mulroney took all questioning and criticism very personally.

Not only did Mulroney have a thin skin—a serious liability in politics—but his relationship with the media changed quite dramatically after the election. He was popular during the campaign because he was accessible and friendly with the press and he was "good copy." He was an effective politician on the hustings who could always spark a reaction from a crowd. It made for good pictures and Mulroney always made the news.

But after the vote, both he and the media became more wary. He mistook the friendly camaraderie of the campaign for support. But that's not how it works. Once in office, any leader is subject to more intense scrutiny because it's no longer just what you promised but whether you intend to practise what you preached. Before too long Mulroney was getting a rougher ride. He often gave the impression of being "on the make," politically speaking, that is. He now spoke in a way he thought sounded prime ministerial. His voice would drop an octave or two; he would look down as if he were in deep thought as he replied to even the simplest query. On the screen, these actions often looked contrived and rehearsed and left the impression of insincerity. When he was speaking on the record I often felt he was mentally punching up a cassette of prepackaged pontifications designed to give away as little as possible. However, no one could ever convince Mulroney that the image he was projecting was problematic. Apparently a u.s. "tv doctor" had once declared Mulroney was a tv natural and he believed that advice above all else. In private and off the record, however, when he wasn't trying so hard to impress, I found Mulroney a very different—and much more likable—man.

In 1985, when he and u.s. president Ronald Reagan and their wives sang "When Irish Eyes Are Smiling" together at the Shamrock Summit in Quebec City, there was a suspicion that, whatever might be true about our need to repair or enhance our relations with the Americans, Mulroney was just too darn close to them already to speak for us to our best advantage. There was a certain comfort, even among anti-Communist Americans, when President Nixon had made overtures to China in 1972 because his credentials as an anti-Red were impeccable (dare I say unimpeachable?).

There was no such comfort among Canadians, who were leery of galloping Americanism when it was Mulroney who was galloping to meet it.

It was a time of major change in the way news was being reported—especially on tv—and the result was frequently a polarization of comment. Television technology had become smaller, more portable and considerably cheaper by the mid-eighties, and there was still some money around. Opening an Ottawa bureau became possible for almost any news-gathering organization that wanted one. And increasing competition in the industry made it necessary for us to do more stories more often.

But there was, it seemed, less time to *tell* the story, even though you might have to tell the same story more frequently. So there was a need to simplify, which often meant painting positions as being black or white, rather than the shades of grey that were more honest.

Free trade was a complex concept and there were so many unknowns that the issues, as they were translated onto television and into the press, often became secondary to the personalities involved. As is often the case, the personalities become the shorthand version of the story.

If Brian Mulroney is in favour, count on Bob White or Maude Barlow to be opposed. Run a sound bite of each, *et voilà*, the news. And, for similar reasons, positions in turn hardened into slogans. Free trade was either going to save the country or destroy it.

Mulroney, who had put so much of his individual prestige into the cause, was presented as a demon by those opposed to the initiative and as the courageous saviour by its fans.

Then there were those who, exclusive of the issues, just didn't like the man. That makes reporting even more difficult because many of the judgments about Mulroney were in the eye of the beholder (read viewer), not the reporter. And Mulroney exacerbated the problem. Whenever he would see less-than-flattering poll results, he would often blame the messenger, never the message. In other words, he thought reporters were distorting the facts and as a result the public was coming to the wrong conclusion.

It reminded me of a story that was folklore around Ottawa. Pierre Trudeau had been reportedly bemoaning the low collective IQ of the press corps and his party's equally low standing in the polls.

If the media would only explain the Liberal agenda fairly, he reckoned, then the public would embrace it. The rather outspoken and astute cabinet minister Don Jamieson apparently shot back, "The problem is not that we are having trouble communicating, sir. The problem is that people are mad as hell at the message." I thought at the time and still believe that Mulroney might have diffused some of the personal attacks if he had been more forthcoming about the real costs and likely consequences of the free trade deal instead of resorting to sloganeering himself. If he'd conceded the fact that whatever deal his negotiators hammered out with the Americans would have a cost, and if he'd stated a concrete intention to mitigate those consequences and delivered on that promise, we—the press and population at large—might have gone easier on him and trusted him more. It was simply not credible for Mulroney to argue, in a country with many protected industries and sectors, anything else.

Mulroney's other public relations error was in not making clear what had changed in his thinking between his warning about the consequences of the Canadian mouse getting into bed with the American elephant and his subsequent immodest race to get us all under the covers. The (Donald) Macdonald commission (a.k.a. the Royal Commission on the Economic Union and Development Prospects for Canada or, colloquially, a Commission on Canada's Future) had been appointed by the Liberals to investigate, among many other issues, just the type of trade alliance later proposed by the Conservatives. As a Liberal initiative, it had raised doubts among the Tories, but when the report came down in 1985 Mulroney used it as a springboard to leap over his own previous objections. It is popularly considered a weakness—and here the media must bear much of the responsibility—for a leader to flip-flop on an issue, though you'd think we would put more value on a willingness to keep an open mind and even to change it from time to time. There is a distinction between a politically expedient reversal and a legitimate change of heart. So, while Mulroney should have been

more careful to explain his change of position, we too should rethink our refusal to let leaders change their minds and be prepared
to accept a genuine conversion based on a persuasive argument. Pre-
sumably, we should reward our political leaders for thinking! Of
course, we should have world peace as well.

I must have filed hundreds of free trade stories over the years I
was in Ottawa and I tried my best to deal with substance rather
than flash. But I think Mulroney, in an odd way, viewed this kind of
reportorial nitpicking as a personal insult.

Dalton Camp, a Conservative Party insider since the Diefenbaker days, told me that Mulroney had once suggested to him,
"Maybe I should just appoint Wallin to the Senate." He hoped that
would stop what he saw as a relentless attack on the free trade initiative. Camp reports he quickly squelched Mulroney's joking or ill-
considered plan by reminding him what an even bigger pain I could
be inside the fold as a Tory-appointed senator.

In fact, the point I, and many others, tried to make time and
again throughout the trade negotiations was simply that there were
areas that needed a great deal more attention and clarity.

In his book *Wrestling with the Elephant,* Canada's deputy trade
negotiator Gordon Ritchie, Simon Reisman's second in command,
confirms that many of the concerns were legitimate. American in-
difference to or contempt for Canadian needs is precisely why it all
took so long. In the end what Canada "won" was the highly touted
dispute settlement mechanism to settle differences over how and
when punitive American laws would be enforced. What Mulroney
had unrealistically promised was exemption from those discrimina-
tory laws and so when it became clear that American trade laws
would remain firmly in place and that Canadians would have to
pay penalties, it's hardly surprising that critics and reporters called it
a loss. But it was by Mulroney's own definition.

The largest issue was, of course, jobs. The free trade deal was
supposed to create thousands of them. So in the course of the nego-

tiations, and in their wake, every time a job anywhere, in any town or industry, was lost the blame fell on the trade deal. Every time one was created, it was proof the deal was working.

Both sides soon lost credibility as we all reeled with the dislocation caused by the concurrent move toward internationalism and an economic recession (which had nothing to do with the free-trade deal). A decade later, the global economy is reality, and while many have prospered, others have also paid a personal price for the "adjustments," as they were so benignly dubbed at the time.

Mulroney had first risen to prominence as a labour negotiator. He was a dealmaker—it was in his genes and in his temperament. His appointment of Simon Reisman to do Canada's negotiating was in keeping with that view of how things work. Reisman's approach was brinkmanship and that provided me with one of the most exciting situations I'd faced since the old *As It Happens* running-full-tilt-to-the-studio days. It started with a call from my old friend and mentor Bruce Philips.

I was at work one night, having already filed my piece on free trade for that night's newscast, when the phone rang. It was Bruce and he had a big story for me. I knew, given the hour, it was too late for the CBC *National* (which ran at 10:00 P.M.) and that meant CTV at 11:00 would have a national scoop. I asked him for details. "Trust me," he said, "it's big. I'll call you back."

I might not have taken the chance with anyone other than Bruce, but I trusted him completely and it was obvious that, whatever the story, it was in the government's interest to make it public. I knew Bruce could distinguish between the kind of story we would want and the self-interested kind that would wind up alienating one of the largest news outlets (and his alma mater) in the country.

In other words, it had to be a legitimate news story and not just a "press release" extolling the virtues of some partisan act. Politics and the media play the same symbiotic game and each needs—and uses—the other. But there are rules.

I called Toronto to explain the situation. Would they be willing, I asked, to stand by with my original piece for broadcast with the understanding that if I got the last-minute call we could shift seamlessly to Plan B? They agreed.

Plan B involved getting the bureau hot (as in "wired"), and ready to do a live insert into the newscast. I would be standing by on the set. If Bruce's call came through in time, then we would signal Toronto off air to introduce me. If the call didn't come, or if it did and I judged that it wasn't a story, then Lloyd, who was anchoring, would simply read the prepared intro to the taped piece I'd already filed.

The call came with less than two minutes to air. Simon Reisman, Canada's chief negotiator, had decided that the only way to get what he wanted from the Americans was to threaten to take his toys and go home. He had walked out of the negotiations with great bluster and bravado. It was indeed a good story and it was especially satisfying to have it first and get it on the air. That's what we call breaking news.

I appreciated that the desk in Toronto had trusted my judgment enough to take the risk. They knew I was able to make such a quick story-to-story pivot because I understood the free trade file inside out. Once I'd heard the headline from Bruce—Reisman storms out of free trade talks—I could put the story into some context.

Of course, a series of facts does not necessarily the truth make and the problem with stories like this is that I had only the official Ottawa version and no American take on the event. So while it served the government's purposes and mine, there was more heat than light. But what makes good TV is not necessarily good for the country. High-stakes poker is rarely the best way to negotiate or to handle the complexities of choosing a path for the nation's future.

Those of us who cover Parliament Hill have a ringside seat to history in the making. We have a privileged, up-close and personal look at our leaders both inside and outside their comfort zones. I had the opportunity to see Mulroney in a wide variety of situations because I did so much travelling with him. Often the decision was whether or not to expose the small moments of insight that occurred on those trips that were so full of content but didn't quite qualify as "news." We usually kept them to ourselves and they were great fodder for late-night dinner conversations after the working day was done. But sometimes the temptation was almost irresistible.

When Brian Mulroney, his wife, Mila, and a troop of journalists were on a tour of Beijing's Forbidden City, the awe-inspiring complex of centuries-old, imperial Chinese buildings that few Westerners have been privileged to see, there was one such moment. There, as we stood surrounded by all the mystery and magnificence of a culture older than Christianity, Brian's off-hand comment to Mila about one of the marble and lacquered chambers was "It would make a hell of a cabinet room, eh?" The face of the Chinese interpreter, who had showed little emotion throughout the tour, betrayed real confusion as he struggled to translate the puzzling comment to the Chinese hosts.

But while it spoke volumes about the prime minister's sensibilities, it wasn't news so it wasn't reported. Neither was Mila's comment after visiting the Great Wall of China, the twenty-four-hundred-kilometre structure, some of it over two thousand years old, that snakes through the country's northern frontier: "I thought it would be bigger." When we got to Seoul, South Korea, the next step on the prime minister's Asian itinerary, the CTV contingent went into one of the city's we-can-make-just-about-anything-in-an-hour shops and had satin baseball caps made that said: "The PM's Asia Tour. We thought it would be bigger."

The Mulroneys didn't think that was very funny. But the hats sold like hotcakes on the PM's plane.

My point in relating these stories here is that Mulroney's early suspicions of being the butt of personal attacks were overblown. It's always possible for the media to make a person look foolish merely by selective reporting or editing, especially of what is said in the midst of the kind of historic moments that inspire nervousness, even in the seasoned public figure. I don't think any of us went out of our way to make him look bad, at least not initially.

On the other hand, there was also much that went unreported about his good side. To his friends and colleagues he was remarkably loyal, and it often cost him in terms of credibility when some of the less scrupulous of them used promises of access to the prime minister's ear for personal gain. Once in power Mulroney was always accessible to those who'd helped him achieve it and he was known among insiders to be approachable and generous. Marjorie Nichols wasn't the only person he invited to his home in an act of warmheartedness. My friends Bill Fox and Bonnie Brownlee were married at 24 Sussex Drive. Bruce Philips, whose opinion about just about anything is usually spot on, always declared that despite some bad politics, Mulroney was, at heart, a "decent guy."

Although Mulroney was the prime minister during my entire time as CTV Ottawa bureau chief, he was by no means the only prime minister with whom I've come into contact over the years. One, British prime minister Margaret Thatcher, passed through my experience quickly but with a major impact.

It was the mid-eighties, after her post-Falklands War election win and we were to meet at the British high commission in Ottawa for an interview for *Canada AM*. I had been forewarned by other journalists that she was not an easy subject. She was used to running things and didn't give up control easily.

All my anticipatory reservations were verified when Mrs. Thatcher arrived and began ordering every person in the room to do something and almost every object in the room, including cameras, to be moved around. The word *imperious* might describe her manner.

I could see we were headed for trouble. If she, and not I, did the questioning, then this was not going to work and I wasn't going to get the answers or the interview I needed. The situation was not about winning but about control. If an interviewer sets out to compete with the guest to prove who's tougher or smarter, everybody loses, particularly the audience. But neither is the audience served if the guest is totally belligerent or dismissive. I knew I needed to connect with Mrs. Thatcher on a personal level.

We spent about fifteen minutes together, on set, with me trying to make small talk while we awaited our slot. It became clear she was not going to engage. I tried everything from her success in the Falklands and my experience there to the weather here in the colonies. Nothing worked. Finally, out of desperation, I suggested that she looked a little pale. Would she mind, I asked, if I had the make-up lady put a bit of blush on her cheeks?

She instantly dropped her taut manner, looked into the monitor at her face and agreed. At that moment something in her—and between us—changed. We were two women with tough jobs to do. We began to talk about exactly that—the common difficulties all women face if they live and work in the public eye.

Imagine: hairdos and make-up with the formidable Maggie T. She still wasn't an easy interview, but she did me the courtesy of at least answering my questions, which was more than I had reason to expect.

There have been seven Canadian PMs (Trudeau twice) in the course of my reporting career and I've had the opportunity to meet with, and form an opinion of, each of them. That's why it was a policy of mine when I was working in Ottawa that I didn't cast a vote in federal elections. There was nothing in the journalist's book of ethics that compelled that course of (in)action; I just felt better that way. As a supposedly objective questioner, I didn't want to face elected leaders on election night—or any other time for that matter— knowing I had voted for or against them. I would have felt compromised when I was so intimately involved in reporting and analyzing the personalities and the issues for others. Most journalists would

disagree with my decision. But a face-to-face interview, and I conducted them regularly, is a different situation from the daily cut and
thrust of a scrum. I don't pretend that this gesture made me more
objective than others or that I had no opinions. Objectivity doesn't
mean having no opinions; it just means not acting on those opinions in the course of your work. However neutral one tries to remain as a journalist, there are no reporters, certainly none who
choose to spend their life reporting political news, who are without
personal feelings about issues as large as who becomes the next
prime minister of the country.

Joe Clark was the easiest of the list for me to empathize with personally because his roots were in the same type of prairie populism
that my father had made a continuing part of my childhood. Prairie
populism reduces the importance of party affiliation and machinery
while exalting the concerns of common people. In my father's case it
produced a staunch supporter of the provincial Social Credit Party,
when there was such a thing, and the Diefenbaker Conservatives
federally, although Dad has been known to cast a Liberal vote if the
candidate was, in his considered opinion, the best person for the job.

When Joe Clark said something about the country I always felt
he believed it, even if it wasn't always the most politically astute
comment. Recently I was asked to introduce him at a luncheon in
Regina. I was on my way home to Wadena for a fund-raiser, a silent
auction to raise money for a new Legion hall. The first thing Joe did
was reach into his pocket and make a contribution. I asked for an
autograph and that too fetched some additional cash for the hall
fund. This is the boy from High River, after all, so he knows what
small towns in this country are all about. Conversation was comfortable. I've interviewed him dozens of times and several years back
we decided to invite Joe and his daughter, Catherine, on together
as guests on my program. Catherine was poised and confident in
front of the camera. Joe Clark, according to his daughter, is a great
father and a man from whom she has learned a great deal about pol-

itics. It's a tribute to him that she is not cynical about the process (and obviously neither is Joe, who has placed himself back in the political ring).

Kim Campbell, the third of the Conservative prime ministers I've crossed paths with, was first elected as an MP in the 1988 election. I met and interviewed her just after that election as one of the most noteworthy rookies of that parliament and found her bright, feisty and personable. That impression of her was obviously shared by Brian Mulroney because she was very quickly appointed to his cabinet, first as minister of state for Indian Affairs and Northern Development, later as minister of Justice and then minister of Defense during the tense time when the Somalia scandal first broke. She took on the contentious issues of abortion, gun control and the protection of rape victims from irrelevant probing of their sexual pasts and was often credited with bringing at least a little feminist perspective to the Justice portfolio.

But Kim wasn't an insider and didn't want to be. With only a single term in Parliament under her belt she ran for the leadership of the Conservative Party, and became Canada's first woman prime minister when she won.

But in the election campaign that followed she faltered, partly for not doing the usual. First, she tried honesty, but both the press and the public punished her. When asked about the persistent unemployment problem she made it clear that it wasn't something she—or anyone—could solve in the course of a campaign or with the wave of a prime ministerial pen. It would be with us, she said, for years. She was attacked for being honest because we, the media, said it showed how naive she was. And the pubic wanted to hear good news, not the straight goods. Imagine the audacity of trying to win an election without lying to the voters.

Campbell also extolled the virtues of what she called "the politics of inclusion," an alternative, she believed, to the old way of doing political business. The promise was to include more real people in the process at the expense of backroom boys. But we all had a hard time figuring out exactly what that would mean in practice. And the backroom boys who tried to manage her campaign charged that the politics of inclusion didn't appear to include doing all the necessary work required to win. In her autobiography, *Time and Chance*, she says she was often treated rudely by the media during the campaign and she cites my election interview with her as an example. I was surprised because I asked her the obvious, questions such as whether she thought she was ready to run the country with only four years' experience in Parliament. When she was thrashed and her party was reduced from 154 seats in the Commons to 2—neither of them her own—I felt badly for her, but I wasn't surprised at the public's verdict.

She had tried desperately but unsuccessfully to separate herself from the name and approach of her predecessor. Mulroney's legacy left the party essentially unelectable. And her new lone-wolf approach to the party politics meant she had no machine or cadre to get the job of getting elected done. She was unable to convince her party or the public that her approach was an improvement.

Both Joe Clark, who didn't move fast enough on patronage for the party faithful who had been so long out in the political cold, and Kim Campbell would have benefited from Mulroney's intuitive sense of politics. Politics is often about who owes you and whether the politician remembers he or she owes you. Or as Mulroney used to say, "You gotta dance with the ones what brung ya."

About Pierre Trudeau, who both preceded Joe Clark and followed him, I can only echo the consensus. It was impossible not to feel the man's intellect, self-possession and ironclad control over any situation in which he found himself. He also unwittingly taught me a lot about my craft. He was the prime minister for most of my formative years as a journalist. He'd become prime minister in 1968— he won the job along with the leadership of the governing Liberal Party that year—and he retired in 1979 when Joe Clark's Conservatives formed the government after a slim electoral victory. But his retirement was brief. Three weeks after Trudeau's announcement that he was leaving public life, Clark's minority government unnecessarily lost a confidence vote, albeit on a very unpopular budget, by mistakenly thinking that without a leader the Liberals would never call their bluff. Bad call.

This was exactly the scenario the Liberals needed to lure Trudeau, their most powerful weapon, back. The caucus asked Trudeau to reconsider. He reversed his previous decision and became prime minister again after a federal election in early 1980. He passed the leadership of the party and the prime ministership of the country to John Turner in June of 1984, but not before orchestrating the major constitutional showdown of this century. He threatened to unilaterally patriate the British North America Act from Britain and bring in a controversial Charter of Rights. He was determined and his views prevailed, fundamentally changing our country and the political balance of power.

My first television interview with Trudeau occurred shortly after I'd started at *Canada AM* in the early eighties after his return from brief retirement. He demolished me. I remember saying to him, with the brazenness that inexperience often begets, "Mr. Trudeau, your popularity is so dramatically low in the polls that surely you have lost the moral authority to govern." This to a man who was not only a lawyer, political scientist and a historian, but who detested the shallowness of the contemporary slavery of politics to the polls, although he wasn't above using them. He smiled not so patiently, as though dealing with a person who was not only uneducated in political theory but also a bit dimwitted, and replied, "Miss Wallin, what an interesting concept of democracy you have. If I were very high in the polls, then would you suggest I ought to simply suspend elections?" Perhaps, he went on, we could simply dispense with the parliamentary system altogether and leave all important matters for journalists or pollsters to decide.

The political science lecture continued until I changed the topic to what I thought was safer ground, at least for me.

At the time, Trudeau had just shown the digital gesture of contempt to a crowd of angry unemployed workers as his train passed through Salmon Arm, British Columbia, and I asked him about the incident. Did he think it was an appropriate thing to do?

"Were you there?" he countered.

"No," I conceded, "but cameras were."

"Let's have a look at the film," he suggested, knowing that I didn't have any, at least not with me. We were conducting this exchange on Parliament Hill. It was clear that only if I produced witnesses and videotape at that instant—and perhaps not even then—would he address the issue of the action rather than spar in courtroom style over whether the gesture itself was real and if it was, what it had meant.

That interview felt like a lifetime. Trudeau was amusing himself teaching a cocky and inexperienced young journalist a lesson. Though it felt very personal at the time, I consoled myself with the knowledge that it wasn't. To Trudeau there were very few minds in the land he couldn't treat as cocky youngsters.

As for the question of whether I liked the man, it seemed then and it seems now irrelevant. Just as one knew about Mulroney how important it was to him to feel liked, it was apparent about Trudeau that it didn't matter to him at all. Whether that's true or not we'll never know, though several people who worked closely with Trudeau said he read almost every word written about him. He simply wouldn't give reporters the pleasure of showing them he had bothered.

However many times I might interview the man it would still come as a surprise to me when he recognized me or remembered my name. But then again, his own staff at the time would say the same thing.

Several years ago I attended a testimonial dinner in Trudeau's honour in Toronto. It was hosted by Rob Prichard, the president of the University of Toronto, and the room was full of Liberal bigwigs and assorted academics and media types.

Partway through the meal Rob came over to me and said, "I've just been looking over the speaker's list and I notice that there aren't many journalists and almost no women. Would you please say a word or two?" The prospect filled me with anxiety, but I couldn't refuse.

Perhaps having no time to prepare was actually a gift. I remember saying that, from a journalist's perspective, "On his bad days he hated us. On his good days he treated us with contempt."

I was gratified to see that Trudeau liked the honesty of the sentiment, especially in the context of the unending effusive praise he was receiving. But I added my own tribute by recounting that first interview. "I will forever be in your debt," I said, "because you taught me more about journalism and how not to do an interview in half an hour than one would normally pick up in years on the job."

Jean Chrétien, our current prime minister, was first elected to Parliament in 1963 at the age of twenty-nine and, with the exception of only one brief period, he's been there ever since. In 1967, he became the youngest cabinet minister in this century. I've interviewed him on numerous occasions over the years. Our paths have crossed many times at everything from press conferences to state dinners. But, oddly enough perhaps, my favourite memory of time spent with Chrétien is of a meeting we had when he was out of politics.

In 1984, Chrétien's leadership bid was stopped by John Turner and two years later Chrétien left the political life to return to the practice of law.

One night while I was commuting between Toronto and Ottawa I ran into Chrétien on a plane. After a brief greeting we prepared for take-off, only to find that the plane was grounded due to the bad weather. So Chrétien and I had a chance for a *tête-à-tête*.

Given that he was out of politics, we could talk like any two people confined on a runway, and not like two people on opposite sides of a microphone.

At various different points in his political career Chrétien had been the minister of National Revenue, Finance, Indian Affairs, Industry and Trade, Justice, Energy, and Mines and Resources. He had also been Trudeau's pointman for the federal strategy on the 1980 referendum on Quebec sovereignty and was instrumental in dealing with the constitutional and patriation battles over implementing the Charter of Rights.

But that stormy night, Chrétien talked about his life, not his work. He claimed to be happy to be out of the political arena, though my sense was that he had more than a bit of regret and anger about the last leadership campaign, where he'd been painted as past his prime.

As many were to learn later, Chrétien has a long memory and a vengeful streak. And it is also true that very few politicians can actually ever leave politics behind.

The flight finally took off and when we landed in Ottawa I asked him if he wanted to come with me to my quite delayed dinner at the home of my friend Bill Fox and his wife, Bonnie Brownlee. He agreed, warning he could only stay a moment, as his wife, Aline, was waiting.

Bill and Bonnie were pleased to see him, and even though Bill was now working for Mulroney, Chrétien and he were the veterans of the constitutional wars that Bill had covered—every move, utterance and nuance.

It was there, as we sat for several hours, that Chrétien, the politician, re-emerged—not in a partisan way, but as a man who lives and breathes politics and who would not be satisfied until he had another shot at the top job. It was a unique insight into a prime ministerial mind because, at that time, with the prospects of a comeback dim, he had little to hide and nothing to protect.

It's an unfortunate side effect of the journalist's work that she hears too many guarded words and not enough that are spoken frankly, candidly and without guile.

A few years later, when Chrétien had become prime minister and I had just lost my job in a highly public way so familiar to politicians, he phoned me to say a few kind words and that he would miss our interviews. It was a very generous and classy gesture. But, as things have unfolded, we've had a chance to meet again across a microphone.

Last on my roster of prime ministers I have known, former and practising, is John Turner. We are linked in history because of what I think of as "the Question"—an event that took on a load of meaning it didn't have. I'd like to set the record straight because everyone else's version of this has been, to say the least, inaccurate.

My term in Ottawa as CTV bureau chief there, as I said earlier, was bracketed by federal elections. It was after the Conservative victory in 1984 that I replaced Bruce Philips as bureau chief, and it was just after the Tories' second win in 1988 that I moved back to Toronto. During that time I logged close to half a million miles following the prime minister around the country and the world. But if my name lives on in media lore for anything from that period in my life it will be, no doubt, for a single exchange with the leader of the Opposition on *Question Period.*

The fall-out from the exchange left me both unsatisfied and with an angry sense that my motives had been greatly misrepresented. Though the televised encounter was the moment that caused the controversy, the story, at least in some people's minds, began much earlier. It didn't, but let me retrace the events.

One wet spring night after I had returned to Ottawa to take up my duties as bureau chief, John Turner gave a party for the press at Stornoway, the official residence of the leader of the Opposition. A canopy was set up in the spacious backyard. Turner and I were among a group talking politics under the canopy.

At some pause in the conversation, well trained as I am, I jumped in to fill the dead air with some innocuous comment like: "Given the rain, it's a good thing you thought to get this canopy. Even those of us in high heels can stand here without sinking out of sight.

John responded, "You know, Pammy, I bet those shoes have been under a lot of beds."

The look on the faces of my male colleagues was one of horror. I gauged the moment, looking for malice. I scanned his face for a hint of intended insult. There was none, so I smiled and countered that I always wished I actually had as much fun as everyone thought I was having.

This is not to say I was not a little taken aback, but as a woman journalist I had had much worse said about me and to me so I wasn't really offended. Surprised, yes. But, as it turned out, others were offended in my name.

This comment was, according to the current wisdom, quintessential John Turner. He had been out of politics for a decade and the examples of his lack of sensitivity to the current climate of political correctness were common.

That said, I don't believe John meant it as an affront. We had always gotten along and I believe it was his equivalent of a slap on the back between colleagues, a gesture to show he thought I was one of the guys, which in his terms would have made the comment a backhanded compliment. So I'd taken it as such.

But within hours I began to get calls from women—many of them Liberals, including senators and MPs—who were indignant at whatever version of the story they'd heard at whatever length from the original. To each I said the same thing: a) I considered the remark not worth getting upset about and—more important—b) it was at an off-the-record gathering anyway, a social event where people who work too hard should get to unwind without checking for bugs.

It was Turner's unhappy lot to attract, repeatedly, the wrong kind of attention with regard to his perceived old-style relationship to women.

There had been a huge debate inside CTV over whether to air the "bum pat," Turner's friendly and firmly felt hand on the rump of Liberal Party president Iona Campagnolo, captured by a TV camera. It finally aired at CTV under mysterious circumstances and garnered more ink (and reruns on Christmas-party funny reels) than many people both in and out of the party thought it deserved. But it was, given the nature of the debate about his ability to deal with women, newsworthy and should have been aired, although the alleged sin seems to pale in the current climate. Think Bill Clinton.

For John Turner, the moment will likely be remembered as long as his years of dedicated work in both the Finance and Justice portfolios under Pierre Trudeau. As Brian Mulroney discovered with his off-the-cuff "There's no whore like an old whore" reference, nothing is ever really off the record these days.

Turner had left politics in 1975 supposedly over a policy dispute with Prime Minister Trudeau, and waited until Trudeau resigned the leadership for real in 1984 (after teasing in 1979) to get back into government. Turner was relentlessly pursued by the party and the press during his years out of politics. Any sighting of Turner talking to another Liberal or even facing toward Ottawa was front-page news and would unleash yet another round of Turner-mania. He won the Liberal leadership in 1984 against major contender Jean Chrétien but lost the ensuing election badly, not least because Trudeau had left behind him a residue of anti-Liberal feeling from sea to sea to sea.

As well, Turner had agreed to make a flurry of Trudeau-ordered patronage appointments just before calling the September '84 election and self-inflicted a wound with the words "I had no option," in response to a very effective calling to account for it by Brian Mulroney in a pre-election TV debate. Ironically, Mulroney was to leave his successor, Kim Campbell, with an equally decisive and fatal load of rancour when he left office in 1992.

Turner was, according to the pundits, out of political practice from his years away from the public eye and had lost the sense of urgency regarding public perception and how to play to it. Times had also changed between 1975 and 1984 in terms of the relationship between press and politician and in the gender-relations arena. There were many women, many Liberal women, who bristled at his apparent jock tendencies. His quarterback's gesture to Campagnolo only confirmed their fears.

All of this is to say that when the word circulated of the rather bizarre little exchange between Turner and me, I started to hear from others that I intended to get even. What they meant, I guess, was that they would have been offended in my position and would have set out to settle a score.

Let me make this clear: I wasn't and I didn't. It was with this history in the minds of Hill insiders that John Turner and I met face-to-face a couple of years later on *Question Period*. I was the host and he was the leader of the Opposition, looking toward the next federal election.

I had changed the program in two important ways after taking the reins from Bruce. Since television was emerging as a medium with its own practices and practitioners, I had begun to use TV reporters instead of print people as panelists. And occasionally I did a simple one-on-one interview with a newsmaker. The Turner interview was one of these occasions, and after long and difficult deliberation, I discovered there was a thorny question I needed to ask him.

At the time, there were rumours even more damaging to his image—and therefore to his chances of leading the party to an election victory—than gender clumsiness. More and more he was being described privately as a man who "liked his drink." Not that he was alone in his alleged affliction. About the only people I met in Ottawa who didn't like a drink had stopped altogether for medical reasons.

But Turner was leader of the Opposition and the only alternative for the people who wanted the Mulroney Conservatives out of office. Displacing Mulroney would be no small task and the Liberal ranks were split over whether Turner was the man for the job. That made him vulnerable. He therefore attracted more than his fair share of criticism any time he was seen as dropping the ball in the anti-Mulroney game.

There was a nasty and growing movement inside Liberal ranks to dump Turner and the rising chorus of whispered accusations of alcohol-induced untrustworthiness played directly into the hands of those forces.

But there were other, less self-serving, sources, including incidents witnessed by my own reporters, so it was my intention to give him a chance to answer the whispered accusations. I felt he deserved the opportunity.

About midpoint in the half-hour interview I asked him "the Question." It should be mandatory for all journalism students to study this tape as a case in point of how *not* to ask a question. Here's the verbatim exchange from January 13, 1988:

PW: I think everybody has been looking south of the border this year, and we have all watched what's happened with Gary Hart and the seemingly endless stream of Democratic candidates who for one reason or another, upon scrutiny and examination of their lives, have been forced to or have willingly stepped aside or out of the race. We've in this country been starting to examine people's personal lives and certainly Sinclair Stevens went through an awful lot with the inquiry. I want to bring this question around to you. There have been suggestions, I guess is the best way to put it, in the town of Ottawa—and this is a very small world in a little fish bowl—that you have, or potentially have, a drinking problem, and people are saying you want to be prime minister of Canada—

you're making a bid for that—and that we should have the right to know and to ask you about that.

JT: Well, I think Canadians are entitled to know about their public figures, about the personal lives of their public figures, insofar as our lives reflect our ability to perform. In response to your question, yeah, I like a good party and I've enjoyed myself over the years, but I have never allowed any pleasure or distraction to interfere with doing the job, whether I was a lawyer or a businessman or now a politician. I mean I keep my eye on the ball.

PW: Does it distress you that here we are discussing that—or what we've seen in the U.S. in the last few months—that I'm sitting here asking you this question?

JT: Well, I think, as I said, that personal character is important. I think personal conduct is important as it relates to a man or a woman's ability in public office to fulfil the responsibility that people give us and if anyone wants to make a legitimate case against me that any of my personal habits, including playing tennis . . .

PW: The long lunch hours . . .

JT: Oh . . . the long lunch hours when you have to get back at 1:30, for goodness' sake, to be in Question Period. I put more questions into the House of Commons than any other member of Parliament. Insofar as that's relevant—fair ball. But I would hope that we don't get into a spate of anonymous-sources journalism and rumours. And I would think, you know, you mentioned Sinclair Stevens. It wasn't his private life that involved us in his problems.

PW: But we began to scrutinize, and the whole issue there was . . .

JT: Well, it was the fact that he mingled his public and private interests and this is what Mr. Justice Parker said in his report. But insofar as his private life, or impact upon the public, well then, I think it's irrelevant.

PW: But it's fair ball if somebody thinks you're making the wrong decision or a bad decision, because they think you have a drinking problem. It's fair ball to put that question?

JT: I think if I . . . I wish there were a little more evidence.

PW: Yeah?

JT: Yeah. I mean and rather . . .

PW: It's been discussed. I raise it because, of course, in the biography of the prime minister by Ian Macdonald the whole issue of his drinking was raised and dealt with. But it's not something we generally talk about in this country, about private lives.

JT: Ah, yes. We're still trying sell Jack Cahill's book about me. If we had won the election we would have sold it, but I think Jack probed pretty deeply into my life, and while he suggested I was convivial and loved sports and companionship, . . . nothing interfered with what I had to do in life. I keep my eye on the ball as I said.

PW: So it's a . . . I guess there's a public right? You agree with that, but you don't want to go the American route. Is that true?

JT: I think that I . . . (pause) Gary Hart, of course, there was a course of conduct there that might have affected his judgment. There was a direct challenge to the media. But I would think, in every individual instance, when you put a question like that to me and I respond to you, it's a question of your judgment—should the question be posed—and it's a question of my judgment—is it a relevant question—and, I think, you and I have been around long enough to know how to handle it. And so I think, I have no hesitation in responding to you the way I have.

Although it's hard to tell from the transcript, we did have a fair airing of the issue, although I should have been more direct. From there we moved on to other topics. From the response to that fleeting few moments of television you'd have thought we'd done a mini-series on drinking problems complete with videos of barroom brawls. And if I'd thought our exchange in the garden had produced troubling interpretations, this televised exchange turned out to cause a great deal of debate not to mention anger and soul-searching in me.

There was an opinion circulating within a large-enough group to be disconcerting that the event was my payback, that I had set about, in response to his comment under the canopy, to hurt Turner personally and professionally, that I was accusing him of having a drinking problem in such a public way that there was no escape from that slur. In my own mind the facts were exactly the reverse of that.

The press gallery was split over whether or not the question should even have been asked. My own regret was never that I'd asked the question, but that I'd asked it so clumsily. Any deserved demerits would have been for my waffling.

The aftermath of the interview was especially galling for two reasons. First, I liked Turner as an individual and when he was on his political game he delivered some of the most eloquent, humane and thoughtful speeches I've ever heard in the House of Commons. I was sorry that the exchange created a weapon in the "dump Turner" arsenal. But that is a real consequence of political journalism. For every winner there is a loser in the zero-sum game of partisan politics.

And second, I had formed the opinion along the way that remains unchanged today that personal behaviour of politicians is only the proper stuff of public investigation when it interferes with public obligations. Drinking, illness, womanizing, patronage are all fair game if they compromise the actions politicians take on behalf of the citizenry or if they have a negative impact on the person's ability to carry out his duties or make wise use of public money.

One of the several allegations made against Turner to me and others by Liberals was that he had, against the wishes of many in caucus, locked the party into a hard-line anti-free-trade position because of loose lips after a long lunch. Turner disagrees. For others, in and out of the Liberal Party, it was a moral concern that leaders must lead by example and some had doubts Turner could. I raised the issue of drinking to allow Turner a forum to refute or respond to the accusations, not so I could watch him squirm. I have passed up more chances than I've taken over the years to raise personal proclivities, and I've never done it just for the drama.

He did not, wisely, challenge me to explain the reason for asking the question or what evidence I had to support it. But he also knew this was not an edition of *Geraldo*, and we were both delicately treading on new ground.

Turner and I spoke many times about the incident and we finally put it behind us. But then yet another version of this story appeared in a colleague's book and in a magazine story and I now feel obliged to set the record straight. Raising this issue again here won't help matters, but with "gotcha" journalism on the rise these days, it's important that we come to some kind of understanding about when personal information is relevant. It's worth noting that by the 1988 election, though the Liberals lost again, Turner had, in fact, rebuilt the party significantly—though his old rival Jean Chrétien, who won the leadership after Turner resigned, was the main beneficiary of the resurgence in Liberal popularity.

I mentioned before that there were two reasons that this whole episode was so troubling. There was a third reason and it has become even stronger over time: that one haltingly asked question in the middle of a TV program should stand out from my years of non-stop work on the Hill. But that, I guess, is just evidence of the power of television, and sometimes its pettiness.

It was the second of the three times I've been most present in public consciousness, and since the first, the Falklands War, was in the end a personal and professional benefit, I guess I shouldn't complain. Especially when I compare the Turner incident with the third time, still to come, when I was fired in (or out of) prime time and became the news instead of reporting it.

12

Settling Down

I have always been driven by some distant music—a battle hymn
no doubt—for I have always been at war from the beginning.
— BETTE DAVIS

IN EARLY 1985, when the dust had
settled from the 1984 election
and Bruce Philips had taken up
his post in Washington, I was on my way back to Ottawa, expecting
the good stories and good times to roll. At thirty-one years of age I
was exactly where I wanted to be. I had the job of my aspirations
and a man in my life who loved me. In my estimation I've enjoyed a
charmed life. Add to that the fact that I've been blessed with self-
confidence, an assertive (some might say aggressive) personality, a
quick mind and a visceral pleasure in hard work. These all seemed
to combine with an equal measure of right place–right time to pro-
pel my career forward.

My move back to the capital was a professional triumph—first
female Ottawa bureau chief returning to the place where I'd begun
my career as a rank rookie less than a decade before.

The irony of my situation was that after a year of long-distance
relating, with Malcolm living in Washington and me based in Toronto,

we had finally figured out a way to live in the same city and things were going well.

After the end of the Falklands war Malcolm came to stay with me for a while in Toronto instead of immediately heading back to his home in Washington. We both talked to Don Cameron to let him know about our situation and he agreed to try to find a way to get Malcolm to Toronto. It took nearly a year, but Don finally offered Malcolm a position as a producer on CTV's program *W5*. In theory it was a promotion, but Malcolm loved his camera work and the travel that was part of it, and taking the new job was more a concession to our desire to have a relationship and our own home. It was also a concession on Don Cameron's part, because he hated to lose such a good cameraman, but Don took some pride as the father of this new relationship. Malcolm uprooted himself and came to Toronto and for the next year or so we lived happily.

We had a great little house on Borden Street that I'd bought one day on a whim. As soon as I knew Malcolm was being transferred I went on a house hunt one lunch hour, just to get a sense of the market, and wound up buying a place before I went back to work for the afternoon. I have always been a bit of a leaper before looker.

Malcolm and I both had work to keep us busy. His new position with *W5* gave him enough opportunity to do road trips that compensated, at least partially, for having to forgo his love of the lens. But it seemed that if there were ever any danger that my life might actually settle down, fate would intervene, and I'd be on the move again.

A federal election was called and with it the prospect of more change. Brian Mulroney and the Conservatives formed the federal government in 1984 and Bruce Philips moved to Washington to work in the Canadian embassy. Bruce had come to talk to me when he received the offer from Mulroney to become second in command to Ambassador Allan Gotlieb. In typical Philips style he had taken himself off the air as soon as the offer came to him, wanting to head off even the slightest glimmer of conflict of interest in his "Brucegrounders" or his other duties. He told me that if he went to Washington he was going to strongly suggest that I get his Ottawa bureau chief job. He took the Washington assignment and I replaced him. As if a nomadic existence was an inescapable part of our lives, Malcolm and I were once again living in separate cities, only meeting on weekends. It certainly wasn't what Malcolm and I had planned for, but we knew that this was an opportunity I couldn't possibly pass up without facing a lifetime of what-ifs.

Malcolm stayed in our house in Toronto and I took an apartment in the same building I'd lived in during my last tour in Ottawa, the one across from the museum. Newspaper colleague Carol Goar, to whom I'd passed the original apartment, had in turn passed it on, so I had to settle for a different apartment, not nearly as nice. I set up what was essentially a second home, and lived like the MPs who commute home on the weekend.

The decision to give up my high-profile place at *Canada AM* in return for the bureau chief job, hosting *Question Period* and reporting for the national news, puzzled my mother. First, she wouldn't be able to keep tabs on me with such ease. She always knew when I was tired or living through a migraine on the air and she would call and warn me to take better care. But why was I giving up a whole show in favour of short little items on the news? Others were mystified by the career choice that forfeited celebrity in favour of journalistic power. I had to explain to Mom that she didn't need to worry; this was a promotion.

When I arrived to take up my post as bureau chief, it was with some trepidation—a new government, high expectations of the first woman ever put in charge of a bureau of this size, sceptical reporters with years of experience, budgets and bottom lines to consider.

Don Cameron's parting shot upon my departure for Argentina about not screwing things up for women reverberated. There was a whole lot more riding on this assignment.

I remembered the words of Charlotte Whitton, the first female mayor of Ottawa: "Whatever women do they must do twice as well as men to be thought half as good. Luckily this is not difficult."

I certainly hoped she was right, but I wasn't convinced. My only advantage was that fresh off the morning shift I was still waking up at 3:15 A.M. so I had a jump on the day. By nine, I'd watched the morning shows, read the papers and the wires and was impatiently awaiting the arrival of the troops with a game plan for the day already in mind.

I was learning on the job. I'd never run an operation this size before. I had my heart set on making the bureau both fun and productive. I may not have had Bruce Philip's years of experience, but I had learned from him what was important about doing good TV and I knew from earlier experiences what a good bureau should feel like.

I'd inherited experienced reporters like veteran Bob Evans and pit bull Robert Hurst as well as Bruce's wonderful assistant Victoria Terry, without whom *Question Period* would never have made it to air week after week. Laine Drewery was hired as the bureau producer. Laine was an experienced reporter who had followed his father, John Drewery, a longtime Hill reporter, into the business. We then brought in Alan Fryer from the Montreal bureau, a reporter with a flair for writing and a feel for a story, and later Mark Sikstrom, a good western boy, filled out the team when Roger Smith left for the Beijing bureau.

The cameramen and editors were a talented, fun-loving and hard-working group and together we made the CTV Ottawa bureau a force to be reckoned with. And, as usual, Jack Fleischmann was in the picture, running the news operation in Toronto.

The stories were ready-made. Brian Mulroney had just been elected with a massive majority. The Liberals, the natural governing party, were out in the cold and out of steam. A leadership rivalry was inevitable. The tainted-tuna scandal would erupt and Brian Mulroney would do a policy pirouette and embrace free trade.

Most of the newly elected Tory caucus members had no chance of winning when the election had been called, but they'd ridden to Ottawa on Brian Mulroney's coattails. And within months, a half-dozen new cabinet ministers would be down for the count, due to inexperience and bad behaviour. We were serious about our work and irreverent about all else. Nothing was sacred or off limits.

The bureau complained good-naturedly about how hard I worked them and once bought me a whip as a gag gift. I remember one sunny afternoon going down to the Sparks Street Mall, whip in hand, to herd them back to work as the crowds on the pedestrian mall sat eating lunch and gawking in wonder at the scene.

We took any excuse to organize a get-together and when one of the guys at the bureau had a vasectomy and foolishly shared that information in an attempt to buy sympathy and some relief from a boring assignment we teased him relentlessly and at the staff party made him sit with a bag of frozen peas on his private parts as we snapped photos to capture the moment. Political correctness was in short supply.

I still tell a story about Laine Drewery, the bureau producer, and reporter Alan Fryer. Now, for the record these were and are two happily married men with wonderfully understanding wives who know their husbands are essentially harmless boys at heart. So nothing said here will result in divorce.

But one day, after the three of us had been out to lunch, they coaxed me to join them for a drink at a local strip club in the Byward Market. Confident in their innate charm and irresistibility, they set out to prove that they would be able to convince one of the women to entertain them tableside for free. I doubted their abilities, said so, and in we went to settle the bet.

They soon learned the rules. To woo the young dancer to our table they needed more than charm. They'd have to dig deep and spring for a bottle of champagne. They did. Refusing to admit their obvious defeat, the two of them carried on brazenly, trotting out all those compelling lines like "What's a nice girl like you etc.,

etc. . . . ." They knew no shame and she showed no interest.

Wanting to rub a little salt in their wounded egos, I tried a different tack. "Watching you dance," I said in all seriousness, "it looks as if you have had professional training. Did you take ballet?"

Her eyes lit up. Most of the patrons couldn't have cared less about her actual abilities. It was the bare skin they were interested in. She took my genuine comment as a compliment and it sparked an animated conversation between the two of us about why she was there. The boys sat silently by. She had, she confessed, a young son and the money she made dancing at tables was a damn sight better than what she would have made waiting on them. It was an interesting detour from Parliament Hill and the boys have never forgiven me my superior communication skills.

But Alan and Laine always did have a flair for the dramatic. At my wedding several years later, they caused quite a scene by drinking champagne from my shoes.

My life in Ottawa, with the obvious exception of my long-distance life with Malcolm, was good. Though the days were long, the work was rewarding and the bureau was a tightly knit unit. Even when the ten- or twelve-hour day was done we'd carry on at dinner or at someone's house, drinking wine and reinventing life and politics. But over time, the long hours at work and the increasing pull of the hospital where Marjorie spent so much time resulted in even more than the usual sleep deprivation.

I was losing a friend and perhaps that's why there was so much living in and for the moment. One of the lingering effects of Marjorie's illness on me was that in the quiet, small hours of the morning I found myself facing questions of my own future and mortality. I knew this reaction was purely emotional, but it forced me to find an equally rational approach to justify it. I began to count air miles and I don't mean for frequent flier rewards. I started to think, for the first time, that maybe thousands of kilometres a month in the air was using up my luck.

I was commuting to Toronto every week and during the first three years as bureau chief I followed the prime minister to economic summits in Bonn and Tokyo and toured the Far East, including China and South Korea, with him and his entourage, not to mention his frequent domestic forays back and forth across this great, huge country of ours.

Slowly, as the novelty of the travel faded, a nagging new and radical idea was taking hold in my mind: perhaps there's more to life than work. That's a serious breakthrough for a serious workaholic. Along with that idea, perhaps causing it, was a new understanding gained through Marjorie's situation that there also may be less to life than one expected. Marjorie's illness put the question of balance in life forward in an unavoidable way.

As bureau chief it was one of my duties to match personnel with tasks. Everyone in the bureau liked to travel and vied for the right to take the next tour of duty, so given that I was feeling less inclined to continue tempting fate, I actually started travelling less, which of course delighted the reporters who volunteered willingly for the road trips.

I also began to think a great deal more about settling down. *Carpe diem*—the dictum "Seize the Day," which I had first heard from seventeenth-century poets in university texts—began to take on increasing urgency and poignancy.

It was on my thirty-fourth birthday in April of 1987 that Malcolm proposed marriage. This gesture spoke volumes and said exactly what I'd hoped to hear. To this day I'm surprised at how excited I was at the prospect of finally formalizing our intentions. I phoned parents and girlfriends and giggled, not a common behaviour for Ms. Newshound. The proposal caught me so off guard—in spite of the fact that we'd been theoretically moving toward this for years— that I actually quizzed him before saying yes. "Does this mean what I think it means? Or is it just a ring?" We decided that we should get married sooner rather than later. And implicit in the agreement was my permanent relocation to Toronto, which consequently meant relinquishing my bureau chief job. I had thought about children before but always with a certain ambivalence, believing there would be time for family later. But I could no longer deny that in the back of my mind, my biological clock was quietly ticking.

Don Cameron was resigned when I told him I wanted to leave Ottawa. All he said was "Too bad. We all knew someday you'd want a life, but it leaves us in a bit of a bind." I understood his resentment.

So Malcolm and I started to make plans for a life together in the same city and under the same roof. I had agreed to stay in Ottawa through to the next election so that the network wouldn't be left in the lurch and would have time to find a replacement bureau chief. I set to work planning the wedding, which we'd decided to have in the summer.

I wanted something fairly traditional—no eloping—but not the whole church package. There's an old castle in Toronto called Casa Loma, which was brought over from Europe early in the century by an industrial magnate named Sir Henry Pellatt. Some of its rooms were available to rent for events. I phoned there, only to discover that they needed about three years' warning. I soon realized Toronto wasn't Wadena and it wasn't going to be easy to find a venue on such short notice. My good friend Peggy Taylor leaped to the rescue.

I first met Peggy, a story producer at *Canada AM*, when I arrived as the new host on the block. She is truly one of the funniest people I've ever met. Letterman and Leno have script writers. She doesn't need them. Peggy lives, works, talks and thinks on fast forward. And watching her book a story was worth the price of admission. She could convince a guest to fly, drive or even run to the studio with her sob stories that their presence was crucial to her very survival. If the guest didn't agree, she would plead that she would be summarily fired or that her children (of course she had none then) would surely starve.

Peggy's specialty these days is public relations and she's the kind of woman who gets things done. And by the way, she does have two children now, honest. I know because her eldest, Hillary, is my godchild.

She told me that her family—she's related to the branch of the Taylor family tree that includes E. P. of Windfields Farms and Northern Dancer fame—belonged to a Toronto club, and she thought she could get us a booking there, even on short notice. When she told me the name of the place, The Badminton and Racquet Club, I wasn't thrilled. I wanted a certain degree of informality but getting married in a gymnasium wasn't exactly what I'd imagined.

Peggy was shocked at my ignorance and informed me quickly that the club included a good deal more than squash courts. With the wedding date set and the location arranged I launched into action.

I was still living in Ottawa and running the bureau and, in retrospect, I realize that although I wanted our wedding to be meaningful for us as well as for our friends and families, the pressures of time and the long-distance commute meant that I ended up managing the whole affair and the run-up to it as if I were planning election coverage or a news special. I am very task-oriented.

I remember that we had difficulty finding a minister who would perform the ceremony at the club rather than in his or her own church, and even when we did find one, she requested that we meet with her for some premarriage consultation at her church.

We drove out to the suburbs to get together with her one evening, but the only thing on my mind was the amount of time we were spending performing what I considered a placating task. I had a plane to catch to get back to Ottawa to prepare for *Question Period*.

I chose a wedding dress design, but grew more and more unhappy with it as the wedding date approached and the dress neared completion. Serendipity to the rescue. Malcolm and I went home to Wadena to celebrate Mom and Dad's fortieth wedding anniversary, and our imminent wedding, at an event at the Legion hall. While at home, my sister and I discussed my wedding dress crisis. She suggested I consider wearing Mom's wedding dress. I didn't think for a moment I'd fit into it, but it was worth a try. We dug through an old trunk and when I saw the dress, which I had seen only in photos, I knew it was exactly what I wanted to wear. It represented family and continuity. The discovery of the "right" dress joined the two celebrations, my parents' marital longevity and Malcolm's and my hopes to follow their example.

Our wedding was a wonderful event, a happy coming together. My entire family was there; my nieces Erin and Meaghan were flower girls; even my uncle Don and his family made the trip. Malcolm's mother came from England. My oldest and best friend, Shelley, and Malcolm's brother Graham stood up for us. The Grays, in tandem, gave a funny and affectionate speech. The Badminton and Racquet Club turned out to be the perfect place for a summer wedding except that, although it's on a busy downtown corner, it's hidden away behind several other buildings. Most of the Ottawa contingent who flew or drove in for the festivities got lost and arrived too late to witness the ceremony.

At first it looked like our marriage was going to be one of the lucky ones. But, as we soon discovered, it is difficult to make a marriage work in the glare of the public spotlight. The invitations always arrived addressed to Pamela Wallin and "guest." Malcolm was often ignored by people we met on the street or at a party as they paid attention only to the TV personality.

And then there was the house. Even if all else had worked for us, that alone might have ruined our marriage. We were still living in the Borden Street house and it had one wonderful attribute. Our neighbour Lynne Delfs. I first met Lynne early one morning when I was heading off to work at *Canada AM* and she was still partying in her backyard. She has a wonderful, infectious laugh and her spirit is like a magnet. But good neighbours aside, the house was not the home I wanted. The one I wanted was about two blocks away.

Settling Down

In Toronto there's a street called Palmerston Boulevard and I've always been drawn to one particular stretch of it. It's not particularly upscale now, but it was three-quarters of a century ago. The houses are large and old, covered in the lovely brick and wood detail that makes a prairie girl think of history and gentility.

So many of the largest houses are subdivided into apartments now that the neighbourhood no longer boasts the city's nobility as residents, but the street still has two reminders of its previous glory: the stone pillars marking the entrance as you turn onto the street and globe-topped street lights that look like Victorian London. From the first time I saw the street I wanted to live on it. Though Malcolm was very happy to stay put, I was bound and determined to move and Malcolm reluctantly went along to keep the peace.

The house deal was closed before the wedding. We didn't have a honeymoon—that came the next summer when we headed off for Thailand and ended up covering a coup attempt against Cory Aquino, the president of the Philippines.

Instead we took the post-wedding week off work to visit with family and move into our new home. We spent two years renovating it virtually from scratch. The house needed so much work inside that when my dad first saw it he assumed we intended to knock it down and build something new. Malcolm lived through renovation hell on a daily basis. I was still commuting, running the Ottawa bureau until my successor was in place, so I had to deal with the disruption only on weekends.

Ripping out walls or taking a sledgehammer in hand to bust up old sewer pipes is not my idea of fun. But, then again, this project had been my brilliant idea!

For months we never prepared a meal at home because we had no kitchen. Lynne, a wonderful cook, would rescue us regularly by offering an evening meal. My brother-in-law, Steve, who's a professional plumber, spent that winter in Toronto on a job and lived in the house while he and fellow Wadenian, Orst, helped us with the work.

We did it all ourselves because we could barely afford the enormous mortgage as it was, never mind pay to have the whole place redone.

With the November 1988 election finally behind us, I moved back into the chaos. It was a full year before we had a house where we could stay home in any comfort. When it was over I was so relieved that the rubble had finally turned into my vision of home that my gregarious side kicked into high gear and I began to have friends over just about every weekend. It wasn't always Malcolm's idea of a good time, though he didn't complain. Instead, he indulged his love of cooking so that when the house was full he could keep his own company in the kitchen while I entertained.

We'd been together nearly ten years and married almost five of those, when the end came. Our life together had its good times certainly, but the strains upon it were obvious. I was once again doing the morning shift on and off throughout the entire period. When I left Ottawa to return to Toronto I was aware that the network had only so many places for me to go and that *Canada AM* might be one of them. My early risings caused extra stress because our schedules were essentially in opposition. The truth of the matter that I see so clearly in retrospect is simply that Malcolm and I were very different people with very different needs.

Thankfully, the final act now plays in my memory more like comedy than tragedy, though, believe me, it's taken a while for the shift to occur. On the way home from work one day in 1992 I picked up a shirt for Malcolm that I thought he would like. Two days later I noticed it, still in its original wrapping, sitting on the stairway to the second floor. During dinner I asked him if there was a problem with the shirt. "Don't you like it?" I asked. His response was simple and to the point. He said, "No, I don't like the shirt. I don't like our life. I don't like the marriage." A man of few words. There would be no negotiations or reconciliation.

The next day after my *Canada AM* shift I had a meeting with John Cassaday, CTV's president, that had been made well in advance of the previous evening's events. I made it through the broadcast looking a bit worse for wear but was visibly upset when I arrived for the meeting. "Please bear with me," I told John, "I'm quite upset about some personal matters." He asked me what the trouble was and I blurted it out. He was shocked that I had even shown up for work and said as much. The truth was that if I hadn't had a job to go to that morning I would have been in much worse shape. Work has always been a source of strength for me.

It was a difficult time, but as I always do in crisis I turned to family and friends. The friends rallied around and my sister came from Saskatchewan to stay with me for a while. Unfortunately, the break-up was as public as the marriage. *Frank* magazine printed the real estate ad complete with a picture of the house now up for sale, with the address and a convenient reference to the schedule of the hours I'd likely be away at work. I actually phoned the editor to explain that his decision to print that information left me extremely vulnerable. Living alone is always risky for high-profile people, as we attract not only fans but fanatics.

Anyone in the public eye, me included, has had to deal with stalkers and crazies. Handing them a road map to your home strikes fear into your heart. But the magazine didn't seem to care about such consequences. I installed a makeshift security system and put bars on the windows as a safety precaution. It's at these moments that you long for the privacy that you no longer have. It's part of the trade-off you implicitly make when your work puts you on the public stage.

There's always a perverse interest in someone's failure or loss, especially if that person is perceived to be successful. Perhaps people need to know that professional success doesn't guarantee personal happiness.

In retrospect, I believe that if I had done at home what I do so well at work, things might have been different. I should have been a better listener. But privacy and private time are precious commodities and necessary to make a relationship work. And they are hard to come by when you live in the public eye.

Malcolm and I run into each other occasionally and it's always cordial. I still remember Argentina like it was yesterday, but the details of a disintegrating marriage thankfully have faded. It's a difficult task to succeed at marriage with a man who keeps his own counsel and a woman who runs so fast that you have to flag her down like a taxi if you want to tell her something. I don't know if Malcolm has changed in the intervening years. I only hope that I have.

13

Prime Time

The obscure we see eventually, the completely apparent takes longer.
— EDWARD R. MURROW

B Y 1992 I'D BEEN BACK in Toronto for more than three years and it would be understatement to say that things weren't working out particularly well for me on any front. My response to the marriage break-up was to immerse myself even further in my work. But even that was giving me less and less satisfaction. I was anchoring the CTV weekend news, covering special events, and I was back on the morning shift all too regularly. Each time a woman co-host at *Canada AM* would leave her chair vacant, I was seconded to fill it. By that time Norm Perry had left too. After fifteen years of getting up before dawn he decided it was time to sleep in. Don Cameron eventually retired as well. In fact it was more a golden handshake than a desired departure. There were new powers in charge and a new philosophy. After heart attacks weakened Don's system and his spirit, it was cancer that finally killed him.

Without Don, the newsman, at the helm the network shifted direction. *Canada AM*, a news-based program, lost the political edge that had always satisfied me. So hosting the show now held less appeal, but I made the best of it.

And I had, by this time, mellowed on the issue of whether entertainers were appropriate interview subjects. I was actually having fun flying off to Los Angeles from time to time to interview the stars. Until, that is, the morning I was set to head south for an interview with Warren Beatty. His co-star and lover, actress Annette Bening, had just announced her pregnancy, causing the following non sequitur, live on air, from J. D. Roberts, my co-host. "Have a good trip," he offered, "and make sure you don't get knocked up." I was stunned by both the inappropriateness and the stupidity of the remark. He thought it was a joke and looked surprised when I explained, off air, why one could not and should not use such phrases on air, never mind imply that I was off to sleep with an interviewee.

Unfortunately this was not an isolated incident. Other on-air comments—like asking the Dalai Lama, the religious leader in permanent exile from his troubled homeland, "So, how are things in Tibet?"—made it difficult to share the set. I felt it was an embarrassment to all associated with the show and an insult to the viewers.

Before long J. D. was wooed back to the u.s., where today he's a successful reporter and anchor at CBS. In what seemed like a trade in our favour, Keith Morrison, a former colleague from CTV who had spent a decade stateside, decided to move back home to Canada and took up the co-host chair.

In March of 1992 Barbara Frum succumbed to the leukemia she'd lived with for years. Her dedication and her courage had made her so much more than a television star. She was revered. For many Canadians, including me, her death was an event of sorrow and loss. For the managers at the CBC it was both a major blow and a programming conundrum.

No one could follow Barbara so the program that had become indelibly associated with her had to be reinvented and it wasn't clear how that could be accomplished.

The *Journal*, the interview program Barbara had moved to from *As It Happens* and that she'd hosted since its inception, had followed the national news anchored by Peter Mansbridge. But the two halves of the hour were run by different departments—news and current affairs. The CBC's new plan was to consolidate the hour, mixing the news with interviews, documentaries and features, and to place the entire program under the jurisdiction of the news bosses. The resulting machinations, power struggles and turf wars were, of course, waged behind closed doors.

My first entry into the scheme was, oddly enough, a phone call from my friend Patsy Pehleman. We'd known each other since *As It Happens* days and she was, at this time, executive producer of *Morningside* at CBC Radio.

I'd been out for dinner with my old friend and colleague from the CTV Ottawa bureau, Alan Fryer. As usual we were gossiping and talking politics. Because I was now separated and soon to be single again, Alan suggested to me that maybe it was time to consider my professional options. We debated the pros and cons of foreign bureau postings and, of course, a move to the States. Quite seriously, I told him that I was probably too old for either option, especially the latter. The American networks continually scout Canadian talent because our training is good and our passports are valuable. But they also tend to seek out younger candidates who are ready to go anywhere, anytime. I wasn't, as the expression goes, hungry enough to go for an American job, which would involve hiring an agent and rolling the fame and fortune dice.

My decision to remain in Canada meant forfeiting the financial rewards and the obvious appeal of an audience ten times as large as any I could reach here, but I had made that call much earlier in life. I had always been suspicious of the editorial freedom an individual reporter would have there. I am also hopelessly and happily Canadian and have always found our domestic narrative totally involving. I liked international travel, but I also liked coming home.

Still, given my new circumstances, a change felt like a good idea.

Canada is a small country when it comes to any single industry. The journalism business is no exception. I'd had my first journalistic job at CBC Radio in Regina and it was there that I'd first met people like Craig Oliver, Peter Mansbridge and Ivan Fecan. Fecan was now back in Canada and at the top of the CBC power structure after a time as an executive at NBC, when I ran into him one day at Toronto's trendy Prego restaurant.

"Why don't you come and work for us?" he queried. "Because nobody's asked," I tossed back. Perhaps it was coincidence but just days later I took the call from my friend Patsy that would set the change in motion.

She told me she'd received an odd request from John Owen, a news honcho at CBC. He wanted her to convey a message to me. She was to call and ask me if I would call him. Why, I asked, didn't he just call me directly?

His roundabout way of handling the situation was unusual, but I'd been in the business long enough to know that large corporations like the CBC have their own culture. Much of what insiders take for granted in the operations of such an enterprise appears odd to the uninitiated.

Patsy and I speculated that given sensitive internal politics, if pressed they could claim "truthfully" that I had actually approached them first.

With hindsight, perhaps the first alarm bells should have begun ringing right then. I was about to discover that this was only an introduction to the twists and turns of a bureaucratic, almost tribal, culture that, in many ways, was incompatible with both my temperament and my experience.

Lines of communication with management at CTV had always been pretty straightforward. As often as Don Cameron would have stormed into the *Canada AM* office demanding a radical rethink of the show on any given day, I would have walked into his office to bluntly share my views and opinions with him. If someone wanted something, one said so. That frankness was what I'd been used to for over ten years.

And then the oddness became even odder.

I called John Owen, we chatted and he asked that in the future I was to use—no kidding—a code name to identify myself. When I phoned John's office I was to call myself by this assumed name so his secretary would know to put me through to him. Of course I knew there would be sensitivities in the hiring process, but this bordered on the bizarre.

Owen told me they were overhauling the entire news hour in the aftermath of Barbara's death and that the CBC was interested in having me on board. I said I too was interested.

But first, John told me, before we could proceed, there was some business I had to clear up with Peter Mansbridge before any substantive details of any potential working relationship could be discussed.

Mansbridge and I met on a crisp autumn morning at a small café in Toronto's Little Italy. It was about ten o'clock, after my shift at *Canada AM*.

I'd known Peter for twenty years and I couldn't imagine what sin I had committed. It turned out he was convinced I had made a cruel comment about his all-too-public marital meltdown with CBC journalist Wendy Mesley. I simply reminded Peter I was in the middle of a marital meltdown myself and any public musings on his misery versus mine would have begged the obvious "pot calling the kettle black" references. We were both taking our lumps and adding insult to injury wasn't a thing I was likely to be insensitive about. With that issue dealt with, we turned to the nuts and bolts of sharing one of the most important hours in the CBC schedule.

Mansbridge had been the solo anchor of the national news and I knew he probably wouldn't be keen to share those duties. On the other hand, he'd always been excluded from *The Journal*, the interview segment of the hour-long program, because that was the journalistic real estate Barbara Frum had made her own. It was not run by the news department but rather by the firm and powerful hand of Mark Starowicz under the aegis of the current affairs department. Competition between two different departments doing the same hour-long broadcast had always seemed a costly and counter-productive concept to me. At CTV there was no such distinction between news and current affairs and there had been neither the time nor money to build separate operations. So I had no idea just how powerful and entrenched these warring fiefdoms at the CBC were, nor how brutal the battles would be over who would be left standing.

The result was a camel. Or, to use the Hong Kong analogy, one country, two systems.

The new amalgamated hour was formatted as a complete entity under one supreme command—news was in control but current affairs loyalists were grafted on and appended to the structure. The plan for the new *Prime Time News* was that both anchors would read the news and do the interviews. Both Mansbridge and I had experience in both areas, though he obviously was more skilled at anchoring and I had more experience with the interviewing side. At that time, Mansbridge appeared to think our teaming up was not only workable but an idea whose time had come.

For my part, being part of a team was what I was used to. I had had nothing but easy co-operation with Norm Perry and most of his successors. My second-in-command role with Lloyd on news specials had always been equally pleasant and easy. But I tried tactfully to say to Mansbridge that teamwork wasn't just about two people sitting side by side, and he tried, equally tactfully, to remind me that while we were contemporaries with equivalent years in the business, he had a special role at the CBC that his tenure and title as chief correspondent reflected.

Our conversation was friendly and candid in a mildly guarded sort of way. We commiserated over our private lives being too public and we looked forward to the possibility of an amiable and mutually successful association.

In early October of 1992, with no final details nailed down with the CBC, I went home to Wadena to officially cut the ribbon on The Special Effects Spa, the beauty salon that my sister, Bonnie, and I were opening. Sparked by the fact that our mother was driving to a nearby town to have her hair done, Bonnie and I had dreamed up the idea one summer afternoon.

The spa opening was a big event in Wadena and the salon was buzzing with local women. At the same time I was doing makeovers, I was also juggling negotiations and phone calls to and from Toronto. Before I returned to Toronto the deal was done.

The CBC wanted me on board almost immediately because the Charlottetown referendum was to be held on October 26 and they wanted me to be there to cover it. The problem was, I was an integral part of CTV's plans for the referendum coverage. Even the publicity had been done so it was agreed that I would stay at CTV through referendum night. It was the only fair thing and was agreed to by all parties.

There were the inevitable rumours that I was jumping ship because CTV wouldn't give me Lloyd Robertson's job, but anyone who knew me would understand that while I had nothing against reading the news, it wasn't something I wanted to do to the exclusion of interviewing. And there was one small technical point—the job wasn't available. CTV had always been good to me. It was just that there wasn't much for me to do there but return to *Canada AM* indefinitely.

I was leaving a great group of people, but you don't leave friendships behind, just workplaces. I still talk regularly to the people there, including Lloyd.

I reported for work at the CBC the day after the Charlottetown referendum, and a week later we officially launched *Prime Time News*.

The CBC promoted my arrival as "coming home." It's true I had started at CBC Radio, but it sounded as though my entire television career at CTV had been some kind of short-term aberration in my professional life. Still, every story needs a headline.

One of the reasons I had been looking forward to going to the CBC was that, as much affection and respect as I had for the institution and the people of CTV, the idea of becoming part of an organization with money, resources and a sizable staff held a certain appeal, even though it was not to be reflected in a larger paycheque for me. Money has never been a great motivator, although now that Boomer angst is setting in, I wish I had cared more. The CBC for years had been seen as being rich to the point of wastefulness, especially by some of the politicians who had to approve the Corporation's budget. Stories of the number of different CBC crews and reporters who would show up at a press conference or an MP's office for an interview were legendary. I certainly didn't support waste— after all I'm a taxpayer too—but I sure liked the idea of sufficiency.

At CTV everyone did several jobs. The upside of that was that you learned a lot, and because there was too much for everyone to do to waste much time or sit through endless meetings, there was very little editorial second-guessing. We were hired for our journalistic skills and were permitted to practise them without layers of hands-on management.

The downside was that everyone did several jobs. There was never enough staff or money at CTV to be free from pinching pennies and, even working double-duty, there were never enough hours in the day. With no income except advertising revenue at the network, the bottom line was an essential issue. "Beg, borrow or steal" was our *modus operandi*. It was, on one level, a challenge to figure a way to do more with less. But it was also a constant source of frustration and, I have to admit, presentation sometimes suffered, though, thankfully, the content seldom did. I was looking forward to more ease in getting the journalistic job done.

In my imagination the new *Prime Time News* was being designed by troops of skilled planners, piloted, tested on audiences and fine-tuned. I reported for duty to find that the program concept was not yet settled, and that no one had asked audiences whether or not a 9:00 news package was of interest to them. The devil is, as we know, always in the details.

Planning for *Prime Time News* was complicated by the sad circumstance of Barbara's death and the power struggles raging around control of the program.

But there were also other complicating factors. The CBC in Toronto was right in the middle of amalgamating the dozens of radio and television offices and studios around the city and planning their consolidation into the new Broadcasting Centre. Resources were half in one location, half in another, as were crews and technicians.

I was more than a bit surprised that I had been hired to do a program that had not yet fully formed. When it did finally emerge from Mother Corp's womb it would still have to fight for audience against an ingrained national routine of entertainment till 10:00.

Personally, I liked the idea of a 9:00 P.M. integrated news hour as part of a new Canadianized CBC. The time shift was a major component of revamping the CBC schedule to become more truly like a public broadcaster and less like a subsidized competitor of private Canadian networks. The overall vision was to make the network unique and recognizable by presenting a 7 to 9 family viewing time block, and a 10 to 12 adults-only zone, each separated from the other by the 9 to 10 news program.

Unfortunately, that conception depended on two shaky premises. The first was that people have loyalty to a particular television network and will plan their lives around the changes that a broadcaster offers. The second was that there was enough worthwhile Canadian programming to fill the schedule, including the after-the-news spot. The jury was out on both counts.

The television industry had been undergoing radical change. All the new cable and specialty channels were providing more choices for consumers but fewer dollars for broadcasters. Market fragmentation was the buzzword, and all the new channels were also fragmenting the major source of revenue available to private networks—advertising revenue. For its part, the CBC had a government stipend that was still close to a billion dollars, so despite the restraint at the CBC, they were rich by comparison. However, it was apparent that federal funds for the Corp were not going to continue growing. The necessary and inevitable restraint dictated a more prudently streamlined and co-operative use of resources. Restraint in the private sector had been a way of life for some time for me so I came with very useful experience with doing more with less. My hopes were high that the new plan would therefore succeed.

But old habits and old fiefdoms die hard and the forced marriage of the news department with the current affairs department turned out to be strained, even hostile.

From the outset I felt like a lightning rod. Tim Kotcheff, a former head of news and current affairs at CTV, was now back at the CBC. He'd left and gone to CTV with Lloyd Robertson when Lloyd had left the Corp over his right to edit copy, and Tim had "gone home" to the CBC before my arrival there. To many CBCers it seemed too coincidental that both he and I were suddenly on the scene. It became a convenient hypothesis that we were there to import heretical private enterprise ideas into public broadcasting, that would subvert the system.

There was also an institutional snobbery at the CBC. CTV was considered by many CBC lifers to be like a farm-team network. I have nothing against hometeam pride and a belief that where you work is the most important place to be, but the sense of superiority that pervaded the CBC was offputting.

My CTV television experience appeared to count for less because it had been private network experience. That I had a wide range of TV journalistic experience, on air and off, doing everything from research and interviewing to bureau chiefing, wasn't given a lot of weight. And then there was the ghost of Barbara Frum.

Among the reasons for the complete rejigging of the hour was that no one wanted to try and fill her shoes. The new format and the new time, everyone hoped, would leave Barbara's and *The Journal*'s place in broadcasting history undiminished and intact and would prevent comparisons between one of Canada's most beloved broadcasters and whoever and whatever came next.

When I reported for duty my first day, the actual move to the new Broadcasting Centre hadn't begun and the program's headquarters were still in the old television studios on Mutual Street, where Barbara had worked.

I was shown to her dressing room, which was to become mine. I privately wished that some other space could have been found, but I was not about to make a fuss. Anne Emin, who had been Barbara's longtime friend and associate, had unlocked the door for me and there were tears in her eyes as she showed me in. Clearly the room had been locked and left untouched since the last time Barbara had used it. I felt I was trespassing on sacred ground. Anne sincerely wished me well but at that moment I felt the intense weight of Barbara's mantle.

Even after I'd been doing *Prime Time News* for months, there were frequent comments about how Barbara had handled this person or that subject. I understood the emotion and loyalty that surrounded Barbara. I too had worked with and learned from her and I felt just as strongly. But the effect of the repeated messages was a constant reminder that I could never be Barbara, and that I wasn't a CBC type. Still, I was bound and determined to make a go of the new job. My first season was filled with optimism and enthusiasm and with bitter internal battles over how the project was evolving and what was expected of whom.

The executive producer, Ron Crocker, was eventually reassigned. David Nayman, the second in command, was a respected journalist who had been enticed away from *The Fifth Estate* and he hung in bravely managing the day-to-day crisis. Freddie Parker, the director, did his best to accommodate me. Tony Burman, who was then chief news editor, was eventually brought in to take the helm. And in spite of the musical chairs and turmoil, we managed to do some good programs.

A certain amount of chaos and adjusting was inevitable, given that we were experimenting and discovering on the air what worked and what didn't. But change does not come easily in any large, bureaucratic organization. Some were trying to streamline a cumbersome system, but it could still take two days and a half-dozen signatures to get an airplane ticket to Ottawa. And there were silly demands like filling out time cards. This was not nine-to-five with overtime. News can happen anytime and we had to respond night or day—that's the way the business works. Why waste the paper and the trees? Well, a rule was a rule.

There were many truisms, both bureaucratic and editorially speaking, that were followed because that's the way it had always been. That nagging feeling of being out of step with the CBC's corporate culture and editorial biases haunted me constantly.

As I marked my fortieth birthday in 1993, in spite of tensions at work, I had a feeling of at least some security and stability in my life. My income was good, I had a three-year contract, I was dating again and I finally sold the house on Palmerston and bought myself a new one in a different part of the city.

My so-called dating was an endless source of amusement for my friends. There had been, until my divorce, the happy gang of six, three couples who, on a rotating basis, hosted one another's birthdays and other causes for celebration. Now there was a gang of five, which, as Peggy Taylor was quick to point out, ruined her seating plans at dinner.

So my friends tried to "help." There were a series of disastrous blind dates and fix-ups. Peggy, jokingly, had placed a name card in front of the plate of one such "date" and simply left it blank. She suggested that any new man could fill out his card upon arrival.

The gang of six-turned-five have a very peculiar collective sense of humour and camaraderie and any newcomer could easily conclude that the barbed and no-holds-barred exchanges meant we didn't like one another. They would be wrong but could have no way of discerning that. Stories of Rick and Peggy's sex life told over dinner were always wildly amusing to their friends, but for new and uninitiated "dates" it could kill not only their appetite but any chance of a return visit.

My mother and father came to celebrate my birthday and it was quite a posh, black-tie affair organized by my friends at Splendido restaurant. I must say I was expecting something much ruder. In the little spontaneous speeches and toasts there were actually some kind and loving offerings and good wishes that were quite out of character for this group.

Mom and Dad stayed on knowing I needed help with the move and Dad could amuse himself doing all that necessary stuff around the new house that only dads can do.

In the divorce, I gained custody of the precious chocolate-point Siamese cat, creatively named Kitty, who was not only warm comfort but embodied my confidence in being able to care for another living thing. Up to this point in my life, it had been a risky proposition to have even plants. Once again, the thought of children began to cross my mind.

All options considered, I concluded that adoption was the only reasonable alternative for a single working woman. Up front I was told by an adoption counsellor that a single mother giving up her baby would prefer a couple rather than another single woman to raise her child, so I'd better not get my hopes up.

But by the time all the interviews, letters of reference and background checks were completed, enough time had passed that my feeling of stability at work had disappeared. A year or more after I began the process of trying to adopt a child I finally gave it up because my circumstances no longer seemed right for it.

At work, the forced triumph of hope over experience was waning. My optimism about a future at *Prime Time News* was replaced by a constant feeling that it just wasn't working out. The word that best sums it up is *estranged*—I felt disconnected from the work I had always loved. The decision-making process about what was news or what was appropriate programming was often puzzling. There seemed to be agendas at play, politically speaking, that skewed the decision-making.

Constrained and restrained in my role, I no longer felt comfortable in my professional skin. There was no single event or crisis that precipitated this, just a non-stop succession of tiny frictions and tensions.

And what troubled me most is that the viewers could sense it too. The person they knew spoke her mind, said what she believed in an honest straightforward way. Now they could sense my discomfort as things came out of my mouth that seemed forced or contrived.

At the start, in the fall of 1992, Peter and I were a team, both reading the news and both conducting interviews. We were high on the energy it takes to get a new program on the air and we were allies. We didn't really socialize off the set, although we shared many friends and acquaintances over the years. What we had in common was both our new and ambitious enterprise and the need to make it succeed—and that meant working all day and through the evening. It doesn't leave a lot of time for a fun-filled nightlife.

Peter and I had tried every possible permutation of sharing the anchoring, but it was hard to overcome the stiltedness of trying to hand back and forth between stories. We tried reading a story each and alternating; we tried doing groups of similar stories together— Peter would do three international stories, for instance, then I would do three national ones—but nothing made the dual anchoring seem less stiff.

Even the "throw" to Peter—what I would say in handing over to him—was scripted and I felt robotic saying "Peter?" when it was apparent that some kind of more human rapport was called for.

Once at the end of a story on a baldness cure (I knew from the script that Peter's next story wasn't a serious one), I said, smiling as I threw back to him, something like "I guess that story is of particular interest to you." He replied also with a smile and an agreement before continuing with his copy. It felt like a breakthrough, a bit of humanness that couldn't hurt. But it sparked a debate in the control room over whether my comment had been appropriate. An hour later, when we redid the show for the eastern time zone, it was clear that the comments were not considered appropriate for a newscast. I wasn't suggesting that we become Regis and Kathy Lee, simply human beings.

When *Prime Time News* began, it was agreed that Peter and I would be announced in tandem each evening and given first billing alternately. One night we'd be ". . . with Peter Mansbridge and Pamela Wallin" and the next ". . . with Pamela Wallin and Peter Mansbridge."

The alternating billing wasn't something I had specifically requested, but I understood it was the Corporation's way of trying to present us as co-hosts. I appreciated the rare gesture because I'd made it clear from the outset that I preferred not to be presented as Peter's helper.

Still, on big events, Peter was the main man. When the 1993 election rolled around, I discovered at a rehearsal the night before that each half hour of the cross-country marathon broadcast would start with Peter on camera alone on another part of the set.

It was, I suppose, a reasonable decision. It's just that I was not given the courtesy of being told in advance. This wasn't a big thing, but it was a clear indicator to me of who was an insider and who wasn't. One in a series.

By the second season I was taken off the news portion of *Prime Time News* and was anchoring, though not exclusively, the second half of the program—or the "bottom end," as it was so respectfully described. As a person whose work is on par with breathing as an essential of life, this was a setback—but there was a silver lining. I actually preferred doing the interviews; it's just that there weren't many to do. There's no doubt, however, that hosting the bottom end, the current affairs portion of the hour, was seen by some as a demotion, though I tried not think of it that way.

And while I enjoyed doing the few interviews there were to do, I certainly wasn't thrilled with all the prerecording and editing and our slowness to react to that day's events. Double-enders—in which it looks to the audience as if the host and guest can see each other while talking but in reality can't—also quite literally take the people out of the equation. Those guests would often be wired twenty feet away or in some other part of the building for that big-screen effect. I just wanted to have them sit down across from me so I could see their face and feel their mood. But all I had to look at was a blank screen.

There were some interesting diversions, however. I was dispatched to Israel, once again a witness to history, as the elusive peace accord was signed. I suggested that I use my downtime to make a quick trip to Gaza. I thought a look at the grim reality of the place that was to be the Palestinian homeland, with its sewers running open in the streets and starving kids huddled under pieces of tin they called home, would help to balance the euphoria of the peace deal. However, my efforts caused nothing but trouble and hard feelings, as I was apparently encroaching on someone else's editorial turf. This was seen as the purview for the documentary or specials units, not the host.

There was a *PTN* crew shooting a documentary in the region and I thought I might be able to use their services, but I was told, they didn't "do news." Fortunately, Paul Workman, the Israel-based CBC news correspondent at the time, came to the rescue by offering to share his crew and knowledge of the area and we cobbled together a special report from the Palestinian front. But my instinct to try to get more bang for the big bucks CBC had spent sending me there was not seen as enterprising but problematic. The bad days were definitely beginning to outweigh the good; the frustrations on the job beating back any sense of accomplishment and satisfaction.

I've mentioned before that my habit of saying what I mean has caused me some grief over the years. At CTV, saying that I didn't like to turn my back to viewers or making a spontaneous criticism of an idea was a thorn in the side of some but acceptable in a newsroom. At the CBC this habit was seen, according to my sources, as evidence that I was powerhungry and a meddlesome bitch.

In the environment in which I was now working, it seemed my suggestions were supposed to be the concerns of others, not of the "talent." If I had an opinion, I was considered obstructionist. I've always thought of it as having high standards and wanting the best possible result.

By this point in my career I'd learned a fair amount about the business of television, having spent my professional life in an environment where lines between duties weren't very clearly drawn. I knew how to write and edit. I knew how cameras worked and how to ensure continuity in a studio setting. I had informed opinions on what worked best in communicating with an audience and tried to ensure that connection survived all the reconstruction. But more and more of what I was doing was taped and edited, with re-asked questions and elaborate openings and special effects added after the fact.

The other problem for me was that I had to please so many producers. Sometimes I would be briefed by four or five of them before an item, each of them wanting something different from the piece.

There were other conflicts of interest. I had been told that I was shifted to the bottom end because of my ability to do interviews. But then documentary producers began to complain that my "insistence" on doing interviews was cutting into the time they wanted for their work. In the last stage of my disintegrating relationship with *Prime Time News* I often spent a ten-hour day at the office and appeared on air just long enough to say, "And now, a full-edition documentary by. . ." Even that one line could take ages to shoot. I came home from work some days twice as tired after twenty-five seconds on air as I had from a day and a night at CTV in which I might have hosted *Canada AM* and still been at work for a live hit on the news that night. It was hard to understand why wanting to work was a bad thing.

By the third season, maybe even earlier, I had the sense that conversations stopped when I walked into a room. On a day-to-day basis, relationships with some of the story producers and crews I worked with were okay, but I was painfully aware that I had few allies where it counted. I had the feeling that people around me thought they should keep some professional distance between themselves and me in case it counted against them.

When the 9:00 time-slot appeared not to be working out, Tim Kotcheff took much of the heat, even though he hadn't even been at the CBC when the decision to change was made. Such details didn't matter—and I was associated with him and he with me so it counted against both of us.

I limped through that fall without the comfort that I was used to deriving from the satisfaction of having done good work. Many friends tried to convince me that I had to leave the show just to protect my health if not my reputation. I was also aware that I was losing my own sense of self and professional confidence.

In many ways, it was sheer obstinacy that kept me from resigning: I felt pushed so I resisted. Quitting was counter to my own instinct as someone who doesn't give up a job just because the going gets hard. But I have to say, the going was extremely hard.

In the spring of 1995 the decision was taken out of my hands. I was informed that my three-year contract, which was to end that summer, was not going to be renewed and that I had done my final show at *PTN* as of that day. I'm forbidden by the terms of my leaving to tell you what those terms were, but I had to fight just to get what I considered to be a fair settling of what was owed.

Ironically, the last program I did at the CBC was a special entitled "Job Security in the 90s," focusing on a book entitled *The End of Work.*

So that was it. Out of work. I was forty-something, unemployed, no savings, a pension that would fit in a piggy bank and, though I love my parents dearly, no chance of inheritance. But, as the old saying goes, there's nothing like a hanging at dawn to help focus the mind. Fortunately, the gods were smiling on the personal front. I had a new man, Michael Decter, in my life who was warm, passionate, smart and determined to see me through this chaos and confusion.

Though it didn't feel like it at the time, my firing would prove to be the best thing that could have happened. I had been desperately unhappy and I wanted to be doing work I could be proud of, in a situation in which my experience and skills could be put to use. I was intent upon finding, or creating, a work situation free of cliques and power politics and personal agendas masquerading as journalism.

I have to confess that the very public nature of my parting company with CBC wound up accruing to my advantage in the long run, though I certainly felt little but anger and humiliation at the time. The way the CBC handled my firing immediately caused quite a stir. Many viewers were displeased by the events, and it was their response and their unfailing support that made it possible for me to do what I did next. Start again.

14

From Prime Time
to My Time

*One's prime is elusive. You little girls, when you grow up, must
be on the alert to recognize your prime at whatever time of
your life it may occur. You must then live it to the full.*
— MURIEL SPARK, *The Prime of Miss Jean Brodie*

T HE INITIAL PERIOD of time
after my exit from *Prime Time
News* was filled with an excep-
tional mixture of highs and lows. First I had to bury the past, then
reinvent the future and move toward it. And through it all there
were a lot of feelings to reconcile. The worst moment was the phone
call to my mom and dad. I couldn't bear the idea of them hearing
about it on the news, especially if it was delivered by my former co-
host. And I had no intimation of how the CBC was going to handle
or explain the whole nasty business.

My parents were wonderful. My mother, in a spectacular show
of solidarity, raged against the unfairness of it all. My father waited
for a moment of calm in the conversation and asked, "Sweetheart,
are you angry or hurt?"

I paused a moment and said, simply, "Angry."

"Good," he said. "Now just remember to keep it ice-cold, not red-hot."

I said I would, without quite knowing what he was telling me. As soon as I'd hung up the phone I understood him. "Keep your cool," he was saying. "Don't even think about getting even. It's a loser's game. Think about getting on with your life." He was right, of course.

If telling my parents was the worst of it, there were a couple of other lows that came in at a close second. The one that angers me most, even today, is the image of a young woman, a story producer, who watched with tears in her eyes as I made my last pass through the office after cleaning out my desk. I knew what she was thinking: If they can do this to you, they can do this to any woman. What chance do we have? I was bound and determined from that moment on to show that young woman that I, and in turn she, could beat the odds. I felt both angry and somehow to blame for the message that young women—in and out of the media business—might be reading from my firing. I hoped they wouldn't shrink back or bite their tongues or lose their enthusiasm.

I wondered too if gender played a part in what happened to me. Then, women—friends, colleagues and many complete strangers— began to call.

There were even calls from women who worked or who had once worked inside the Corporation to say it was not a female-friendly place. I appreciated their sympathies but was saddened at how fearful they were of being caught getting in touch with the exile. One woman called me from a pay phone so there would be no trace of the call.

They bemoaned the fatal odds against an aggressive, opinionated woman in shrinking work environments. When I gave my first public speech a while later I joked that when I wrote my book, the chapter about the whole *PTN* situation would be titled "None of This Would Have Happened If Only I'd Played Golf." Women, especially those in the business world, knew exactly what I was talking about.

Then there was the embarrassment I felt I had caused the people back home. Just the year before, the stretch of Highway 5 that cuts through Wadena had been renamed Pamela Wallin Drive, complete with street signs on each corner. It was an honour for me above all others.

The whole event had been planned and executed without my knowledge. When I arrived back in Wadena supposedly to attend an anniversary party for my sister and brother-in-law, what I found instead was a tribute night that included speeches from teachers, friends and family. It was a wonderful surprise and the conspiracy of silence was well executed. I am a subscriber to the *Wadena News*, the weekly newspaper, and for the month before the event Jim Headington, the publisher, had printed a special edition of the paper without the ads announcing the event and sent that version to me in the mail.

I had made them proud and this was their thank-you. And now I was afraid the people who'd done me the honour might feel shortchanged. I should have known better. They didn't feel let down by their native daughter, but rather by the institution that they felt had let me, and them, down.

Apparently, a deluge of angry telephone calls flooded the CBC after the broadcast, but the recorded messages somehow vanished. A network spokesman said at the time only that there were over a thousand calls that night, ninety percent of which expressed anger at my firing. Someone else told me that my photograph had instantly disappeared from the wall in the Broadcasting Centre, where it had hung among their on-air personalities. My exit felt more like a purge than a parting of the ways.

I knew I was going to be the subject of a rumour campaign, but, as my father had made clear, there wasn't much I could do about it. The insinuation that I was impossible to work with, however, wasn't exactly going to help launch a bidding war for my future services. In the field of journalism, we have only our reputations and our track records to offer, so for me, quite literally, everything was now at stake.

I called friends for advice and everyone I spoke to recommended that I get a lawyer and quickly. By Sunday, Terry O'Sullivan, then at McMillan and Binch, had accepted the task and his first instruction was clear: say nothing except thanks for the good wishes. No details, no allegations, no accusations. Not to the press, not to callers, not even to my family or friends. It was extremely difficult for me to keep quiet, especially when what I needed most was a chance to set the record straight.

It's also hard for a journalist to use the phrase we all detest, "No comment," when responding to colleagues. It leaves the reporter writing the story little choice but to present the views of those who will be quoted, either on or off the record.

Reluctantly, I followed my lawyer's advice as best I could, even when, as I'd expected, the word started to circulate that I'd gotten what I deserved.

In the beginning at least, I had the feeling that wherever I went people didn't quite want to meet my eyes. Awkward silences lingered everywhere. I remember going for a manicure—with all that time on my hands I wanted them to look good—and noticing that the staff seemed embarrassed.

These were people I saw several times a week because I went there regularly to have my hair done. I laughingly assured them that though I didn't have a job I still had a credit card. That broke the ice, permitting us to get things back to where they had been just the week before. But the feeling of being the cause of discomfort and even gossip was unnerving. And once the rumour mill started to churn, fuelled by the Corporation's side of the tale, I actually found myself snubbed by people who weren't immediately involved but who were intimates of those who were.

Even if I hadn't received advice from both my lawyer and my father, I would have realized that there was no way to fight the whisper campaign. I certainly didn't stop going out in public, but there was a time when I felt completely comfortable only among my closest friends.

The highs, thankfully, compensated. The ground swell of support was immediate and immensely gratifying. I received hundreds of calls, letters and faxes, especially from points west. Many people felt insulted, as if the very attributes they prided themselves in—determination and level-headedness—were being attacked. My sister, Bonnie, called to say that the open-line shows in Saskatchewan had taken up my case. I am quite proudly public property in that province.

They felt that an affront to me was an affront to the prairie population at large. Keith Morrison, fellow Saskatchewanian and my former co-host at CTV, had also been fired the same week I had, so the response was intense.

Yet, in the context of the many thousands of others around the country being downsized or fired, outplaced or whatever other euphemisms you might want to use, my own circumstances seemed trivial. I did not have young children to support and I had a fabulous network of friends.

I gave my sincere thanks to everyone who wished me well, but when asked for "my side of the story," I demurred. When *Maclean's* put me and my firing on the cover in April of 1995 it was one of the best-selling issues of the year.

Then, in May, the Royal Canadian Air Farce invited me to make a surprise guest appearance on a show they were taping in Regina and I agreed, believing that the time had come to let the folks at home know I was alive and well. It would give me a chance to say thank you as well.

Both my lawyer and my merry band of advisors cautioned against my participation, but I felt I had to do it and this was a good time, a great way and the best place.

The first script the Air Farce sent me to review was very funny but brutal in its references to both Mansbridge and the Corporation. So I had to tell them that I really couldn't participate in a sketch that harsh. Aislin's cartoon depicting Peter looking into the camera and saying that coming up was an investigation ". . . into why the CBC treated Pamela Wallin so shabbily" was gentle compared with the Air Farce bit.

The rewritten sketch had me back in Wadena running a one-woman television station where I did everything myself. In between the news, weather, sports and business reports, I also did commercials for The Special Effects Spa on Main Street. The script struck a chord and reminded me of the things about myself that I needed reminding of, such as where I'd come from and why community is of such fundamental importance in my life.

When my name came up during the performance the audience expected Luba Goy to appear—she portrays me when the Farce is poking good-natured fun at me. But when I appeared as myself, the entire crowd stood and cheered. Two thousand people letting me know in no uncertain terms that they weren't about to write me off as yesterday's news. My parents were introduced from the audience and received an equally warm response.

That night was an important turning point for two reasons. The first was that I was presented with unequivocal evidence that my work and my ability to do it mattered to a lot of people. You can forget that when you're busy working and living in the media capital of Toronto. You're aware that many people know your name and your face. They may stop you in the grocery store to tell you they watch you on television, but what you can't know for sure is whether it's your celebrity or your work that matters to them.

The audience in Regina left no doubt. Their warmth was both comfort and reward.

The second reason that the Air Farce performance was a pivotal moment for me was that even though the revised script was just a send-up, it did remind me that, despite the obvious downsides, I was now free of a situation that had been very destructive in terms of my career, not to mention my psyche. While I was not really going to become a one-woman TV station in Wadena, it was my experience, my skills and aspirations and the trust of the viewers that would allow me to reinvent the future.

As a workaholic it's terribly difficult to get up every morning and have nowhere to go. My work had given my life definition. The public response added to my growing resolve to return to what I was best at, to return to the airwaves in whatever effective way I could.

I received a flurry of interesting job offers, but nothing that seemed right for me. Newsworld suggested I move to Halifax to host their morning show. I think that suggestion was made largely so the CBC could then say I had been "reassigned" and not fired. It might also conveniently divert attention from all the negative public opinion.

For all the anxiety and uncertainty that kept me constant company through the spring and into the early summer of 1995, thankfully there was an equal amount of sustaining energy. My lawyer, Terry O'Sullivan, used to remark on the amazing people who would show up with me for meetings. To protect the innocent I won't name them, but you know who you are.

They all had the same advice: get on with it and get back to work. My network of friends was more important than any television network, more important even than any old boys' network. I'll never be able to tell them how much I love them or how crucial they were to my professional resurrection.

And there were several others who also provided a crucial psychological hand up. The first was Adam Zimmerman, and he probably has no idea of the role he played. A well-respected business tycoon, Adam ran Noranda for many years. We had first met a few years earlier when, as a friend of John Turner, he had called to tear an angry strip off me for raising "the Question" on national television. A few days before my firing, Adam called to invite me for lunch. But his invitation had to go unaccepted, because my schedule was just too overloaded. The news of my ejection from *Prime Time News* had barely hit the papers when Adam called again and, with his characteristic dry wit, renewed his lunch proposal, noting that I certainly couldn't claim a full calendar any more. It might have been the first time I'd laughed in a few days and I was happy to arrange a meal with Adam, although I made him promise to buy.

When we met he was his usual forthright self. "What do you want to do?" he asked me, "and what can I do to help?" I told him that I'd thought before about producing my own television program and that I would need to start my own company if that was to happen. The only problem was I didn't have a clue how to run a business. I'd been a boss and a manager, but meeting a bottom line and balancing that with journalistic imperatives is a very different mission from trying to fund a bottom line. It was essential, I added, that the programming be thoughtful, centred on ideas and people and offer a forum long enough to explore them fairly. I was tired of sound-bite journalism.

Because Adam wasn't a media insider like most of the people I was meeting with, he focused on specifics and promised to answer my calls, no matter how trivial the questions seemed. My outlook had changed dramatically by the time that lunch was over and as I left the table I was looking squarely into the future with less preoccupation with the recent past. I went home and did something I'd never even considered before: I drafted a mission statement for an independently produced television program and a plan to set up my own production company that I hoped would mark the next step in my life. The harsh reality in TV land is "out of sight, out of mind." So the next step was obvious. Phone Jack Fleischmann.

Jack had been on call for me, as he has always been, throughout this latest crisis of career and confidence. He'd left broadcasting several years previously at that point and was running his own media consulting firm. He was quite generous, if not a little crazy, with his commitment to help me in any way. Always a man of ideas, he had something even more important to contribute—practical knowledge of the world of business. Jack knew, for example, how to rent office space and create a budget.

Together we began to hatch a plan that contained only a single given. All we knew for sure was that we wanted a forum for the most interesting minds around us to engage in serious conversation. By serious we meant in-depth, not humourless. We weren't in the business of educating, but that's not to say the entertaining couldn't give thinking people something to think about.

The cable and specialty industry in Canada has exploded in the last few years, but as recently as 1995 there were still very few real alternatives for an independent television producer trying to sell a thinking person's talk show in prime time. Big private networks would have had to kick profitable U.S. sitcoms or movies off their schedule to make room for what we were proposing and a quick canvass of the possibilities led us straight to the CBC's all-news network, Newsworld. Their schedule was quite elastic, but there was the small matter of my ongoing legal negotiations with the CBC main network and their lawyers, which seemed to be dragging out what should have been a pretty simple business. Finally, under the deft guidance of Terry O'Sullivan, matters were resolved, and Jack and I went to see Slawko Klymkiw, the head of CBC Newsworld.

Newsworld is separate entity from the CBC main television network. Their operation—and this is one of the things I liked about it—was more reminiscent of CTV than of *Prime Time News*. Financially, Newsworld is a close-to-the-bone operation, so the type of show they would be most receptive to—meaning cheap—was really the type of show Jack and I knew how to create: clean and lean with not a bell or whistle in sight. I didn't really want the costly satellite facilities because I liked the idea of a live face-to-face, unedited encounter. Every guest would be within touching distance, every gesture, mannerism or nuanced smile obvious to me and to our audience.

This was the kind of journalism I preferred and the Newsworld budget made it a necessity. It was a happy meeting of needs and minds. And the program would be seen, in most parts of the country, in prime time—and that mattered.

While Canadian politics remained a passion, the program Jack and I had always envisioned—whatever its final form—would have a much broader-ranging focus than holding the Hill under a microscope five nights a week. There were plenty of other shows trying to do just that. We certainly intended that politics would play a part in the new show, but not in predictable ways and not at the expense of the physical and intellectual landscape that produces interesting ideas.

I have no doubt that the fact that Jack and I were proposing an independent co-production must have pleased Klymkiw as much as the fact that we were prepared to do a season of television for very little money. We would succeed or fail on our own merits and Newsworld would not have to take responsibility. My company would produce the program and I would hire my own staff of producers, who would be responsible only to me. We would use CBC technical staff and facilities and David Nayman would be our liaison with Newsworld. But Slawko Klymkiw was the kind of person you could pick up the phone and just call and he didn't seem to have any problem dealing with the "Pamatollah," as some *PTN* staffers had dubbed me.

By the time Jack and I left Klymkiw's office we had struck a deal to go on air on Labour Day—less than a month away. I was excited by having a new project to throw myself headlong into, a new vision to realize. And best of all, it was our own vision. No longer would I have to try to squeeze myself, against all my instincts and experience, into an oversized labyrinthine scheme.

The downside was that we'd agreed to do 201 live, hour-long programs for a bargain-basement price. When we sat down to deal with the reality of what we'd promised, Jack and I saw clearly that next to our budget, "lean and mean" looked positively opulent.

It was obvious that once we'd rented and equipped an office and hired a staff to go with it, there'd be almost nothing left but the opportunity to test my views about programming with the Canadian viewing audience. I couldn't wait.

I have long believed that Canadians want intelligent programming. That's not to say that we don't want to be entertained or amused. There's no rule that says informative and interesting programs have to be dull.

People have always felt comfortable enough to approach me and share their views on everything from politics to last night's program. I'm like a walking public opinion poll. If you listen carefully you'll hear all the advice and insight you need to create programs that people want to watch.

What I heard was that viewers wanted to learn about and come to understand the complicated stories and people that shape their world. And implicit in their frustration with the daily offerings served up by the media was an appeal for a venue devoted to full, frank and fair exchange.

I was convinced if we built such a place, they would come: a meeting place where people with talent or ideas or views on life's lessons learned would engage their minds. Viewer and participant alike would be treated with respect. No staged encounters, no contrived debate and no editing. Our vision was simple—conversation not confrontation.

15

Pamela Wallin Lives

I believe the second half of one's life is meant to be better than the first half. The first half is finding out how you do it. The second half is enjoying it.

— FRANCES LEAR

I T WAS AN OMEN. Actually, it was a typo. At the new *Pamela Wallin Live* office, our *Globe and Mail* subscription arrived addressed as "Pamela Wallin Lives." It seemed to capture the moment. I was indeed alive and well, but we would need a sense of humour if we were going to survive the near impossible task we'd just agreed to: 201 hour long programs, five nights a week.

Within just a couple of weeks' lead-time, Jack and I set about putting together a television program from an idea and a business plan from the back of an envelope. What we had to work with was a vision and about half a century of combined experience in the media. Despite his denials, TV is in Jack's blood.

A direct result of all my years of journalistic work in radio, print and television, from prisons to Parliament Hill, from Wadena to the world's war zones, was that I could now envision a place where the experiences and the accumulated knowledge could meld into a new project: a meeting place of minds and a marketplace of ideas. It was counter intuitive in the contemporary world of high-tech TV. We simply wanted to see and hear people talking to people about things that mattered. And we would need a special group of people to help make it happen.

When the announcement hit the papers that I was setting up *Pamela Wallin Live*, we immediately started to hear from producers who wanted to join our fledgling unit. Since much of what plagued me about the PTN experience was the fear that the allegations made about me would make it difficult to find good people, it was extremely gratifying to discover how many of television's best were eager to take the risk.

We interviewed potential candidates, trying to warn them without scaring them off that the task wouldn't be easy due to the relentless demands of a daily show and a host with exceptionally high standards. Even though time was short, it was evident that we had to find the smartest and most energetic producers in the industry, since brains and dedication were going to have to fill in the gaps that can often be papered over with cash.

Jack and I conducted interviews in my living room, since that was the nearest thing we had to an office. We talked to maybe a dozen applicants and chose our roster on nothing but instinct. We picked those who had the three things we were looking for most: creativity, enthusiasm and a sense that they understood and shared our vision. You can't have a program based around smart, creative guests unless you've got a smart creative staff to find them.

It was a stroke of luck that Anne Bayin, who became our senior producer, was between jobs. In the nomadic fashion of freelancers, Anne spent her working life going from project to project in television, radio and print, as her interests or the exigencies of the industry dictated. She started planning for the first show within minutes of our agreement.

The flamboyant and wonderfully persuasive Mary Lynk came to us from radio, where she'd been a producer on Peter Gzowski's *Morningside* for several years. Wendy Bryan was fresh off a stint with an afternoon talk show, which obviously played to a very different audience than we hoped to appeal to at night. But along with TV experience she had also worked at polling and PR firms and in party politics in England and her interests were eclectic. And there's one more person who has been with us almost since the beginning. Rebecca Eckler was a student when she came to do her practicum with us. I knew within days she had the right stuff. She's smart, sassy and has a sense of humour.

We knew that it took a certain depth of thought to produce segments that ran an hour rather than the few minutes most programs permit for even the most complex issues and ideas—and these women seemed to have it in full measure. The choices all-around—ours to choose them and I hope theirs to choose us—have been justified.

Graeme McCreesh, who works for the CBC, has been our director fairly consistently since we went on the air, and despite the fact that he doesn't wear a skirt, his talents and his willingness to roll with the punches have been invaluable and have earned him honorary status in the "not so old" girls' club. Through Graeme we met Janine Blanchard, who followed Larry St. Aubin in the impossible task of production manager. That means she's in charge of everything—from mood swings to making sure the guests arrive on time. Her insights and her laugh help us all get through the endless work-day.

And also with us from the beginning is our greeter and assistant, Mark Landells, who has performed more miracles than anyone bearing wings.

The team worked then as it does now at fever pitch. Unfortunately for them, I have always considered that normal. But their presence, for me, is a kind of affirmation as important as anything the reviews might contain.

I'm always asked why my staff are almost all women—is it deliberate or political statement after my experiences at the CBC? No, I can truthfully reply, it's not discrimination. I just hire the best and the brightest.

When we embarked on this project we wanted a studio setting mixed with a feeling of warmth and intimacy. *Pamela Wallin Live* was not going to be a bear pit where guests had to feel guarded and defensive, but neither did we want the simulated living room look.

One of my must-haves was a desk that didn't separate me from my guests by an expanse of tabletop. I don't like the feeling, as host or as viewer, of an interviewer sitting like a business executive at a fortress-sized desk that screams of self-importance and distances him or her from the person on the other side. We found the prototype for my desk one night a bar called Acqua, where Jack and I had gone for a meeting. As soon as we were seated I said to Jack as I nodded toward the bar, "That's it! Look at the indentation that brings everyone close together."

We careened onto the air on Labour Day with our first guest—Pat Conroy, the author of *Prince of Tides*—and by the end of the program I knew that this newest adventure in my life was going to turn out even better that I had hoped. People I knew or had interviewed or had encountered over the years supported our project by willingly giving of their time and making up the early guest list. Others were enticed by our novel approach.

The luxury of an hour's conversation with a thoughtful person, an hour with no attack and defense, with no attempt to get a ten-second news clip was, with no exaggeration, wonderful.

The eloquent and thoughtful editor of *Harpers* magazine, Lewis Lapham, arrived on our set one night, sat down and irritably inquired as to whether we'd have a grand total of five or six minutes for the interview. "No," I replied, "we have an hour." He sat back in his chair and when the program was over he volunteered to be at our beck and call because nowhere in his country would he have the opportunity to delve into a topic for an hour.

I've always believed that if you give people a good substantive Canadian alternative to American fare, they will, in significant numbers, choose it. I don't mean cod liver oil TV, "Here, take this, it's good for you because I say so" kind of programming I've seen practised. Nor would I pander to the lowest common denominator, counting good ratings above good taste. I had to put my program and my beliefs to the test and there would be no one to blame but me if it didn't work.

The program certainly didn't ignore my first love—Canadian politics—but it certainly more often wanders much wider afield in our attempt to give our viewers an unusual luxury in the television world, time to develop ideas.

Our conversations with politicians, whether it's Paul Martin or Jean Charest, are not just about the news of the day. But rather they look at what forces and factors guide their decisions.

As the season progressed we found a mix of the political with the non-political worked best. The former included everyone from Segal, Kirby and Caplan to the president of the World Bank. But interviews with everyone from country star Garth Brooks to Sarah MacLachlan to Patrick Watson with his magic tricks were just as intriguing.

I can do an hour on politics or with a personality with very little in the way of prep time. On other nights, gaps in my knowledge of the world need filling as I grapple with areas of thought and endeavour as diverse as the astrophysics of Hubert Reeves and the cutting-edge rap music of Ice T. Since we've started the program, I've put in enough reading, background research and listening to new ideas to earn another university degree. It has been, and remains, a mind-broadening experience.

The mail immediately, both its volume and the praise it contained, gave us evidence that we were hitting an audience who felt underserved by television, and by the end of our first season on air we were pulling in some of the highest audience ratings on the Newsworld network.

We are, as I write, into our fourth season on air and the education of Pamela Wallin continues nightly. We now have more than 700 programs to our credit and though we don't do the show live anymore because we were moved to a spot an hour later, we do do it "live-to-tape," which means that we still do not edit. What you see is actually what occurred, mistakes and all. That's the way I like it best.

Whether it's listening to some of the best minds in the world meandering through an hour of conversation, or experiencing the roller-coaster ride of *Canada AM*, over the years I've learned a little about this biz. Let me tell you about the interview as I've come to understand it—and it's no different whether the person opposite me is singer Tony Bennett or the prime minister of Canada.

It's often a nerve-wracking, sometimes awkward, adrenalin-producing affair. Sometimes the intellectual connection, the give and take, the reading of signs and signals, rivals a romantic encounter. The interview can be a very intimate experience. The contrary is, unfortunately, true as well.

A bad interview is like a bad blind date. You've invited him to your house so as the evening progresses you can't flee, however much you might want to. If only it were his place—you could sneak off into the night, leaving no forwarding address.

Over the years, when the red light goes on and a floor director like Gerald or Paul or Kevin gives me my cue—I make a commitment. I am focused on the person across the desk. Many other things are happening—in my head, in my ear and in the studio in general, and I must deal with the environment as well as I can. Is there lipstick on my teeth, did the microphone pick up a growling stomach, what shot are we on, what's left on the clock, did the audience see the smirk on the guest's face or was the camera on me at that moment? If the audience *didn't* see the smirk and I ask a pointed question in response to it, anyone watching will think I'm just being rude. How do I avoid a misunderstanding? Can I use humour or is this guest unlikely to respond well to it? The questions in my mind are endless, even before I've asked the guest anything.

The first rule is to always interview someone who's worth the time and energy. For everyone's sake. The second rule is to not ask questions so much as advance ideas that your guest can respond to. Give him or her thoughts to finish.

The third rule is to know your ground. It's the minimum show of respect for the person you've invited. You should know as much about this person sitting across from you as it takes to make him feel flattered at your investment of time. The last thing you want is a guest screaming silently to himself that you just don't get it, that you've missed the point completely. Though no studio microphone will pick that up, you can bet that an astute audience will hear it.

The fourth rule is don't be afraid to admit that you don't know something. And don't be afraid to say that you do. Next, rule five, keep your biases and preconceived notions fully intact, but always be ready to shed them when the evidence challenges you.

Every interview is a balance between your role as the viewer's surrogate and your own interests and indulgences. And every interview is a Rorschach test. Each viewer sees a different personal and unique exchange.

That's a fact of the business that's beyond my control and I've stopped pulling out my teased hair when a viewer charges bias or favouritism. If the accusation is of incompetence or error, though, I'm ready to read that letter twice and write rule three on the blackboard one hundred times.

Conducting an interview comes with a large dose of responsibility. People's careers and reputations are at stake. But seldom is the bargain between journalist and guest stated plainly. For me to feel that an interview has succeeded, I have to come away feeling that it contained something for everyone—me, the guest and most importantly you, the viewer.

I stand in your place, ask the questions I expect are on your mind and try to find a path into each guest's individual truth. I like that I now spend less time trying to get someone to let a tidbit slip from unguarded lips and more time exploring ideas. Sometimes it is a congenial process, sometimes it makes the blood boil, but the conversation continues at a more leisurely pace than our soundbite media normally permits.

In the end there's no magic formula for a good interview except to be prepared. There's chemistry to consider. If you click with someone, great. But even anger can sometimes be a catalyst, though disdain never works. There has to be a reason to want to connect and contempt, like bad hair or gaudy earrings, just gets in the way.

To be awestruck doesn't make for an engaging encounter either. In fact, it's seldom anything but an embarrassment for the awestruckee, and for the interviewer it can be professionally fatal. Although I did propose to Tony Bennett, I think, or was it he who proposed to me?

There have been moments of surprise, disappointment and reward. Carl Bernstein was one interview I was really looking forward to with anticipation. Any journalist growing up at the time was shaped and inspired by Woodward and Bernstein's work. With the help of Deep Throat they brought down a sitting president and raised the cachet of journalism as a profession of which to be proud. I met him in the green room a few minutes before the interview was about to begin, to explain that although his book was about the Pope and the end of the cold war we wanted to spend a few moments retracing the steps that led him to his historic claim to fame. He turned to me and barked, "Save it for the studio," then turned away. I was disappointed.

This man, once a journalistic icon, showed me in a flash that he was not worthy of the mantle. The interview was a bit testy and he remained unpleasant in his approach all night. There will be no return engagement, unless, of course, he brings Deep Throat with him.

But other nights I have been witness to examples of true spirit and generosity that restore my faith in humanity enough to forgive even a Carl Bernstein.

There was the conversation with George Chuvalo, a boxer who was dealt his most deadly blows outside the ring. Two of his five children died of heroin overdoses. His wife and youngest son committed suicide. Now the former champion spends his days going from classroom to classroom trying to convince kids to be wary of drugs. Musical legend B.B. King talked about his love for women and the fifteen resulting children. And he shared the story of how music helped him survive a childhood from hell. Many people were reassured when Michael Wilson, the former Finance minister, emerged from behind the political mask to talk about the death of his son. Others were inspired by five-year-old Wesley Chu, a piano prodigy who has the talents of a musical genius and the curiosity of a kid in a TV studio.

Tom and Melissa Gallant were two who brought tears to my eyes and in the same moment a real sense of hope. Melissa had been severely brain-damaged in a freak car accident. Through four years of trauma, Tom stayed with her, despite her repeated request that he leave and find another life and love. No, he said, and he told us why. There's too much emphasis on the beginnings and ends in life. We, as a culture, are so obsessed with births and deaths, weddings and divorces, that we forget about the middle—the part that is all about for better and for worse.

There was not a trace of the martyr in his voice. And not surprisingly, his faith in Melissa and his love have helped pull her back from the brink. It's not just a love story or the tale of a medical miracle. It's the story of how two people cope with the lousy hand that life sometimes deals.

Without sounding too clichéd, we seek out people who have triumphed over disaster and who are able to translate life's lessons for others. It's a contribution we can make. Of all the twenty-four-hour days there are available, on all the dozens of channels, I think we can afford one hour each night to find the good in the human spirit.

Pamela Wallin, the program, is an indicator of who Pamela Wallin, the person, has become. I still run through my life at a clip that many find tiring just to watch. I wouldn't have it any other way.

I always wake up early. I spend my weekdays and nights at the office and in the studio and, since I've never lost my taste for good conversation, weekends are spent, as often as possible, with friends. I truly enjoy, and still feel flattered, when I'm asked to chair a symposium, give a speech or referee a debate. My speeches—which are almost invariably about the power and the responsibility of the media—and the audience response sessions afterwards keep me in touch with the most important group in the media equation: the viewers. I'm always moved when strangers stop me on the street to tell me I've made a difference in their lives. And since I'm a firm believer in giving back to your community, I also do my fair share of charity work.

As well, I am an investor in and sit on the board of a company that Jack Fleischmann now runs called NewsTheatre. This facility is a television studio, where we tape Maclean's TV, a project we do in cooperation with the magazine and CTV. And our Friday night program is taped there as well now. NewsTheatre is also a movie set and a venue for corporate press conferences and events. And it has its own TV network, feeding the events at NewsTheatre into every cash-strapped newsroom in the city. It was another one of those ideas that Jack and I discussed over endless lunches for months, if not years.

I am, at forty-five, better than halfway through my career, but I take great hope and inspiration from both demographics and Gloria Steinem, the journalist and feminist crusader.

The former shows me that an aging woman is less likely to be put out to pasture today because millions of Baby Boomers are heading into their fifties and they want to see themselves reflected on the screen.

As for Gloria, she inspires me because she makes a compelling case that, despite all the fears and the stereotypes, aging is a liberating experience. When she turned forty, some well-meaning friend commented with kind intention, that she didn't look forty. In true fashion, Steinem retorted, "This is what forty looks like. We've been lying so long, who would know?" A frontal assault, as is her style, on the age-old double standard about aging. Millions of women, myself included, breathed a sigh of relief and gratitude.

As she continues to age gracefully she becomes even more compelling in her belief that aging is another country. "The older I get," she writes, "the more intensely I feel about the world around me . . . and more able I am to use my own voice, to know what I feel and say what I think." The last time we met I interviewed her and we talked about this very issue on air. Later that evening I queried her again, privately. Was it really true? Did she really mean it? Her serene smile and quiet nod, and her simple answer—absolutely. I believe her.

So here we are at what I hope will be the midpoint of a life. The great writer Evelyn Waugh once said that only when one has lost all curiosity about the future has one reached the age to write an auto-biography. Well, I haven't lost my curiosity or my common sense. So I may have disappointed some of you because there is little juicy gossip about battling egos, anchor wars and old boys' networks. Much could not be said in this book in order to protect the living and the sensitive. And, besides, I have good legal advice!

Still, I trust I've answered the questions that so many of you have asked over the years: what is your life and work really like? What drives you? And I hope I've helped you see the world a little more clearly from my side of the screen. You see, I want to recruit you to the cause of making TV wiser, smarter and better and of making us all more critical users of it. As the old saying goes, if an ass peers into a television screen, you cannot expect an apostle to peer out. In other words, only your high standards ensure ours.

TV is an industry that everybody loves to hate, even those of us in it. We stand accused of being intrusive and unfair, of making people fat, lazy and stupid and promiscuous and violent. We are blamed for everything from moral decay to family breakdown, from alienated Gen-Xers to untrustworthy politicians. Yes, according to the experts, TV is even responsible for declining male sperm counts because guys spend too much time in front of the tube with their legs crossed, eating junk food. There are some truths in all those accusations, but I've tried to make our work and the forces that shape and restrain it a little more understandable.

I, too, am one of those forces. Like all of us who are catapulted into the public consciousness by television, I am in some ways a product of the sheer number of eyes that see me—a creation of mass media just like some of our guests. The power of television is like nothing we've seen before in its ability to promote celebrity, its power to etch a face onto the public imagination, its capacity to imbue the question-asker with the same phenomenon of celebrity as the people of whom she asks her questions. Along the way I've learned that you can't please everyone and, more importantly, there is no good reason to want to. But I'm satisfied with the work I've done and I've never forgotten that it's the journalist's job to give everyone access to the few who make decisions for all of us.

One of the crazy characters in Jane Wagner's book *The Search for Signs of Intelligent Life in the Universe* asks herself this imponderable: "What is reality anyway?" She answers herself with this little gem: "Nothing more than a collective hunch." It leaped out of the pages at me like a fundamental truth. And I have used it ever since to try to explain what we do: explore that collective hunch about what matters most to the most number of people on a given day.

We are simply in the business of collecting and transmitting facts and information, but it sometimes takes much longer for the truth to emerge.

Journalism at its core is about reporting on all those obvious collective hunches that we share as a citizenry and either confirming that the reality you know is still intact or reporting that it is no longer what you once believed.

All we can do is follow the sage and succinct advice of one of the high priests of journalism, Edward R. Murrow:

To be persuasive, we must be believable. To be believable, we must be credible and to be credible we must be truthful.

This is increasingly difficult in a era that has unleashed changes and technology no one could have conjured up, even in a work of science fiction. But I'm not some high-tech Pollyanna here proposing that if we just love one another and tell the truth the world will be a warm and fuzzy place.

Perhaps the challenge is not so much in discovering and mastering all the new frontiers as it is in looking inside our heads and our hearts to rediscover some old values and old truths to help us navigate in this New World. The cornerstones of my beliefs have not changed much since my days as a story editor in Ottawa: the need for accountability of the powerful, the necessity of an energetic press in a free society and the crucial value of an educated public. And maybe at the top of the list is that we *are* our brother's keeper.

We have to ensure our kids are TV literate in the same way we care about whether they can read or write. The television screen is how they ingest and understand the world. We must give them the tools, to become critical viewers and not opt for the v-chip or raise our voices in a cry for censorship. It's hardly fashionable these days, but I am a believer in free speech. It is a basic tenet of our democracy. And I can't just believe in free speech when if suits me. The laws against libel, slander and hate protect us from the worst sins. But, I must defend the right to vile or offensive speech or ideas that I disagree with or that may even be dangerous because I want the freedom to express my own ideas and hear new thoughts and think thoughts other than those I am used to thinking. If nothing else this is simply enlightened self-interest. We need new thoughts to evolve as a civil society.

I was struck profoundly by this when I was invited by the Swedish embassy in Canada to be Canada's "cultural representative" at the Nobel Prize ceremonies in Stockholm in December of 1997. Given my own Swedish roots, it was a marvellous experience to see the homeland. But over the course of several days, as I sat listening to some of the world's leading thinkers, I was struck by what they all had in common. For years, regardless of their respective disciplines, each had struggled away, often in obscurity, bearing the brunt of collegial ridicule and guffaws because people with new ideas are too readily dismissed as crazy, nutty professors.

Decades later, as they stood in the international spotlight to have their theories and research recognized with the most prestigious of honours, I sensed the profound satisfaction that their work and that even the humiliations suffered had, in the end, been worth it.

On a daily basis journalists face ethical and moral dilemmas and the question of accountability. Can you be both an accountable and a free press? It's frightening, but journalists are still struggling with this most basic question that has plagued and perplexed us since the fourth estate emerged.

We may have come a long way from the days when Pierre Elliott Trudeau declared that the state had no business in the bedrooms of the nation. But what about the boardrooms or the courtrooms or the chatrooms on the Net? And if not the state, what about the media?

I will leave as my last defense and explanation of journalism the words of one of the keenest observers of the human race, Charles

Dickens. Dickens wrote that what is meant by knowledge of the world is simply an acquaintance with the infirmities of man. In other words, to be truly knowledgeable, we must recognize human frailty. And that's how I see my work, as the art and craft of telling stories of the human condition. That's my mission; that's my life's work. Now do you see why I love it?

Index

A

Allmand, Warren, 90
Aquino, Cory, 239
Arciuch, Peter, 154, 156
As It Happens, 97-110, 111, 117, 141
Atkinson, Mac, 80
Austin, Julian, 43
Axworthy, Tom, 177

B

Banadygas, Perry, 10
Barlow, Maude, 204
Barnett, Barry, 154
Bauch, Hubie, 140
Bayin, Anne, 276-7
Beatty, Warren, 244
Bélanger, Nicole, 92, 94, 102
Bennett, Bill, 121
Bennett, Tony, 280, 282
Bening, Annette, 244
Bergman, Ingrid, 94
Bernstein, Carl, 282, 283
Bernstein, Howard, 169

Bishop, Heather, 75
Black, Conrad, 131
Blaikie, Dave, 122
Blanchard, Janine, 277
Bouchard, Lucien, 189
Brooks, Garth, 279
Brown, Tina, 125
Brownlee, Bonnie, 210, 218
Bryan, Wendy, 277
Bull, Meagan, 30
Burman, Tony, 254

C

Cameron, Don, 140, 146-8, 151, 152-3,
    154, 160, 166, 170, 172, 182, 186, 187,
    230, 231, 236, 243, 246
Cameron, Stevie, 121
Camp, Dalton, 206
Campagnolo, Iona, 221, 222
Campbell, Kim, 213-14, 222
Canada AM, 139, 141-8, 149, 150, 155,
    165, 166-89, 201, 243-4, 246, 280
Caplan, Gerry, 177, 178

Carrey, Jim, 174
Cassaday, John, 240-1
CBO Morning, 76, 78, 79, 135
Chrétien, Jean, 137, 177, 217-19, 221, 228
Chu, Wesley, 283
Chuvalo, George, 283
Clancy, Lou, 111, 113, 114-16, 129, 140, 169
Clark, Catherine, 212-13
Clark, Joe, 109-10, 202, 212-13, 214
Clinton, Hillary, 28
Conroy, Pat, 278
Conway, Fiona, 141
Crocker, Ron, 253
Crosbie, John, 88, 166-7

D
Dalai Lama, 244
Decter, Michael, 121, 261
Delfs, Lynne, 238, 239
Deverell, John, 66-7, 74, 75, 76, 81, 88, 90, 99
Dickens, Charles, 289
Douglas, Marilyn, 47
Drewery, Laine, 232, 233-4

E
Eckler, Rebecca, 277
Elizabeth II, Queen, 150
Ellerbee, Linda, 93
Emin, Anne, 253
Evans, Bob, 232

F
Fair, Mrs., 27-8, 38
Falkland Islands, 151-63
Fecan, Ivan, 246
Figg, Albert, 192
Finlay, Michael, 101, 116

Fleischmann, Jack, 77-8, 90-1, 135-6, 139, 170-1, 173, 174-6, 177, 179-80, 181-2, 186, 187, 232, 270-2, 275, 276, 278, 284
Fotheringham, Allan, 200
Fox, Bill, 120, 121, 122, 140, 169, 177, 202, 210, 218
Fox, Malcolm, 154-5, 156, 158-60, 161, 163, 167, 186, 199, 229-30, 231, 234, 235-42
Franks, Bev, 32
Frum, Barbara, 97, 98, 102, 105-8, 111, 244, 248, 252-3
Fryer, Alan, 232, 233-4, 245

G
Gallant, Melissa, 283
Gallant, Tom, 283
Galtieri, General Leopoldo, 160-1
Gambacorta, Dorato, 181
Gandhi, Indira, 103
George, Bonnie (sister), 7, 9, 10, 14, 15-16, 23, 24, 26, 33, 35, 37, 38, 238, 241, 249, 267
Gibson, Anne, 102
Gigantes, Evelyn, 88
Goar, Carol, 121, 122, 231
Gordon, Alison, 100, 109, 110, 114, 116
Gordon, Anita, 99
Gordon, Barbara, 140
Gotlieb, Allan, 83, 189, 230
Gotlieb, Sondra, 122
Goy, Luba, 268
Gray, Charlotte, 121
Gray, Colin, 90
Gray, Elizabeth, 75-7, 78, 80, 81-3, 85, 88, 89-90, 91, 121, 135, 167, 238
Gray, John, 82, 83, 89-90, 238

Index

Gray, Josh, 90
Gray, Rachel, 90
Gustin, Ann, 55-6
Gwyn, Richard, 121, 122
Gwyn, Sandra, 121, 122
Gzowski, Peter, 102

H
Habib, Patti, 101
Halberstam, David, 4
Hansen, Rick, 88, 89
Harasen, Lorne, 56
Hatfield, Richard, 121
Headington, Jim, 265
Hefner, Hugh, 5
Heller, Joseph, 4
Hepburn, Bob, 122
Honderich, Beland, 121-2
Honderich, John, 122
Hunter, Tommy, 109
Hurst, Robert, 232

J
Jackson, John, 187
Jamieson, Don, 205
Jamieson, George, 101
Janigan, Mary, 121
Jewison, Norman, 109
John (boyfriend), 42-3, 45, 46, 47, 48, 51-2, 54, 59
John Paul II, Pope, 154-5
Journal, The, 247-8, 253

K
Keleher, Terry, 121
King, B.B., 283
Kingwell, Mark, 6
Kirby, Michael, 177, 178

Klymkiw, Slawko, 271, 272
Kotcheff, Tim, 152, 252, 260
Krueger, Lesley, 116

L
Landells, Mark, 277
Lapham, Lewis, 278
LaPierre, Laurier, 92-5, 182
Laurence, Margaret, 182
Levant, Bill, 51
Lévesque, René, 88, 89, 137, 138
Lewis, Stephen, 177
Lloyd, Peter, 151-2
Lougheed, Peter, 2, 125, 126-8, 137, 138
Lynk, Mary, 277
Lyons, Margaret, 102

M
McCreesh, Graeme, 277
MacLachlan, Sarah, 279
McMurtry, Roy, 137
McQuaig, Linda, 101
Maeots, Krista, 102
Maitland, Alan, 106
Mandel, Howie, 166
Mansbridge, Peter, 245, 246, 247-9, 256-7, 268
Medina, Ann, 152
Mendelsohn, Al, 100-1
Mesley, Wendy, 247
Metalious, Grace, 5
Miller, Joan, 42, 47, 56
Milley, Al, 180-1
Milley, Bill, 180-1
Mitchell, W. O., 12
Moore, Sheila, 72, 73, 74, 84
Morgan, Robin, 53
Morrison, Keith, 244, 267

Mosher, Terry, 150
Mulroney, Brian, 173, 189, 198, 201,
    202-7, 209-10, 213, 214, 216, 221-22,
    223, 230, 232-3, 235
Mulroney, Mila, 209
Murphy (cab driver), 180
Murrow, Edward R., 132, 287

N
Nayman, David, 253, 272
Nichols, Marjorie, 84-5, 171, 191-2,
    195-200, 210, 234, 235
Nixon, Richard, 203
Nkomo, Joshua, 105
Noble, Pat, 104

O
Oliver, Craig, 151, 152, 153, 154, 246
Osler, Jock, 121
Ostry, Bernard, 83
O'Sullivan, Terry, 266, 269, 271
Ottawa, 79-95, 191, 201
Ottmann, Wes, 9
Owen, John, 246, 247

P
Pamela Wallin Live (later *Pamela
    Wallin*), 270-73, 275-84
Parker, Dorothy, 59, 131
Parker, Freddie, 253-4
Parker, Rob, 88
Peace, Kelly, 29
Pehleman, Patsy, 245, 246
Perry, Norm, 142, 143, 148, 171-2, 173,
    174, 183, 243, 248
Peterson, Shelley, 28-31, 52, 238
Philips, Bruce, 129, 134-5, 136, 139, 142,
    143, 178, 185, 186, 189, 207, 208, 210,

219, 229, 230-1, 232
Presley, Elvis, 104-5
Prichard, Rob, 1, 216-17
Prime Time News, 183, 248, 249,
    250-1
Prince Albert, Saskatchewan, 62-7

Q
Question Period, 129, 130, 133-7, 145,
    171, 201, 222, 232

R
Radio Noon, 67-71, 91
Reagan, Ronald, 203
Reeves, Hubert, 279
Reisman, Simon, 207, 208
Ridsdell, John, 67, 70
Ritchie, Gordon, 206
Roberts, J.D., 244
Robertson, Lloyd, 142, 147, 183, 184-6,
    201, 208, 249, 252
Rollins, Doc, 13
Romanow, Roy, 137, 177
Rubinek, Saul, 109
Russnel, David, 29

S
Sanders, Larry, 62
Sarnoff, Robert, 130
Saskatchewan Today, 72-3
Sauvé, Jeanne, 124
Scott, Gail, 108, 142, 146
Segal, Hugh, 121, 132, 177, 178
Sikstrom, Mark, 232
Smale, Lily ("Grandma Smale"), 26-7,
    28
Smishek, Walter, 70
Smith, Roger, 232

Starowicz, Mark, 91, 98, 248
Steinem, Gloria, 284, 285
Sunday Morning, 92-5
Szende, Andy, 122

T
Tannen, Deborah, 125
Taylor, Peggy, 236-7, 254
Terry, Victoria, 232
Thatcher, Margaret, 151, 210-11
Thicke, Alan, 165
Todd, Clark, 152
Toronto Star, 110, 111, 113-29, 136, 140, 145
Tory, John, 177
Trudeau, Margaret, 86
Trudeau, Pierre, 40, 86, 110, 121, 125, 137, 149, 172, 204-5, 214-17, 221, 288
Trudel, Chris, 187
Truscott, Steven, 92
Turner, John, 215, 217, 219-28

U
Ullmann, Liv, 175-6
Urquhart, Ian, 122

V
Vellacott, Wilf, 9

W
Wagner, Jane, 286
Wallin, Bill (father), 8, 13, 21-2, 24, 32, 35, 42-3, 47, 66, 90, 193, 194, 195, 212, 255, 263-4
Wallin, Leone (mother), 8, 13, 21, 22, 23-4, 32, 35, 38, 46, 47, 52, 74, 231, 255, 263

Wallin relatives:
Barb (cousin), 20
Bilokraly, Meaghan (née George—niece), 16, 238
Bub (second husband of Nan), 18, 20-21
Deb (cousin), 20
George, Bonnie (sister), 7, 9, 10, 14, 15-16, 23, 24, 26, 33, 35, 37, 38, 238, 241, 249, 267
George, Erin (niece), 16, 238
George, Steve (brother-in-law), 239
Grandfather Wallin (Grandma Piper's first husband), 17
Grandma Piper (paternal grandmother), 17, 19, 20, 192-5
Macfarlane, Colin (Nan's first husband), 17
Macfarlane, Don (uncle), 12, 25-6, 37, 199, 238
Nan (maternal grandmother), 17, 19-20, 26, 38, 44-5, 47-8
Piper, Archie (second husband of Grandma Piper), 17, 192
Watson, Patrick, 92-4, 95, 182, 279
Waugh, Evelyn, 285
Webster, Jack, 195-6
White, Bob, 204
Whitton, Charlotte, 232
Wilson, Michael, 283
Winsor, Hugh, 85
Workman, Paul, 258

Z
Zimmerman, Adam, 269-70